The Anthropocene: Politik—Economics—Society—Science

Volume 41

Series Editor

Hans Günter Brauch, Peace Research and European Security Studies (AFES-PRESS), Mosbach, Germany

http://www.afes-press-books.de/html/APESS.htm
http://www.afes-press-books.de/html/APESS_41.htm

Annet Adong

Armed Conflicts and Forced Displacements in the Anthropocene

Incentives and Consequences in the Great Lake Regions of Sub-Saharan Africa, with a Special Focus on Northern Uganda

zef
Center for Development Research
University of Bonn
Hans Günter Brauch Foundation
for Peace and Ecology in the Anthropocene
Springer

Annet Adong
Center for Population and Applied Statistics
Makerere University
Kampala, Uganda

On this book and Acknowledgements
This book emerged from the author's Ph.D. dissertation at the Center for Development Research (ZEF), Faculty of Agricultural, Nutritional and Engineering Sciences, University of Bonn, Germany. The title of the dissertation is *Armed Conflicts and Forced Displacements: Incentives and Consequences for Food Consumption and Social Preferences in the Great Lakes Region of Sub-Saharan Africa, with a Special Focus on Northern Uganda.* The author acknowledges funding from the German Federal Ministry of Economic Cooperation and Development (BMZ) under the grant 2014-0689.1 of the Deutscher Akademischer Austauschdienst (DAAD) and Eiselen Doctoral Program of the Foundation Fiat Panis.

The cover photo was taken by © Andrew McConnell, PANOS Pictures, London, who granted permission for its use here. It shows the South Sudanese returnee Nyauke Chianjiak, aged 18, who sits with her one-year-old sister, Kuoli, in a transit center in Renk, South Sudan, after fleeing the conflict in Sudan.

ISSN 2367-4024 ISSN 2367-4032 (electronic)
The Anthropocene: Politik—Economics— Society—Science
ISBN 978-3-032-04819-6 ISBN 978-3-032-04820-2 (eBook)
https://doi.org/10.1007/978-3-032-04820-2

Language Editing: Dr. Vanessa Greatorex, Chester, England
Copy editing and layout: PD Dr. Hans Günter Brauch, AFES-PRESS and HGBS, Alte Bergsteige 47, 74821 Mosbach, Germany

This Springer imprint is published by the registered company Springer Nature Switzerland AG
The registered company address is: Gewerbestrasse 11, 6330 Cham, Switzerland

The book is dedicated to my Parents,
Mr. and Mrs. Selestino and Paskolina Okullo.
It is also dedicated to my Daughters,
Abigail Paska Agwai,
Annabel Zione Awor,
Angellica Theresa Agwai,
Alexandra Maria Agwai
and in Memory of
Felicia Auma.

Foreword

Annet Adong explores incentives (and disincentives) for engaging (and disengaging) in armed conflicts in the Great Lakes Region (GLR) of East and Central Africa. Countries of focus include Uganda, DRC, South Sudan, Rwanda, and Burundi. Armed conflicts in the GLR are shown to be driven by control for power to access economic benefits, natural resources and other economic benefits, availability and access to cheap conflict capital, subventions from hostile governments, positive externality from neighboring countries, grievances and discontent arising from high inequality, lack of political rights, grievances from ethnic discrimination and repression and psychic beliefs. Importantly, this dissertation by Annet Adong provides deep analyses of economics and social behaviour of refugees and resident populations explored in the setting of North Uganda in the wider context of the Great Lakes Region. There is very little such research at micro, household and community levels. Furthermore, Annet Adong examines medium- to long-term consequences of the exposure to the conflict. Interestingly, Annet Adong identifies prosocial attitudes between refugees and host communities. She studies this with so-called trust and dictator games in the field. Finally, informal land arrangement between refugees and host communities are studied by Annet Adong. The results indicate that preferences matter, and that trust and experience reciprocity increase the likelihood of host community members being willing to engage in informal land transactions with refugees in the future.

Prof. (em.) Dr. Dr. h.c. Joachim von Braun
Center for Development Research
University Bonn
Bonn, Germany

Joachim von Braun is Emeritus Professor for Economic and Technological change at Bonn University, in the Center for Development Research (ZEF). He is an agricultural economist and his research is on economic development, food nutrition and agriculture, bioeconomy, resource and environmental economics, science and technology policy. von Braun is President of the Pontifical Academy of Sciences of the Vatican, and a member of the German National Academy of Science Leopoldina, the German Academy of Engineering, other academies, and the International Science Council. In 2020 and 2021 he served as Chair of the Scientific Group for the Food Systems Summit 2021 of the UN Secretary General. He was Director General of the International Food Policy Research Institute (IFPRI) based in Washington DC. He has published more than 250 peer-reviewed publications.

Foreword

The eastern parts of Africa have a long and complex history of armed conflict, spanning over five decades. From protracted civil wars to interstate and cross-border skirmishes, including the ongoing civil conflicts in South Sudan and the Democratic Republic of Congo (DRC), the region continues to grapple with crises that pose significant threats to peace, security, and sustainable development. These conflicts have undermined the region's vast potential, despite its abundance of natural resources such as cobalt, copper, fertile arable land, and substantial hydroelectric capacity. According to the World Bank, an estimated 73.5 percent of Congolese lived on less than $2.15 a day in 2024. One in six people living in extreme poverty in Sub-Saharan Africa resides in the DRC.[1]

The root causes of these armed conflicts are multifaceted. Historical grievances, ethnic fragmentation, weak and often exclusionary governance, and unresolved colonial legacies have all contributed to cycles of violence. In particular, the scramble for control over mineral-rich territories, frequently involving both state and non-state actors, has entrenched instability and impunity. These dynamics have created

[1] See at: https://www.worldbank.org/en/country/drc/overview#:~:text=Economic%20Situation,supported%20by%20construction%20and%20services.

conditions in which armed militias thrive, with civilians bearing the brunt through displacement, killings, sexual violence, and deepening poverty.

Forced displacement is one of the most devastating consequences of these recurring conflicts. It is both a symptom and a driver of ongoing instability. Communities are frequently uprooted from their homes without warning, abandoning not just property but also critical social networks and sources of livelihood. This dislocation severely disrupts economic activity, education, and access to healthcare, leaving millions in a state of protracted vulnerability. Host countries, often with limited resources themselves, face the compounded pressure of providing land, infrastructure, and services to growing refugee populations. This stretches already fragile systems.

Uganda, for instance, is currently the largest refugee-hosting country in Sub-Saharan Africa, with nearly 1.6 million refugees originating from South Sudan, the DRC, Somalia, Eritrea, Burundi, Sudan, and Rwanda. More than half of them come from South Sudan, followed by those fleeing the DRC.[2] These refugees are primarily settled in Uganda's northwestern and western districts, as well as in the capital, Kampala. While Uganda's progressive refugee policy is commendable, the sheer scale of displacement has resulted in increased pressure on land, public infrastructure, and social services. This raises important questions about long-term sustainability and integration.

What makes this book particularly timely and important is its dual focus on armed conflict and forced displacement. It does more than recount historical events; it interrogates the structural and systemic failures that allow conflict to persist and displacement to become protracted. The author presents a nuanced analysis that connects localized violence to broader geopolitical dynamics while also examining the relationships between refugees and host communities. This synthesis opens new avenues for academic inquiry, policy dialogue, and practitioner reflection.

This book's contribution lies in its ability to bridge the gap between theory and practice. It challenges the prevailing narratives that often reduce displaced populations to mere statistics, instead centering their lived experiences within broader social, economic, and political contexts. By shedding light on both the immediate and long-term implications of forced displacement in the Great Lakes Region, this work contributes to rethinking durable solutions that prioritize justice, restitution, and regional cooperation.

I believe this book will serve as a valuable resource for scholars, practitioners, and policymakers alike. It addresses one of the most pressing humanitarian and

---

[2] This is as of March 2024, accessed from UNHCR Uganda Refugee Population Dashboard; https://data.unhcr.org/en/documents/details/107753.

developmental challenges in the region and opens space for deeper understanding and sustained engagement. I endorse this book wholeheartedly.

Kampala, Uganda
June 2025

Assoc. Prof. James Wokadala
School of Statistics and Planning
Makerere University, Deputy Principal
College of Business and Management
Sciences (CoBAMS)

Assoc. Prof. James Wokadala is currently the Deputy Principal of the College of Business and Management Science (CoBAMS) at Makerere University and Associate Professor in the Department of Planning and Applied Statistics, and has researched widely in the areas of education and forced displacements. James's interests lie in applying quantitative methods to analyze diverse social and economic situations, with a particular focus on poverty analysis, gender dynamics, education, finance, institutional efficiency, and social and economic issues. He has consulted with the World Bank, DFID, UNICEF, UNFPA, and several Government Agencies in Uganda. He has a Ph.D. in Applied Economics from Kobe University, Japan; a M.Sc. in Quantitative Economics; and a BSc in Quantitative Economics (January 2005) from Makerere University.

Acknowledgements

This book is based on my Ph.D. Thesis on Armed Conflicts and Forced Displacements, focusing on the incentives and consequences for consumption and social preferences.

I extend my deepest gratitude to my Ph.D. Advisor, Prof. Joachim von Braun, whose presence, thoughts, and guidance kept me on the Ph.D. track. Special thanks to my doctoral advisers, Dr Oliver Kiptoo Kirui and Dr Lukas Kornher. Your encouragement and optimism regarding my key achievements were instrumental in helping me complete my dissertation. To Dr Ibrahim Kasirye, I owe this achievement; thank you for nurturing my interest in conflict research while I was at the Economic Policy Research Center. I would also like to express my sincere appreciation to the Bonn International Graduate School of Development Research (BIGS-DR) at ZEF for their administrative support during my Ph.D., as well as to DAAD and Dr Hermann Eiselen's Doctoral Program of the Foundation Fiat Panis for the financial support provided for fieldwork in refugee settlements in Northern Uganda.

My appreciation also extends to the refugee and host communities in Northern Uganda, who generously shared their time and experiences, making this research possible. Their resilience and cooperation were foundational to this work. To the research team that surveyed hard-to-reach places, I am immensely grateful, with special recognition for the dedication of Justine Atima (RIP), your memory lives on through this work. To my dear parents, Selestino and Paska Okullo, I cannot thank you enough. You made this dream a reality by supporting me throughout my life's journey and by being present, including making sacrifices to ensure your daughters receive the best education. To my wonderful husband, Bernard Agwai, thank you for being my cheerleader in all aspects of life, including my career achievements. You wanted this book completed as much as I did, and I will always cherish that.

The manuscript received a significant improvement in clarity, flow, and layout thanks to the guidance of Dr. Hans Günter Brauch of the *Hans Günter Brauch Foundation for Peace and Ecology in the Anthropocene.* My gratitude to him for his unfailing support, professionalism, and efficiency, without which this book would not have been realized.

Kampala, Uganda
June 2025

Annet Adong
Makarere University

Summary

This book explores the twin challenges of armed conflicts and forced displacement in the Anthropocene. The Great Lakes Region (GLR), which consists of Uganda, Rwanda, Burundi, and the Democratic Republic of Congo (DRC),[3] has witnessed some of the most violent armed conflicts in Sub-Saharan Africa, leading to a significant number of forced displacements within the region. This book focuses on three main issues related to armed conflicts and forced displacements in the Anthropocene, namely: (1) drivers of armed conflict in the Great Lakes Region, (2) prosocial attributes in forced displacement, (3) the role of social preferences in improving refugee access to land.

In the second chapter, the drivers of armed conflict are explored using document reviews of case studies. These reveal a mixture of economic and non-economic drivers of armed conflicts in the region. Notably, in the GLR, ethnic divides cannot be separated from the incidence of armed conflict. Unlike theoretical explanations and studies that hinge on ethnic diversity as the likely factor driving armed conflict, in the GLR, the desire for ethnic dominance is one of the most probable sources of conflict. Moreover, as similar ethnicities cut across the borders, one successfully led armed conflict by a given ethnicity in one country motivates the same group to wage a similar upheaval in other neighboring countries. Political leaders have also taken advantage of ethnic differences to drive their motives for gaining power. Ethnic divides cannot be separated, either, from the colonial era, which historically institutionalized divisions, pitting one ethnic group against the other. Lastly, the concept of "market of violence" additionally explains why countries in the region meddled or continue to meddle in the affairs of mineral-rich DRC, due to a ready demand for minerals obtained through violence.

Within the GLR, armed conflicts emanate from the selfish desire to ascend to power and be in charge of the economic benefits of autocratic leadership, a characteristic of most regional governance structures. Prosecution, litigation, disciplinary actions, and penalties have been demotivating factors for engaging in conflicts in

[3] This study also includes South Sudan, which is not amongst the Great Lakes countries but has a significant number of refugees fleeing into the region due to ongoing conflicts.

these areas. Examples include (1) Uganda's self-referral to the International Criminal Court (ICC), which helped to quell the Lord's Resistance Army (LRA) rebellion; (2) the International Tribunal for Rwanda, which silenced any attempts similar to the Rwanda genocide in 1994; (3) the Dodd-Frank Wall Street Reform and Consumer Act in the USA, which is a check to prevent the sourcing of mineral wealth from conflict-affected countries like DRC. Beyond prosecution and litigation, impunity measures include granting amnesties to incentivize individual rebels under LRA to stop fighting and return home. Armed conflicts remain active in South Sudan and DRC. In this chapter, governments are recommended to pay attention to and address drivers that have previously motivated armed conflict in order to minimize the repetition of historical armed conflicts in the region.

The third and fourth chapters focus on forced displacements resulting from armed conflicts. Using the case of Uganda, they investigate refugees' and hosts' prosocial behavior and examine how social preferences affect access to land to promote refugee self-reliance. For refugee integration, discrimination based on the identity of being a refugee or host should be minimal. Chapter Three indicates that refugees do not consider the social differentiation of "us refugees" and "them host" in their interactions as much as hosts do, particularly in areas remote from urban areas. First, refugees will reciprocate trust to hosts more than to fellow refugees in remote areas. Second, refugees will also be more altruistic towards hosts than towards fellow refugees in remote areas. Lastly, refugees do not anticipate that their partners may expect them to favor fellow refugees or support hosts. The non-discriminatory nature of refugees in Uganda illustrates their willingness to integrate with their host communities. The results are important when thinking about refugee integration with hosts' communities. Meanwhile, hosts tend to favor fellow hosts but not in rural areas. They also anticipate that their fellow hosts will expect more from them in trust, and refugees will expect less from them in confidence. Lastly, hosts are not charitable to either fellow hosts or refugees, even in remote areas. These results reveal the need for more constructive interactions between hosts and refugees in remote areas. To a greater extent, this may be due to the closer confines or a smaller radius of interactions due to limited movement. There is also a possibility that the observed results may be attributed to refugees' high density in remote areas. Investments in social development activities such as joint social gatherings and social clubs that increase interaction between refugees and hosts are therefore recommended.

Further, Chap. 4 explores how host-refugee social preferences might affect land transactions. In light of unsustainable and insufficient government land distribution to refugees, land transactions between refugees and hosts offer alternative ways by which refugees can access land from the host and be self-reliant. Contracts are usually informal, might rely on personal relations of trust, altruism, and cooperative norms, and may not require any documentation. Currently, 47.2 and 43.3 percent of both refugees and hosts have been or are willing to engage in land transactions such as giving land for free for a specified period, land labor exchanges, land rent, and other unspecified methods. This chapter shows that the extent to which hosts trust refugees is likely to determine the degree to which they are willing to engage in land transactions with refugees. These results are treated cautiously, given the possibility of reverse causality; engaging in land arrangement increases trust, and trust might increase willingness in return. It is important not to underestimate the extent to which other factors – such as asset ownership, expectations in beliefs, and gender – affect the desire to engage in land transactions. These results are provided here to guide governmental action in order to ensure that refugees access land and become self-reliant. The government can consider encouraging land transactions between hosts and refugees to increase refugee self-reliance by banking and improving positive existing behavioral attributes such as trust and altruism between refugees and hosts.

Contents

Abbreviations

ACLED	Armed Conflict Location and Event Data
ADF	Allied Democratic Forces
ADFL	Alliance of Democratic Liberation Forces
CRRF	Comprehensive Refugee Response Framework
DRC	Democratic Republic of the Congo
FARDC	Armed Forces of the Democratic Republic of the Congo
FDLR	Forces Democratiques pour la Liberation de Rwanda
FNL	Forces Nationales de Libération
GLR	Great Lakes Region
ICC	International Criminal Court
LRA	Lord's Resistance Army
NRA	National Resistance Army
PALIPEHUTU-FNL	Party for the Liberation of Hutu people and National forces of Liberation
RPF	Rwandan Patriotic Front
SDG	Sustainable Development Goals
SPLM	Sudanese People's Liberation Movement
SPLM-IO	Sudanese People's Liberation Movement/Army in Opposition
SSA	Sub-Saharan Africa
UBoS	Uganda Bureau of Statistics
UNHCR	United Nations High Commission for Refugees
UNHS	Uganda National Household Survey

List of Figures

List of Tables

List of Maps

Chapter 1
Introduction and Motivations

1.1 Background

Armed conflicts involving armed forces between two or more organized groups threaten to prevent achievement of the Sustainable Development Goals (SDG). Countries with active conflicts (as of 2019) include Afghanistan, Yemen, Syria, Libya, South Sudan, Somalia, Saudi Arabia, Mali, plus some other countries in the Sahel region. The ten most conflict-affected countries by fatalities from 1989 to 2015 include Rwanda, Syria, Afghanistan, the Democratic Republic of the Congo (DRC), Iraq, Sudan, Sri Lanka, Eritrea, India, and Ethiopia (Table 1.1). The most significant fatalities are from armed conflicts involving the Government, except the Rwandan genocide and Hutu refugee massacres in the eastern region of DRC (Melander et al. 2016). Armed conflicts have led to many unprecedented displacements of people forced to flee their homes to seek refuge elsewhere. From 2009 to 2018, displaced people escalated from 43.3 to 70.8 million, mainly due to ongoing armed conflict (UNHCR 2019a). 67% of displaced people are from conflict-affected countries, and the top five refugee-hosting countries in 2018 included Turkey (3.7 million refugees), Pakistan (1.4 million), Uganda (1.2 million), Sudan (1.1 million), and Germany (1.1 million) (UNHCR 2019a).

Most countries supporting refugees are signatories to global commitments such as the Comprehensive Refugee Response Framework (CRRF) and Global Refugee Impact that provide a framework to guide support for refugee by countries. The CRRF prioritizes the need to ensure that refugees become self-reliant and contribute positively to hosting communities. In this regard, Uganda's refugee policy, which allows refugees to access land and other services accessed by fellow host communities, is heralded for being generous (UNHCR 2019b).

To distinguish armed conflicts from continually occurring conflicts, Wallensteen/Axell (1993) define armed conflicts as: "contested incompatibility that concerns government and/or territory where the use of armed force between two parties, of which at least one is the government of a state, results in at least 25 battle-related

A. Adong, *Armed Conflicts and Forced Displacements in the Anthropocene*,
The Anthropocene: Politik—Economics—Society—Science 41,
https://doi.org/10.1007/978-3-032-04820-2_1

Table 1.1 Conflict-affected countries by number of fatalities, 1989–2015

Country	Total no. of fatalities 1989–2015	Fatalities in state-based conflict	Fatalities in non-state conflict	Fatalities in one-sided violence
Rwanda	520,529	6,521	–	514,008
Syria	188,088	169,603	11,212	7,273
Afghanistan	162,035	150,618	2,517	8,900
Ethiopia	138,440	129,878	6,090	2,472
DRC	100,390	22,258	12,149	65,983
Iraq	95,243	77,931	2,943	14,369
Sudan	89,581	50,114	20,402	19,065
Sri Lanka	65,162	61,234	567	3,361
Eritrea	57,301	57,301	–	–
India	51,011	35,599	4,909	10,503

Source Compiled by Melander et al. (2016)

deaths in one calendar year". Wallensteen/Axell's (1993) definition excludes non-state conflicts between organized rebel groups and communities common in Sub-Saharan Africa (SSA) and has a threshold of 25 battle-related deaths This study adopts the above definition by Wallensteen/Axell (1993) and Collier/Hoeffler (2004) to distinguish armed conflicts from crime, litigation, strikes, and lockouts by having one or more of the following characteristics: (1) the government is a primary actor by engaging directly with rebels or in the repression of its leaders (state-based armed conflict and one-sided violence), (2) both warring parties suffer from the death of its members, (3) there is military action involving both internal and external parties, (4) there is the displacement of people to other countries as refugees. Lastly, the study dwells chiefly on conflicts involving armed ammunition with no threshold of 25 battle related deaths.

1.2 Motivations and Framing of the Study

Armed conflicts and displacements are of policy concern to policymakers, academia, and humanitarian organizations because of the immense negative consequences for economic, social and environmental outcomes. Collier (1999) estimates a 2.2 percentage point difference in economic growth between countries with ongoing civil war and ones with no conflict. Guerrero Serdan (2009) estimates that children born in areas affected by high violence levels during the Iraq war are 0.8 cm shorter than children born in low-violence provinces. Beyond the consequences for economic performance, human capital, and institutional changes, there are other immense long-term impacts of the war, such as diseases and disability, whose effects far outweigh the number of deaths during fighting (Ghobarah et al. 2003).

Past and recent research focuses on the consequences of conflict on child nutrition and health (Akresh et al. 2012; Bundervoet et al. 2009; Guerrero Serdan 2009), schooling (Shemyakina 2011), economic performance (Akresh et al. 2012; Brück et al. 2018; Bundervoet et al. 2009; Rockmore 2017, 2020), social preferences (Bauer et al. 2016, 2018; Hartman/Morse 2018), famine (von Braun et al. 1998), and institutional changes (Annan et al. 2011; Bauer et al. 2016; Bellows/Miguel 2009; Hartman/Morse 2018). Most of the evidence shows immense negative impacts on economic performance, health, and education. Nevertheless, evidence also indicates that experience of conflict may lead to positive outcomes, such as institutional changes for the better. For example, Blattman/Annan (2010) find that abduction from violence increases one's participation in voting and community leadership. Similarly, Bellows/Miguel (2006) find positive correlations between war experiences and involvement in community meetings in Sierra Leone. Bauer et al. (2018) find that child soldiering has no detrimental effects on social behavior. Despite reasonably substantial literature on the causes and consequences of armed conflicts, a few gaps warrant further research and form this study's primary motivation.

First, the study adds to the limited literature on incentives for engaging in armed conflict in Sub-Saharan Africa. The Great Lakes Region (GLR), including Rwanda, Burundi, Uganda, and DRC,[1] and South Sudan,[2] have a history of armed conflict since gaining independence, with some active armed conflicts in South Sudan and DRC. The number of forced displacements from the region has also increased over the last few decades. For example, in 2018, 5.4 million Congolese from DRC, with 854,000 refugees or asylum seekers, were forcibly displaced. The GLR is also characterized by criss-crossing hostilities, including governments supporting fellow incumbent governments to quell a rebellion or supporting rebel groups hostile to sitting governments. The region provides an excellent case study for understanding the incentives and disincentives for armed conflict, especially in SSA.

Secondly, most studies on refugees and host communities focus on livelihoods and less on their behavioral attributes. Refugees and their hosts may face challenges that emerge from differences in their social identity and characterization within and external to refugee settlements. Non Governmental Organizations offering support in refugee communities may already make clear distinctions between refugees and hosts, even when both groups face similar challenges. In the third chapter, discrimination in trust and altruism between refugees and hosts is examined using lab in the field experiments. Lab in the field experiments overcome biases from the endogeneity of preferences experienced with other approaches of measuring trust and altruism, such as using survey data, conjoint experiments, and observational methods. This study also concentrates on the behavioral puzzle of understanding beliefs in trust, reciprocity, and selflessness, crucial for many social interactions that remain largely

[1] The Great Lakes Region is composed of countries that surround the Great Lakes in Africa situated in the Eastern Rift Valley. Other countries in the GLR that are not part of this study include Tanzania, Malawi and Kenya.

[2] South Sudan is not part of the GLR but is included in this study.

informal between refugees and hosts. We examine how discrimination and or ethnic biases and stereotypes vary with remoteness.

Thirdly, Chap. 4 of this book examines bilateral land transactions between refugees and hosts' communities and whether social preferences of trust and altruism matter in these arrangements. Bilateral land transactions allow refugees to access land and provide alternative ways of ensuring refugees' self-reliance. Self-reliance has been at the center stage of global efforts and solidarity in refugee protection. The Comprehensive Refugee Response Framework (CRRF) urges member countries to adopt self-reliance approaches to refugee management. In this regard, Uganda's refugee policy, which offers land for residence and agriculture purposes, is heralded as generous. However, government land provision has proved insufficient and not sustainable. The area given to refugees has reduced over time; free land provision to refugees is a very costly endeavor. Amidst challenges of government land distribution, bilateral land agreements between hosts and refugees offer alternative opportunities by which refugees can acquire land. Bilateral land transactions between refugees and host communities are explored to determine whether social preferences of trust and altruism matter.

1.3 Research Objectives of the Book

The three main objectives of this study, which form separate chapters of the book, are to:

(1) Examine the incentives and disincentives for engaging and disengaging in armed conflicts in the Great Lakes Region and South Sudan. This area has a history of armed conflicts and criss-crossing hostilities between countries, with ongoing active conflicts in South Sudan and DRC which provide a good case study.
(2) Examine prosocial attitudes between refugees fleeing from armed conflict and hosting communities who have previously experienced armed conflict to explore any forms of discrimination in trust, reciprocity of trust, and altruism. The study further examines how these behavioral attributes vary with remoteness from district headquarters. The theory of parochial altruism in psychology literature postulates altruistic behavior towards in-group members and mistrust, hostility, or indifference towards out-groups (Baumgartner et al. 2012; Tajfel et al. 1971). This leads to the hypothesis that there is likely to be favoritism towards people from the same social identity as refugees or hosts (out of tastes for discrimination or ethnic stereotypes) in trust, trustworthiness, and altruism and that such behavior changes according to remoteness from urban areas, such as district headquarters.
(3) Examine the role of social preferences in predicting the willingness to engage in and the previous engagement in land transactions between hosts and refugees. Examples of land transactions include: (1) sharecropping agreements, (2) hosts giving land to refugees in exchange for refugee labor in their plots, (3) land

rental agreements for a specified period, (4) hosts giving refugees land for free for a specified period. It was hypothesized that bilateral land transactions are more likely to be engaged in by the more 'trusting' members of the hosting communities and by refugees who are considered by hosts to be trustworthy. The research also indicates that other intrinsic motives, such as altruism and expectations of trustworthiness, explain previous engagement in land transactions and willingness to engage in land transactions with refugees in the future.

1.4 Ethical Considerations

As part of the ethical considerations, the study received approval from the Center for Development Research, University of Bonn Ethics Review Committee. In Uganda, Makerere University School of Social Sciences and the Uganda National Council of Science and Technology (SS46) assessed and approved the study protocol. Department of Refugees, Ministry of Disaster Preparedness granted further clearance to conduct this research in refugee settlements. At the refugee settlements there was close collaboration with the regional refugee desk office in Adjumani district to access both refugees and host communities. In refugee settlements, the local leadership was used to access households. The sampled respondents were asked for their consent, having explained in detail the objectives and procedures before embarking on the research.

1.5 Structure of the Book

The entire book is structured as follows: this chapter provides the introductions and motivations. Chapter 2 examines the drivers of armed conflicts in the GLR. Chapter 3 explores prosocial attitudes between refugees and host communities living in close proximity. Chapter 4 examines whether social preferences matter in improving refugee self reliance through access to land. The last chapter also provides general conclusions and policy implications.

References

Akresh, R., Lucchetti, L., & Thirumurthy, H. (2012). Wars and Child Health: Evidence from the Eritrean–Ethiopian Conflict. *Journal of Development Economics*, *99*(2), 330–340. https://doi.org/10.1016/j.jdeveco.2012.04.001

Annan, J., Blattman, C., Mazurana, D., & Carlson, K. (2011). Civil War, Reintegration, and Gender in Northern Uganda. *Journal of Conflict Resolution*, *55*(6), 877–908. https://doi.org/10.1177/0022002711408013

Bauer, M., Blattman, C., Chytilová, J., Henrich, J., Miguel, E., & Mitts, T. (2016). Can War Foster Cooperation? *Journal of Economic Perspectives*, *30*(3), 249–274. https://doi.org/10.1257/jep.30.3.249

Bauer, M., Fiala, N., & Levely, I. (2018). Trusting Former Rebels: An Experimental Approach to Understanding Reintegration after Civil War. *Economic Journal*, *128*(613), 1786–1819. https://doi.org/10.1111/ecoj.12503

Baumgartner, T., Götte, L., Gügler, R., & Fehr, E. (2012). The Mentalizing Network Orchestrates the Impact of Parochial Altruism on Social Norm Enforcement. *Human Brain Mapping*, *33*(6), 1452–1469. https://doi.org/10.1002/hbm.21298

Bellows, J., & Miguel, E. (2006). War and Institutions: New Evidence from Sierra Leone. *American Economic Review*, *96*(2), 394–399. https://doi.org/10.1257/000282806777212323

Bellows, J., & Miguel, E. (2009). War and Local Collective Action in Sierra Leone. *Journal of Public Economics*, *93*(11–12), 1144–1157. https://doi.org/10.1016/j.jpubeco.2009.07.012

Blattman, C., & Annan, J. (2010). The Consequences of Child Soldiering. *Review of Economics and Statistics*, *92*(4), 882. https://doi.org/10.1162/REST_a_00036

Brück, T., D'Errico, M., & Pietrelli, R. (2018). The Effects of Violent Conflict on Household Resilience and Food Security: Evidence from the 2014 Gaza Conflict. *World Development*, *2018*. https://doi.org/10.1016/j.worlddev.2018.05.008

Bundervoet, T., Verwimp, P., & Akresh, R. (2009). Health and Civil War in Rural Burundi. *Journal of Human Resources*, *44*(2), 536–563. https://doi.org/10.3368/jhr.44.2.536

Collier, P. (1999). On the Economic Consequences of Civil War. *Oxford Economic Papers*, *51*(January 1999), 168–183.

Collier, P., & Hoeffler, A. (2004). Greed and Grievance in Civil War. *Oxford Economic Papers*, *56*(2004), 563–595. https://doi.org/10.1093/oep/gpf064

Collier, P., Hoeffler, A., & Söderbom, M. (2004). Duration of Civil Wars. *Journal of Peace Research*, *41*(3), 253–273.

Ghobarah, H. A., Huth, P., & Russett, B. (2003). Civil Wars Kill and Maim People Long After the Shooting Stops. *The American Political Science Review*, *97*(2), 189–202. http://www.jstor.org/stable/3118203

Guerrero Serdan, G. (2009). The Effects of the War in Iraq on Nutrition and Health: An Analysis Using Anthropometric Outcomes of Children. *SSRN Electronic Journal*, *14056*. https://doi.org/10.2139/ssrn.1359161

Hartman, A. C., & Morse, B. S. (2018). Violence, Empathy and Altruism: Evidence from the Ivorian Refugee Crisis in Liberia. *British Journal of Political Science*, 1–25. https://doi.org/10.1017/S0007123417000655

Melander, E., Pettersson, T., & Themnér, L. (2016). Organized Violence, 1989–2015. *Journal of Peace Research*, *53*(5), 727–742. https://doi.org/10.1177/0022343316663032

Rockmore, M. (2017). The Cost of Fear: The Welfare Effect of the Risk of Violence in Northern Uganda. *World Bank Economic Review*, *31*(3), 650–669. https://doi.org/10.1093/wber/lhw025

Rockmore, M. (2020). Conflict-Risk and Agricultural Portfolios: Evidence from Northern Uganda. *The Journal of Development Studies*, *2016*, 1–21. https://doi.org/10.1080/00220388.2019.1703953

Tajfel, H., Billig, M. G., & Bundy, R. (1971). Social Categorization and Intergroup Behaviour. *European Journal of Social Psychology*, *1*(2), 149–178. https://doi.org/10.1002/ejsp.2420010202

UNHCR. (2019a). *Global Trends: Forced Displacement in 2018*. www.unhcr.org/5c6fb2d04

UNHCR. (2019b). Uganda Country Refugee Response Plan. *The UN Refugee Agency*, *Jan 2019–Dec 2020*, 72. http://reporting.unhcr.org/sites/default/files/UgandaCountryRRP2019-20%28January2019%29.pdf

von Braun, J., Teklu, T., & Webb, P. (1998). *Famine in Africa. Causes, Response and Prevention*. The John Hopkins Univerisity Press.

Wallensteen, P., & Axell, K. (1993). Armed Conflict at the End of the Cold War, 1989–92. *Journal of Peace Research*, *30*(3), 331–346.

Chapter 2
Armed Conflicts in the Great Lakes Region: Attempts to Explain the Drivers

2.1 Introduction

Armed conflicts pose a significant threat to achieving many of the Sustainable Development Goals (SDGs), with well-documented negative consequences for human development, economic growth, and the environment (Ghobarah et al. 2003). For example, 489 of the 815 million hungry people are in conflict areas, and 75% of the world's stunted children are in countries affected by conflict (FAO/World Food Program 2018). Collier (1999) estimates a growth gap of 2.2 percentage points between countries experiencing ongoing civil war and those at peace; however, several states are currently either engaged in battle or transitioning to post-conflict status. Examples include Iraq, Afghanistan, the Democratic Republic of the Congo (DRC), Somalia, South Sudan, Syria, the Central African Republic, Libya, Ukraine, Pakistan, and Nigeria.

Armed conflicts often arise from irrational or rational decisions and leaders who are ignorant or inconsiderate (Blattman/Miguel 2010; Fearon 1995). Irrational leaders ignore or are biased against the private and social costs and consequences of armed conflicts. On the other hand, rational leaders are aware of the social and private costs associated with armed conflicts, yet they still engage in disputes (Bennett/Stam 2016; Fearon 1995) due to information asymmetry, bargaining, and commitment failure. Meanwhile, ignorant leaders engage in armed conflict as a 'mistake' (Collier/Hoeffler 2004) without considering the costs and consequences beforehand. This chapter explores the incentives and disincentives behind rational, irrational, and misguided decisions made by leaders, communities, and nations to engage in or disengage from armed conflict, specifically in the Great Lakes Region (GLR).

This chapter chiefly contributes to the armed conflict literature by linking theory to existing case studies of past and ongoing armed conflicts in Sub-Saharan Africa. Armed conflict is theorized as a contestation of resources, to maximize benefits, driven by social, cultural, and behavioral factors (Blattman/Miguel 2010; Collier

A. Adong, *Armed Conflicts and Forced Displacements in the Anthropocene*,
The Anthropocene: Politik—Economics—Society—Science 41,
https://doi.org/10.1007/978-3-032-04820-2_2

1999; Cramer 2002; Grossman 1991). This book specifically focuses on five countries in the GLR: Uganda, DRC, South Sudan, Burundi, and Rwanda. GLR countries have a history of armed and criss-crossing hostility from the times when they became independent. The armed conflict in South Sudan is ongoing, while in other countries there are reported pockets and occasional episodes of disputes. Each of the five GLR countries has a history of providing direct support to national armies to quell rebellions or to rebel groups fighting incumbent armies, creating an environment of uncertainty and distrust. Historically, Uganda and Tanzania have had this relationship. In 1971, Tanzania hosted the ousted President of Uganda, Milton Obote, and provided him with grounds for reorganizing and rebelling against the incumbent President.

On the other hand, Uganda hosted Paul Kagame, the leader of the Rwandan Patriotic Army in the 1980s, and supported his efforts to oust the ruling Rwandan President at the time. Uganda and Rwanda supported Laurent Kabila's rebellion against Mobutu Sese Seko of Zaire (now DRC) and successfully dislodged the latter. The Ugandan army has also recently been supportive of the South Sudanese army in dealing with the ongoing rebellion. Lastly, DRC currently hosts Hutu origin refugees hostile to Rwanda, the Allied Democratic Forces (ADF), and the Lord's Resistance Army (LRA) hostile to Uganda. The criss-crossing hostility among countries in the GLR is a good case study scenario for understanding the motives behind the conflicts in the region.

This analysis is conducted at both the individual and the group levels, where considerable variation may exist. Understanding armed conflicts solely from the national level (as is the case for many theoretical propositions) overlooks or undermines the actual characteristics, interactions, and attributes that form the rebel groups (Cunningham et al. 2009). The definition used here follows Collier/Hoeffler (2004) and Ngaruko/Nkirunziza (2000), as provided in Chap. 1, and the primary focus is on conflicts involving armed ammunition.

From the discussion, incentives to engage in an armed conflict emerge from a complex mixture of nonmaterial and material factors. The bush war of 1986 in Uganda, the Rwandan genocide in 1994, the several rebellions in DRC, the armed conflicts in Burundi, and the ongoing armed conflict in South Sudan stem from grievances and the desire for control of power. The autocratic nature of the political systems in the countries in the GLR only aggravates existing ethnic and religious differences. The belief in psychic abilities blinds leaders from reflecting on the actual costs of engaging in armed conflict. Examples of this include Alice Lakwena, the "spiritual leader" who led a rebellion against the National Resistance Army (NRA) and the Mayi-Mayi from DRC. Both groups motivated their soldiers to smear oil as a means to protect themselves from bullets. Other incentives include: (1) the availability and access to cheap capital such as military equipment, (2) support from internal and external sources, and (3) a positive externality from neighboring countries.

Incentives to end armed conflicts have emerged from external interventions in prosecution, litigation, and disciplinary actions against perpetrators and actors in the armed conflict. For example, Uganda's self-referral of LRA's atrocities to the International Criminal Court (ICC) in December 2003 and, subsequently, ICC's issuance of arrest to the five leaders of LRA contributed to some extent towards ending the two decades of armed conflict. For its part, the Dodd-Frank Wall Street Reform and Consumer Act in the United States (US) inhibits US companies from sourcing minerals from war-ravaged countries such as DRC, and thereby disincentives rebel activities. However, further research to explore the impacts of the Dodd-Frank Wall Street Reform and Consumer Act in the United States (US) on armed conflict in DRC is needed. The International Tribunal for Rwanda set to prosecute persons responsible for crimes has been critical in quieting down the likelihood of genocide recurring in Rwanda. Lastly, offering impunities and security guarantees through granting amnesties also motivated former soldiers of LRA to stop fighting and return home. Incentives and disincentives involve a cross-fertilization of economic, social-cultural, and behavioral explanations.

The rest of the paper is structured as follows. The next section is an overview of armed conflicts in the five countries of the GLR. Section 2.3 provides some of the existing theoretical explanations for the incentives and disincentives for armed conflict. Section 2.4 looks at the methodology, including the conceptual framework adopted. Section 2.5 provides a discussion based on case studies. The conclusion appears in Sect. 2.6.

2.2 Overview of Armed Conflicts in the Great Lakes Region of Sub-Saharan Africa

In 2019, the Fund for Peace Fragility[1] Index ranked South Sudan as the third most fragile state globally, DRC as the fifth, Burundi as the 15th, Uganda as the 20th, and Rwanda as the 40th (The Fund For Peace 2019). Most of the armed conflicts in the five countries are state-based, involving government and rebel groups, as shown in Table 2.1. The outcomes have been battle-related deaths for conflicts involving the state and rebel groups, massacres, and genocide for one-sided violence and communal violence between rebel groups. Unique armed conflicts include the Rwanda genocide of 1994, some non-state armed conflicts in DRC, and the Karamoja raid in Uganda. A map of armed conflicts and fatalities in GLR is in the Appendix, Fig. 2.1, of this chapter.

2.2.1 Conflicts in Uganda

Uganda has an estimated population of 45.9 million, based on the 2024 population census (Uganda Bureau of Statistics 2024a). Since independence in 1962, it has

[1] The Fragility States Index uses twelve conflict risk indicators to assess the vulnerability of states to collapse.

Table 2.1 Nature of conflict in the GLR

	State-based armed conflict	One-sided violence	Non-state conflict
Actors	Governments, rebel groups	Governments, organized groups, e.g. rebel groups	Organized groups, e.g. rebel groups and communal groups
Outcomes	Battle related deaths	Violence against civilians, e.g. massacres and genocide	Communal violence, violence between rebel groups
Examples	LRA, Uganda, DRC, Burundi, Rwanda, South Sudan	Rwandan genocide	DRC, Uganda

Source Author's modification of Wallensteen/Axell (1993)

witnessed several armed conflicts associated with the power transition from one political leader to another. Outstanding armed conflicts include the 1979 liberation war, the Ugandan Bush War, the Lord's Resistance Army (LRA), and the Allied Democratic Forces (ADF). The 1979 Liberation War was an armed conflict between Uganda and Tanzania, lasting about eight months and leading to the overthrow of President Idi Amin Dada in 1979. The Uganda Civil War from 1980 to 1986, also known as the Resistance War, was an armed conflict between the Uganda National Liberation Army (UNLA) and several rebel groups, most distinctly the National Resistance Movement (NRM), under the leadership of Museveni. After the NRM successfully took over the country's leadership in 1986, several armed groups emerged, including the Uganda People's Democratic Army (UPDA), consisting of soldiers from UNLA, the Holy Spirit movement (led by Alice Auma Lakwena), and the LRA under Joseph Kony.

The most significant armed conflict was that led by the LRA insurgency spearheaded by Joseph Kony, which lasted for two decades and has been the most devastating armed conflict in Uganda since independence. The LRA committed several atrocities, including the abduction of children and adults, mutilations of people's body parts, and civilian killings. In 2003, Uganda self-referred the LRA rebels' inhuman activities to the International Criminal Court. Currently, the LRA is active in the DRC and the Central African Republic. Another major armed conflict was the Allied Democratic Forces (ADF) insurgency, led by ADF rebels, which formed a merger between Uganda's Tabliq movement and former National Army for the Liberation of Uganda (NALU) soldiers. The ADF operate within the borders of Uganda and DRC. Their first attempted attack on Uganda was in 1995. In 1998, they attacked Kichwamba Technical College and killed 80 people. In 2002, the group fled to the DRC, where their bases are currently located (Map 2.1).

The graph in Fig. 2.1 shows the number of events and armed battles in Uganda (for which data is available) from 1997 to 2019, extracted from the Armed Conflict Location and Event Data (ACLED) (Raleigh et al. 2010). The number of events and reported fatalities was highest between 1997 and 2001 and between 2001 and 2006. Between 1997 and 2001, armed conflicts included Karamajong ethnic militia, Jie

Map 2.1 The Perry-Castañeda Library (PCL) Map Collection, Uganda Maps. The map was produced by the US Central Intelligence Agency and is therefore in the public domain. *Source* https://maps.lib.utexas.edu/maps/africa/uganda_pol_2005.pdf

ethnic militia, ADF, and the LRA forces. Fatalities between 1997 and 2001 include (1) 624 deaths in 1999 from an armed battle between the Government of Uganda and the Interahamwe military; (2) 720 reported deaths in Kitgum in 2000 due to an armed clash between the Uganda army and the LRA rebels. Between 2001 and 2006, the majority of the reported fatalities were by the LRA. In 2004, there were 604 reported deaths from Karamoja ethnic clashes. Karamoja ethnic clashes were usually

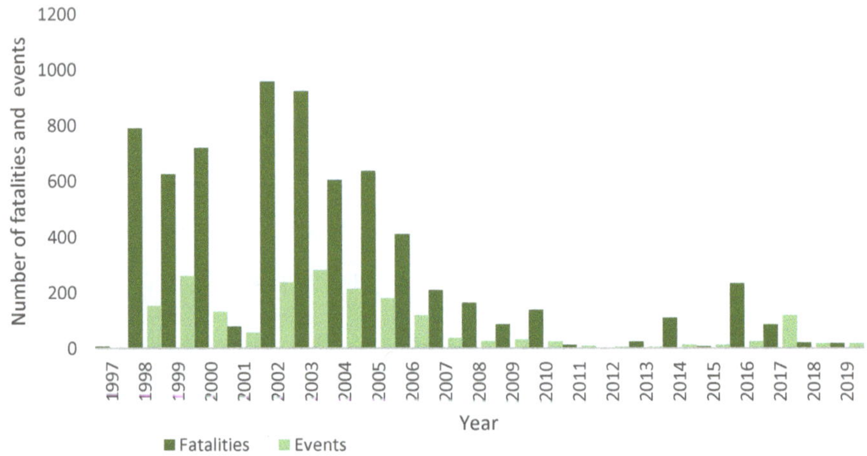

Fig. 2.1 Number of fatalities and conflict events from 1997 to 2019 in Uganda. *Source* Author's construction based on ACLED

armed raids between different ethnic communities stealing, raiding, or recovering cattle (Saferworld 2010). The reduction in the number of armed events and fatalities in 2006 and after that coincides with reduced LRA activities.

2.2.2 Democratic Republic of the Congo

DRC is the second-largest country in Africa after Algeria, with an estimated population of 80 million people. DRC is covered by sizeable dense forests and expansive fertile agricultural land. DRC has a massive endowment of natural resources with one thousand one hundred listed minerals and precious metals and is a world-leading producer of copper and cobalt. Its other minerals include coltan, diamond, silver, and petroleum. Past and ongoing conflicts are linked to mineral endowments (Bloem 2019; Cuvelier et al. 2014). The armed conflicts in DRC have taken the form of secession, rebellions, insurrections, revolts, invasions, and ethnic wars. Examples of armed forces include (1) Armed Forces of the DRC (FARDC) in the Orientale province in North East; (2) the LRA (from Uganda) at the border with the Central African Republic; (3) ADF with Ugandan origins in the North of the Kivu area (DRC) and South Sudan; (4) Forces Democratiques pour la Libération de Rwanda (FDLR): an armed group with Hutu Rwandan origins in the provinces of North Kivu and South Kivu; (5) 23rd March Movement (M23) or Congolese Revolutionary Army with Tutsi Rwandan origins; and (6) Forces Nationales de Libération (FNL) with Burundian roots. In 2016, there were at least 70 active groups and militias in the Kivu area in Eastern Congo (Rufanges/Aspa 2016) (Map 2.2).

Map 2.2 The Perry-Castañeda Library (PCL) Map Collection, Maps of Zaire (Democratic Republic of the Congo). The map was produced by the US Central Intelligence Agency and is therefore in the public domain. *Source* https://maps.lib.utexas.edu/maps/africa/congo_demrep_pol98.jpg

DRC has also been at the center of Africa's world war, which involved several countries, such as Uganda, Rwanda, Angola, Namibia, and Zimbabwe. The First Congo War from 1996 to 1997 emerged due to about two million refugees of Hutu origin fleeing from Rwanda into DRC and antagonizing the host communities. In the refugee camps, the Hutu refugees imposed violence on the hosts' communities, subsequently leading to an uprising of Mayi-Mayi to force the Hutu Rwandans out of Congo. Mayi-Mayi, literally meaning "magic water-magic water", relied on the rituals and symbolism of magic water to protect warriors from bullets (Jourdan 2011). The First Congo War led to the uprising of the Allied Democratic Forces for the liberation of Congo-Zaire (AFDL), led by Laurent Kabila and backed by Rwandan and Ugandan armies. AFDL ousted the Mobutu government and replaced him with Laurent Kabila in April 1997. Despite the change in leadership, anti-Kabila armed conflicts continued in Eastern Congo. Supported by Angola, Namibia, and Zimbabwe, Laurent Kabila turned against his allies – the Rwandan and Ugandan governments – allowing Hutu armies to regroup in Eastern Congo. In 2001, the bodyguard of Laurent Kabila murdered him, and his son Joseph Kabila took over DRC's leadership. In 2003, Joseph Kabila signed a transitional constitution, power-sharing interim government with rebel groups to allow opposition forces and the government's coexistence. In December 2018, DRC held an election, and Félix Tshisekedi replaced Joseph Kabila.

Figure 2.2 shows the number of events and related fatalities in DRC from 1997 to 2019, based on ACLED (Raleigh et al. 2010). The highest numbers of reported deaths were in 1999, 2002, and 2009. The total casualties in 1999 were 4,436, while in 2002, there were an estimated 4,670 reported fatalities, and in 2009, 3,173 reported deaths. Between 1997 and 2009, reported fatalities were as a result of the following: (1) the Mayi-Mayi rebellion, which affected North and South Kivu; (2) the movement for the liberation of Congo; (3) the Lendu ethnic military and Hema ethnic military; (4) the rally for Congolese Democracy (Kisangani); (5) the Military Forces of Democratic Republic of Congo (1997–2001) (Banyamulenge faction); (6) the Military Forces of Democratic Republic of Congo (1997–2001). Between 2010 and 2015, some battle events were from the clashes between Allied Democratic Forces and the National Army for the liberation of Uganda, the Lord's Resistance Army originating from Northern Uganda and currently settled in DRC.

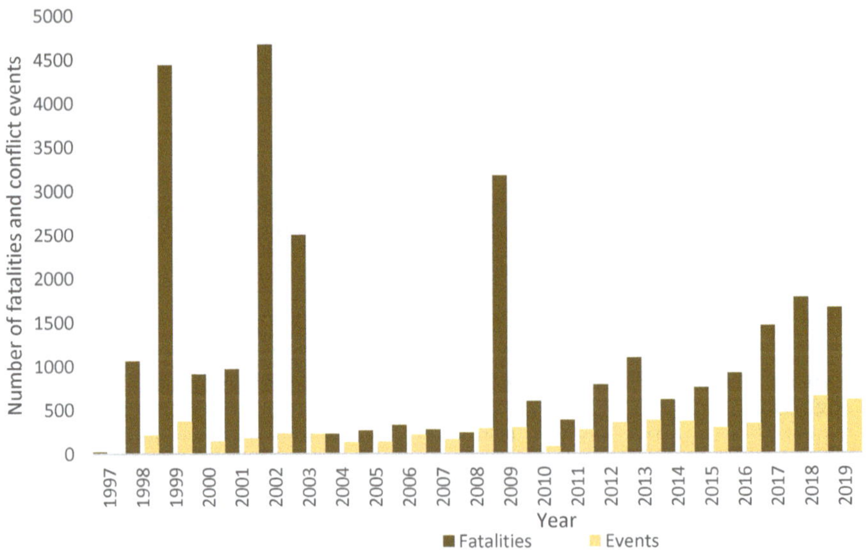

Fig. 2.2 Number of fatalities and conflict events from 1997 to 2019 in DRC. *Source* Author's construction based on ACLED

2.2.3 South Sudan

South Sudan is a new country that got its independence from Sudan in July 2011. Since then, it has witnessed several ethnic and political armed conflicts. The ongoing battle between the Sudanese People's Liberation Movement (SPLM) and Sudanese People's Liberation Movement/Army in Opposition (SPLM-IO) resulted from a political dispute between the ruling President, Salva Kiir, and his deputy, Riek Machar. In 2015, the two leaders signed the Compromise Peace Agreement, and in June 2016, Riek Machar, the leader of SPLM-IO, was appointed the vice president to Salva Kiir. Nevertheless, the peace deal did not last, and armed conflicts reignited with an attack in Juba. Not much has been achieved regarding negotiations between the warring parties, and the South Sudan conflict remains active.

Figure 2.3 shows the number of fatalities and armed events in South Sudan since independence. The highest reported casualties were in 2014 (an estimated 4,473 deaths from 537 armed conflict events) and 2017 (an estimated 3,356 deaths from 618 armed conflict events). Fatalities have been driven mainly by clashes between government forces and SPLM-IO (Maps 2.3 and 2.4).

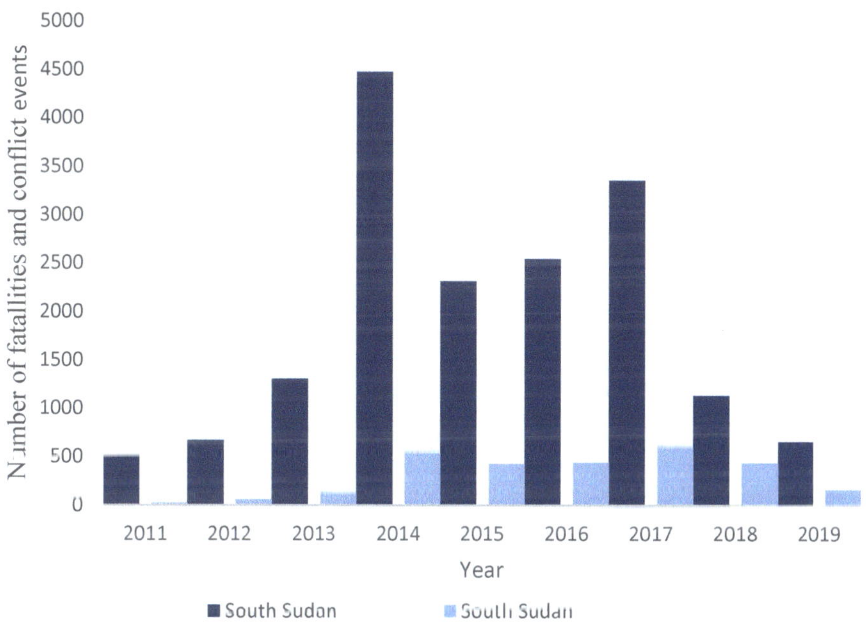

Fig. 2.3 Number of fatalities and armed conflicts in South Sudan from 2011 to 2019. *Source* Author's own construction based on ACLED

Map 2.3 The Perry-Castañeda Library (PCL) Map Collection, Map of Sudan. The map was produced by the US Central Intelligence Agency and is therefore in the public domain. *Source* https://maps.lib.utexas.edu/maps/africa/txu-oclc-219400066-sudan_pol_2007.jpg

2.2.4 Rwanda

Rwanda has about 12 million people and is bordered by Uganda, Tanzania, Burundi, and DRC. It is composed of three ethnic tribes: Tutsi, Hutu, and Twa. Since attaining its independence from Belgium, there have been three major episodes of armed

Map 2.4 The Perry-Castañeda Library (PCL) Map Collection, Maps of South Sudan. The map was produced by the US Central Intelligence Agency and is therefore in the public domain. *Source* https://maps.lib.utexas.edu/maps/cia16/south_sudan_sm_2016.gif

conflicts in Rwanda: (1) the Rwandan Revolution, also known as the Social Revolution or the Wind of Destruction; (2) the Rwandan Civil War; (3) the Rwandan genocide. The Rwandan Revolution took place between 1959 and 1962, marred by ethnic violence between the Tutsi and Hutu groups fighting for dominance and power control. The revolution led to the transition of power from the Tutsi monarchy that had succeeded the colonial rule masters to the Hutu-dominated Republic (Map 2.5).

The Rwandan Civil War from October 1990 to July 1994 was an armed conflict between the government armed forces and Rwandan Patriotic Front (RPF) rebels. Existing tension from ethnic differences between the Hutus and Tutsi led to RPF's emergence, which first attacked the North Eastern part of Rwanda in October 1990 but

Map 2.5 The Perry-Castañeda Library (PCL) Map Collection, Maps of Rwanda and Burundi. The map was produced by the US Central Intelligence Agency and is therefore in the public domain. *Source* https://maps.lib.utexas.edu/maps/africa/rwanda_pol96.jpg

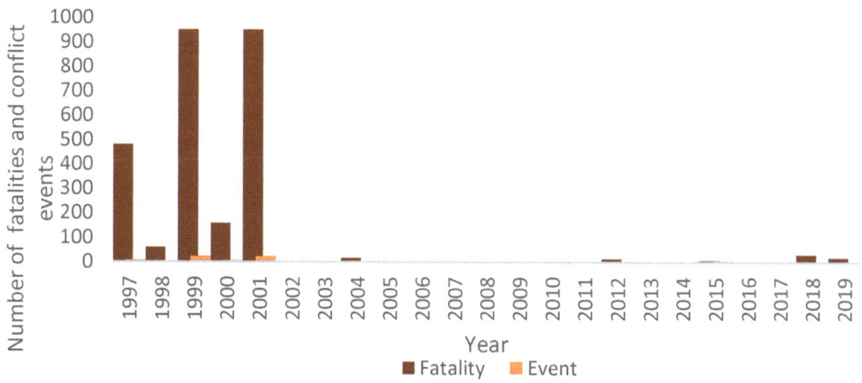

Fig. 2.4 Number of fatalities and armed conflict events in Rwanda from 1997 to 2019. *Source* Author's construction based on ACLED

was halted by the Rwandan Army with France's support troops. Under the command of the current President, Paul Kagame, the RPF then retreated to the Virunga Mountains and reorganized before re-emerging in a guerrilla war that persisted until mid-1992. In 1993, under Habyarimana's leadership, the Government agreed to negotiations with the RPF and signed the Arusha Peace Agreement in August of that year. On 6 April 1994, the assassination of President Habyarimana sparked off the Rwandan genocide over the next 100 days. Between 500,000 and 1,000,000 people were killed in the genocide. The genocide ended with the invasion of the Tutsi-led Rwandan Patriotic Front (RPF), supported by Uganda. Figure 2.4 shows the number of fatalities and armed conflict events in Rwanda between 1997 and 2019. After the genocide of 1994, occasional clashes between the Rwandan army and Hutu rebels continued until about 2000. In 1997, for example, between 200 and 300 people were killed when Hutu rebels attacked a jail in northwestern Rwanda to free their colleagues. In 1998, 250 rebels of Hutu origin were killed by the Rwandan patriotic army in Gisenyi. The clashes between RPA and Hutu rebels originating from DRC in 1998 led to about 2,048 reported fatalities.

2.2.5 *Burundi*

Burundi has approximately 13.2 million people (2023)[2] and no significant natural resources. It comprises three major ethnic groups: the Hutus (85% of the population), the Tutsi, and the Twa. Burundi's turbulent political history, marred by armed conflicts since it gained its independence from Belgium in 1962, provides a good case study for understanding the incentives and disincentives for armed conflict. Six episodes of civil war can be traced, in 1965, 1972, 1988, 1991, 1993 to 2003, and

[2] See at: https://www.worldbank.org/en/country/burundi/overview.

2015. A failed coup by the Hutus in 1965, three years after gaining independence, led to the political exclusion of the Hutu by the Tutsi in power (Nkurunziza 2022). In 1966, the Tutsi from the southern province of Bururi, under their leader, Captain Michael Micombero, seized power. In 1972, a political insurgency led by the Hutu ensued (Lemarchand 2008). In response, the Tutsi army repressed the Hutus, hunting down all the educated Hutus and forcing them to flee into exile. The massacre of the Hutus by the Tutsi army was massive, reducing Hutus to an oppressed underclass (Bundervoet et al. 2009). In 1988, another attempted Hutu insurgency was launched to gain power. As before, the Tutsi army repressed civilians of Hutu origin (Nkurunziza 2022). In a democratic election in 1993, a Hutu was elected into power. However, in October of the same year, the Tutsi's coup attempt cut short his reign and marked the beginning of another prolonged armed conflict, which lasted close to 10 years. Several Hutu armed rebel groups, such as the National Council for the Defense of Democracy and the Forces for the Defense of Democracy (CNDD-FDD), the Party for the Liberation of Hutu people, and the National Forces of Liberation (PALIPEHUTU-FNL), emerged against Burundi's regular army (Nshimirimana 2024). In 2005, through democratic elections, power transitioned from Tutsi to Hutu with a few rebel activities (Map 2.6).

In 2015, armed clashes between unidentified armed groups of people and the national police force took a toll, and several fatalities were reported (Fig. 2.5). From 1997 to about 2003, the number of armed conflicts escalated, driven by clashes between Burundi government troops and Hutu rebels. For example, on 27 February 2001, at least 315 army soldiers were killed by the Defense of Democracy, a Hutu rebel group. The reduced fatalities in 2003 correspond to the signing of a ceasefire agreement between the CNDD-FDD and the government. From 2005 to 2014, there were only occasional escalations of armed conflict following the victory of the leading rebels, who subsequently formed a political group known as the CNDD-FDD.

From the conceptual framework, incentives to engage in conflict can be classified into three broad categories: (1) opportunistic, (2) preference-driven, and (3) selective incentives. Despite this classification, it is challenging to determine which incentives or disincentives provide a more persuasive explanation for engaging in or disengaging from armed conflict and which comes first in sequencing the motives. Most armed conflicts are also path-dependent, dating back a long time, and are not primarily explained by most models.

2.3 Theoretical Approaches

Armed conflicts often stem from irrational decisions, rational decisions, and leaders who are ignorant or inconsiderate (Blattman/Miguel 2010; Fearon 1995). Rational leaders engage in armed conflicts due to information asymmetry, bargaining indivisibilities, the uncertainty of adversaries, and commitment problems which hinder agreements or cause bargaining breakdowns (Blattman/Miguel 2010; Fearon 1995; Powell 2006; Skaperdas 2008). Commitment failure involves one party reneging on

Map 2.6 The Perry-Castañeda Library (PCL) Map Collection, Maps of Burundi. The map was produced by the US Central Intelligence Agency and is therefore in the public domain. *Source* https://maps.lib.utexas.edu/maps/burundi.html

a mutually preferable term (Fearon 1995) to have the first-strike advantage. Commitment failures and reneging on bargains emanate from a lack of contract enforcement capabilities, primarily due to weak institutions (Skaperdas 2008). The presence of institutions and legal representation (local and international), market promotion, and tax levying can facilitate contracting (Acemoglu et al. 2010; Collier et al. 2004) and manage conflict (Besley/Persson 2008a). Besley/Persson (2008a, b) find that

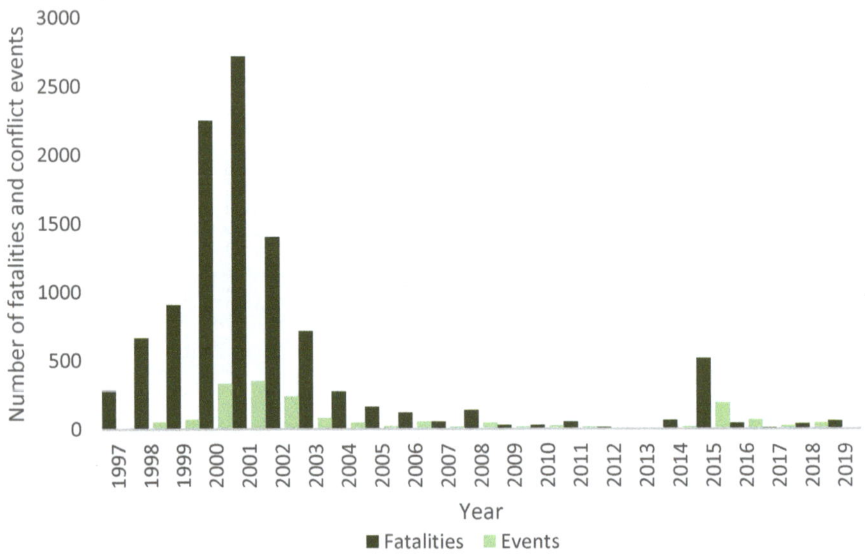

Fig. 2.5 Number of fatalities and armed conflicts in Burundi from 1997 to 2019. *Source* Author's own construction based on ACLED

higher world market prices of exported and imported commodities are significant predictors of civil war. Higher prices of imported commodities reduce real wages and thus the costs of going into conflict, yet high export prices increase the revenue collected by the government and thus the incentive for warring parties to engage in war. International institutions like the Rome Statute of the International Criminal Court are crucial for enforcing commitments and helping competing groups reach a compromise. Factors that make contracting difficult (geographically distant places, ethnic distance) by creating a power vacuum (Skaperdas 2008) or increasing the cost of contracting also explain observed armed conflicts.

Theoretical explanations for conflict occurrence lean towards neoclassical (maximization of benefits) or psychological and sociological theories. Neoclassical conflict theories focus on explaining the emergence of conflict as being motivated by the desire to maximize economic gains. Conflict is theorized as an 'enterprise' or investment that generates profit or has a pay-off (Collier/Hoeffler 2004; Grossman 1991) driven entirely by greed. Engaging in armed conflict is only possible if the utility of participation is positive; otherwise, one would not. On the other hand, the political science literature further explores the role of grievances in initiating conflict (Collier/Hoeffler 2004). The focus on material explanations with little or no regard for nonmaterial answers, such as grievances, is reductionist and simplistic (Cramer 2002). For example, reducing the influence of social relations on armed conflict to only ethnic fractionalization is simplistic (Cramer 2002). Social relations, for example, may explain rebel recruitment and coherence during a rebellion. Beyond materialistic explanations, non-materialistic explanations also suffice. For example, the unequal distribution of resources may cause a section of society which is unfortunate to feel aggrieved and resort to insurgency (Blattman/Miguel 2010).

Contest models for the occurrence of armed conflict: In contest models, two parties, such as the Government and a rebel group, compete to allocate resources for production or appropriation. Production is modeled using standard production function models. At the same time, allocation follows a "contest success function" (Blattman/Miguel 2010), consisting of war artillery or other technologies (such as skill, firearms, training, and rugged terrain) as inputs, and the probability of winning and consuming the opponents' production function, besides their own, as the output. Under information asymmetry, one party possesses private information regarding their pay-offs and military capacity but is unwilling to reveal or misrepresents this information to gain a better position than their adversary (Fearon 1995; Powell 2006).

Grossman (1991) and Collier/Hoeffler (1998) present two economic models essential for understanding the incentives and disincentives for engaging in armed conflict. Both models only consider two players, although Grossman (1991) also considers the case of a ruler pitted against peasants.

Collier/Hoeffler (1998): the decision to engage in an insurgency is to either capture the state or secede from it (Eq. 2.1)

$$R = 1 \text{ if } U_R > 0, \text{ else } R = 0 \tag{2.1}$$

where $R = 1$ if an armed conflict occurs and $R = 0$ in its absence while U_R is the utility function of engaging in the armed conflict set out as in Eq. 2.2 (Hoeffler, 2012)

$$U_R = \int_{t=D}^{\infty} \frac{p(T) \cdot G(T, P)}{(1+r)^t} dt - \int_{t=0}^{t=D} \frac{(f(Y)) + C}{(1+r)^t} dt \tag{2.2}$$

p is the probability of a successful insurgency, T is the taxable capacity of the economy, G is the gain when the rebellion is successful, P is the size of the population, D is how long the insurgency will take, Y is the per capita income, C is the transaction costs from coordinating rebel activities, and r is the discount rate. A war will thus occur when

$$a \cdot p(T) \cdot T + b \cdot P - c \cdot D - d \cdot Y - e \cdot C > \eta \tag{2.3}$$

From Eq. 2.3, the occurrence and duration of war will be affected by the taxable base, per capita income, population size (which captures the desire for secession), and insurgency costs. The cost of rebellion includes the loss of income from a sustained war and the transaction costs associated with coordination (Hoeffler 2012).

Grossman (1991): armed conflict is an equilibrium outcome for competition for scarce resources (contest model). It's a two-person model consisting of a single ruler and the peasant farmers, with no cooperation, resulting in a one-shot game. The ruler seeks to maximize the expected income from his subjects through taxation or rent collection. On the other hand, peasants seek to maximize their anticipated revenue by allocating their labor time to production, soldiering, or participating in a rebellion. The equilibrium for the ruler and the peasant is characterized by the distribution of time among production, soldiering, and insurrection, as well as a probabilistic distribution of income among rents and taxes received by the ruler's clientele, net earnings from productive labor, wages for soldiering, and booty taken by insurgents (Grossman 1991). With a higher tax rate, peasants are willing to engage in an insurrection (the incentive is the booty and the revenue the leader collects in rent or taxes and distribution) rather than focus on food production. Ultimately, the ruler will collect more revenue from taxes but increase the likelihood of a successful rebellion. For the leader to quell any secession efforts by farmers, military expenditure on soldiering and technology is crucial. Grossman (1991)'s model shows that poverty is a critical incentive. As the relative returns of fighting versus production increase, soldiering is likely to increase. Leaders have to motivate their citizenry into soldiering (opportunity costs of soldiering should be low) (Besley/Persson 2008b; Blattman/Miguel 2010). The wealth effect of owning natural resources is ambiguous. On the one hand, the higher the national wealth (taxes, natural resources, or external transfers), the higher the equilibrium effort is to fighting rather than producing. In the absence of resources, production is less rewarding than fighting; however, the incentive for war also reduces due to smaller gains (Blattman/Miguel 2010; Grossman 1991).

Models by Grossman (1991) and Collier/Hoeffler (1998) narrow the causality of war to greed from war pay-offs or profits gained from toppling the Government. The two models also highlight taxation's role in maintaining power and preventing an uprising, income inequality, or ethnic misrepresentation. Political elites will be at the crossroads of maximizing rent through taxation but are also aware of the likelihood of high taxation fueling conflict. The middle ground is an efficient means of taxation that increases the benefits of controlling power but reduces the possibility of engaging in a battle (Acemoglu et al. 2010). Cramer (2002) criticizes both models and other neoclassical models of conflict, which relate armed conflict only to opportunistic explanations, use only two actors, disregard historical factors, and overlook the international dimension of armed conflict.

Psychological, sociological, and historical motivations for the occurrence of armed conflict: the literature seems to suggest that material or economic explanations for the engagement of individuals and/or groups in armed conflicts don't provide complete descriptions (Cramer 2002; Gates 2015). Even in cases where economists have reduced accounts to greed only, psychological and sociological motivations might be the reason rather than material benefits (Cramer 2002). For example, Collier/Hoeffler's (2004) study on greed and grievances as causes of armed conflict found little explanatory power for variables that proxy for grievances, such as inequality, political rights, or ethnic and religious divisions. Cramer (2002) criticizes the simplistic use of proxies for grievances, arguing that they do not capture entirely what grievances entail. Some people might join insurgencies for no apparent material benefit but rather for ideological reasons, religion, or kinship (Gates 2015). For example, the rewards for engaging in armed conflicts may be due to the solidarity of belonging to a group, rather than just material pay-offs. Emotional and ideological outrage might emerge as a result of inequality and fuel conflict. Additionally, behavioral notions of fairness, equity, and reciprocity (Fehr/Schmidt 1999; Rabin 1993) may explain the motivations for individuals to engage in armed conflicts and the glue that holds insurgent groups together. Armed conflicts may also follow a path dependence due to historical factors. Colonial forces may have, in the past, institutionalized relations of force within the population (Cramer 2002), thereby perpetuating conflict in the post-colonial era. Also, diversity or dominance in ethnicity is linked to conflicts (Collier et al. 2004). Powell (2006), for example seems to suggest that war leads to Pareto-inferior outcomes or inefficient outcomes, since war is associated with the depletion and distraction of resources. He seems to suggest that the 'pie' to be divided before war begins is larger than when it starts and warring parties should reach a Pareto-superior agreement before war commences. Instead, factors related to informational problems, bargaining indivisibilities and commitment issues affect the agreement.

2.4 Methodology

The methodology used in this book combines theoretical arguments with the analysis of case studies drawn from publicly available documents, including books and journal publications. Secondary data on the number of armed conflicts and fatalities from ACLED (Raleigh et al. 2010) and narratives from former rebels of the LRA are also used to understand the drivers of conflict in the region.

Incentives can be positive or negative from an individual or a group perspective. When the expected utility in conflict is positive ($(U_t) > 0$) then individuals or groups will be incentivized to engage in conflict. Otherwise, when $E(U_t) < 0$, individuals or groups will be disincentivized to engage in conflict. Collier/Hoeffler (2004) classify the decision to participate in armed conflicts into grievances and opportunities, while Hirshleifer (1995) classifies it into three: opportunities, preferences, and perceptions. The latter is at the intersection of the first two. If wrongly perceived, opportunism and grievances that might have driven armed conflicts in the first place may indeed turn out to be very unprofitable or result in more grievances (Collier/Hoeffler 2004). Opportunistic reasons for engaging in armed conflicts include: extortion of natural resources, donations, subventions, availability of cheap conflict capital, weak government military, loot, future rewards, and protection from harm (Blattman/Miguel 2010; Collier/Hoeffler 2004). Some directly benefit those engaged in armed conflicts, while others facilitate war to be less costly, thereby increasing the likelihood that the expected utility is positive.

Grievances arise from ethnic or religious discrimination, repression, exclusion, and inequality (Collier/Hoeffler 2004). Peterson (2001) lists self-validating beliefs, emotions such as envy, dispositions such as altruism, norms of reciprocity, threshold-based behavior, network diffusion, and relative deprivation as causal patterns or mechanisms explaining individuals' actions in engaging in armed conflicts. A number of these fall within the categorization of preferences suggested by Hirshleifer (1995). Following Collier/Hoeffler (2004), opportunistic motives for engaging in armed conflicts can further be disaggregated into (1) opportunities for financing rebellion, which include extortion of natural resources, donation from diasporas, and subventions from hostile governments; (2) the prospect of low costs, which include recruitment costs (opportunity costs for rebellions are small), and weak government military (for example a favorable terrain for the rebels, such as forests, mountains); and lastly (3) opportunities from social cohesion, including ethnicity (proxied by ethnolinguistic fractionalization[3] or dominance) and religious diversity). Apart from opportunism and preference, a third classification arises from individuals or groups who are unwillingly forced by threat and/or punishment to engage in armed conflicts. These can be classified as selective incentives. From the conceptual framework, incentives to engage in conflict are classified into three broad categories (1) opportunistic, (2) preference driven, and (3) selective incentives. Despite this classification, it is difficult to isolate which incentives or disincentives provide a more persuasive explanation for engaging or disengaging in armed conflict, which comes first in sequencing the motives. Most of the armed conflicts are also path-dependent from a long time ago and are not primarily explained by most models.

2.5 Discussion

2.5.1 Drivers of Armed Conflicts in the Great Lake Regions

In this section, the drivers behind the several conflicts that have historically marred the countries in the GLR are discussed. Three interlinked factors tend to explain the occurrence of armed conflict within the GLR region: the presence of natural resources and other economic benefits associated with disputes, the governance systems that control the resources, and the grievances emerging due to discrimination.

The armed conflict in DRC is primarily attributed to the country's extensive natural resources (Cuvelier et al. 2014; Skaperdas 2008), with minerals such as tin (cassiterite) and tantalum (coltan) characterized as "conflict minerals" (Bloem 2019), and conflict events and fatalities being higher in areas rich in mineral deposits (Bloem 2019). For example, the Katanga region has 70% of the country's copper and cobalt production, the Kasai region is endowed with diamonds, and the Kivu region has vast reserves of gold, coltan, and tin. Armed rebel groups have profited directly from these minerals as "boots on the ground" or indirectly by seeking rent from miners and traders (Cuvelier et al. 2014). Local and external markets for DRC minerals looted through violence have also increased the feasibility of engaging in and continuing armed conflict in the region, as suggested by Elwert (2018), who notes the likelihood of coexistence between markets for violent acquisition of resources and non-violent

[3] Ethno linguistic fractionalization: "is the probability that two randomly drawn people are from different ethnic groups" (Collier/Hoeffler 2004).

trade (Elwert 2018). Since 2000, there has been a growing presence of Chinese companies in DRC, targeting minerals such as cobalt, tin, tantalum, tungsten, and gold (di Montenegro 2017). Armed groups have profited from illicitly obtaining the minerals and selling them to Chinese companies, which process the minerals into consumer and industrial goods, such as electronic products sold to consumers in the USA and Europe (Ma 2009). Rwanda and Uganda's military engagements in DRC have also been attributed to the looting of valuable minerals such as coltan and timber (Titeca 2024). Between 1999 and 2000, Uganda's coltan exports had increased by USD 250 million in 18 months, which Venugopalan (2016) attributes to the involvement of Uganda's army in militaristic activities in DRC.

Despite the evidence of armed conflicts in areas of high mineral deposits in countries such as DRC and South Sudan, natural resources have not been the solemn initiator of conflicts in the region, nor have they been the only factor in sustaining battles. The governance systems that control the natural resources and other economic benefits also explain the conflicts in the area. The governance pattern in most African countries has been associated with neopatrimonial tendencies that characterize different styles of authority, idiosyncratic mannerisms of certain individual leaders, and social practices within states (Mkandawire 2015). Neopatrimonialism is associated with less democratic tendencies characterized by strong presidential rule, patronage-based distribution of power, and state resources for political legitimation (Sigman/Lindberg 2017). It drives the desire to have political power in many African countries and has been an incentive to engage in conflicts. This follows the theoretical presuppositions of Grossman (1991) and Collier/Hoeffler (1998), who postulate that several conflicts have emerged because of the desire to have control over power and to access economic benefits such as revenue raised from taxation. Burundi's neopatrimonialism system is akin to controlling economic power through various rents, including allocating foreign aid, tax revenue, government employment, and awarding public contracts (Nkurunziza 2015). In DRC, Mobutu's regime was characterized by clientelism, in which power and property concentrate in the hands of certain political elites in exchange for loyalty (Jourdan 2011). Armed conflicts in these countries have emerged with the desire for rebelling parties to be at the helm of neopatrimonialism or as vengeance for such power associated with inequalities.

Specifically, grievances and discontent arising from high inequality, lack of political rights, and general exclusion are the sources of conflict in these regions: Grossman (1991) highlights the role of distribution in minimizing insurgency. Social disparities, deprivation of basic needs, and unemployment create fertile grounds for conflict by exacerbating existing grievances and making rebellion less costly. Unemployed youths are a source of cheap labor and can quickly join revolutions. In DRC, the youth's marginalization over access to land (traditional collective land ownership replaced with the Bakajika law) led to youth grievances (UNECA 2016). The Bakajika law transferred control over land to elite Congolese. Further, Mobutu's regime closely relied on clientelism, with power and property concentrated in the hands of only a few politicians and individuals loyal to those in leadership. Marginalization and the lack of proper public education system left many youths disgruntled and lured them into armed groups like the Mayi-Mayi that ravaged the North and South Kivu regions. Several armed conflicts in DRC also emerged out of discontent with how the central government manages revenue from natural resources. Simultaneously, rebel leaders in these mineral-rich areas have taken advantage of the grievances to push their selfish political motives forward. In South Sudan, the ongoing armed conflict is partially attributed to the presence of oil resources in some of its regions (Nyadera 2018). Oil-rich parts, such as Unity, Jonglei, and Upper Nile, are also areas with high conflict occurrence. Other economic benefits are associated with raiding and looting, particularly with small armed groups with the lowest probability of capturing power (Blattman/Miguel 2010). In Uganda, the LRA rebels mostly relied on raiding and looting food from the civilian communities, even when the chances of seizing power seemed slim (Allen/Koen 2010). Similarly, several child soldiers in the AFDL army in Congo joined armed forces for material gains (cited in Jourdan 2011).

Armed conflicts have also emerged in the region due to grievances from ethnic discrimination and/or repression. Ethnicity refers to the identity (tribe, religion, sectarian belonging, social status) and solidarity of a group, which varies with time and interaction and is therefore ambiguous (Bakwesegha et al. 2004). Colonial administrations in many of the countries classified people along ethnic and tribal differences ('Hutu' and 'Tutsi' referred initially to farmers and cattle keepers) (Joras/Schetter 2004) to divide and rule and garner support for themselves. In Uganda, the South, mainly of Bantu origin, was pitted against the North, primarily of Luo origin. In Rwanda and Burundi, the Tutsi were pitted against the Hutu. These colonial and post-colonial divisions paved the way for enhancing armed conflicts along ethnic lines in post-colonial error. According to Allen (1991), the LRA in Uganda and the armed Holy Spirit battalion of Alice Lakwena emerged to protect the Acholi people (Luo ethnicity) from the discriminatory plans of Museveni's Government. Uganda National Rescue Front (UNRF) emerged as a rebellion against Museveni's government in Uganda to fight against the marginalization of people from the West Nile (Refugee law project 2022). In South Sudan, orders from President Salva Kiir from the Dinka ethnicity group (the largest ethnic group in South Sudan) to disarm all presidential guards from the Nuer ethnic group (the second-largest ethnic group) sparked off an armed conflict (Brosché/Höglund 2016). The killing of about 20,000 civilians of Nuer ethnicity in Juba's capital caused grievances and created hatred among the Nuer ethnic group of other ethnic groups (Dessalegn 2017). Subsequently, many soldiers sought revenge, and the White Army fighters did not have to be coerced into fighting but emerged spontaneously in solidarity to rescue and revenge (Young 2016).

In DRC, a massive influx of Hutu refugees from Rwanda to Congo created a delicate imbalance in power relations along ethnic lines and explains the armed conflicts from 1996 to 1997 (UNECA 2015). Ethnic antagonism fueled by the political leadership of Mobutu pitting the Banyamulenge against the hosting communities partly explains the emergence of rebellion by Laurent Kabila of the Alliance of Democratic Liberation Forces (ADFL). The ADFL relied on the support of ethnic groups who were opposed to Mobutu's regime.

In Burundi, several conflicts are ethnically driven. Inferior Hutus often attempted to change their status quo (discrimination and exclusion) through engaging in rebellion. On the other hand, the Tutsi leaders marginalized the Hutus more (Nindorera 2012) to maintain their status quo. Ngaruko/Nkirunziza (2000) describe the conflicts in Burundi as a conflict trap. Rebels of Hutu origin emerged due to killings of fellow high-ranking Hutus by Tutsi politicians or discriminatory acts in government and public sector positions. In response, the Government forced revenge by killing rebels and any Hutus irrespective of whether they were culprits or not, exacerbating existing grievances (Ngaruko/Nkirunziza 2000).

Despite the prominence of ethnically driven motives in fueling several conflicts in the GLR, it is also plausible to think that political leaders used existing ethnical grievances to rally support and push their agendas. There are incidences where the same leaders have committed great atrocities against the very people they claim to fight for (Mkandawire 2002). The LRA rebels in Uganda (Acholi tribe) attributed their fight against the Government to ethnic discrimination of their people. However, they killed, tortured, abducted, and mutilated several of the very people from their ethnicity along the way (Allen 1991).

Armed conflicts also emerge as a result of the moral agency to revenge or reciprocate ill-treatment and behavior. Reciprocating bad behavior with bad and good with good is common behavioral economics (Fehr et al. 2002). Similarly, motives behind armed conflicts in the GLR have emerged from desires to avenge and/or reciprocate ill-treatment, usually along ethnic lines. The armed conflict in South Sudan is between the Nuer and Dinka and follows a historical path dependency of intergroup grievances (Young 2016). The Bor massacre in 1991, in which more than 2,000 Dinka people got massacred, left an indelible historical mark that motivated the Nuer White Army in South Sudan to take up arms and fight the Dinka army (Young 2016). In Uganda, the Karamoja ethnic clashes were often for revenge for the murder of relatives or retaliation for raids inflicted upon them by other tribes (Saferworld 2010).

Several governments in the region also find it a moral agency to protect their borders and thus find themselves engaged in the armed conflicts. Between 1997 and 2001, Rwanda and Uganda often participated in armed conflicts with the Interahamwe military, who had receded to Mgahinga Park bordering DRC, Rwanda, and Uganda. On their part, the Rwandan government was always skeptical of the actions of the Ugandan Government and, at some point, got convinced that Uganda was training the Interahamwe military, which is hostile to Rwanda (Kisangani 2003; Relief web 2002). In 1996, the Rwandan government made the first attack on Kivu's refugee camps with a strategy of preventing the ex-Banyamulenge soldiers who led the 1994 genocide from remustering and attacking Rwanda.

Some armed conflicts in the GLR resulted from psychic beliefs and/or religiosity. Psychic beliefs and/or religiosity may psychologically persuade individuals to ignore the likely negative consequences of armed conflict (García 2020). Many armed conflicts in the GLR in the past enticed local people to join the armed forces through the preaching of rituals and beliefs in supernatural powers that could, for example, protect warriors from bullets. Armed rebel groups like the Mayi-Mayi that fought alongside the ADFL in Congo believed in using magic water to protect rebels against weapons (Vlassenroot/Van Acker 2001). Similar beliefs were held elsewhere in Tanzania by the Maji-Maji Rebellion between 1905 and 1907 by the Lugbara in Uganda and the Dinka and Mundu in South Sudan (Jourdan 2011). In Uganda, Alice Lakwena's Holy Spirit Movement, which emerged soon after the National Resistance Army came into power, relied on spiritual beliefs, such as smearing oneself with oil to protect against bullets and being protected by a supernatural being during combat. Alice Lakwena believed she was a representative of magical powers sent to cleanse the Acholi tribe from their previous acts of murder, looting, and raiding (Allen 1991). Joseph Kony, the leader of the LRA rebellion in Uganda, held Christian mystical beliefs and exhibited religious fanaticism. He referred to himself as the 'spokesperson' of God and led a resistance based on the principles of the Ten Commandments (Allen 1991).

Armed conflict resulting from selective incentives from threat and punishment. In common, most of the armed conflicts in the region involved forceful recruitment of children as soldiers. In Uganda, of the 25,231 children and youths returning to the reception centers following the end of the LRA, 37% were children between the ages of 13 and 18, and 24% were youths aged between 19 and 30 (Pham et al. 2008). An extract below from an LRA abductee gives an account of being abducted by the LRA rebels.

> I am a 36-year-old male abducted in 2003 from a burial ceremony. I spent three months in the bush but managed to escape. My role was to carry looted items from civilians to the base of the LRA within the Lango and Teso sub-region. I was abducted again on 23 October 2004 after I had gone to a marriage ceremony in Aloi Sub-county Alebtong district with one of my brothers, and trained and armed with a gun (*Source* Author's interview with former LRA abductee).

Armed conflicts in the region have also persisted due to the availability of and access to cheap conflict capital, e.g. military equipment, which reduces armed conflict costs. The case of the newly independent South Sudan provides a useful example of how access to and availability of arms can incentivize individuals to fight. According to O'Brien (2009), after seceding from Sudan following a prolonged war, disarmament was not adequately done in South Sudan, so state security agencies and civilians had easy access to ammunition and quickly took up arms in the chaos.

Subventions from hostile governments and support from external and internal sources have also contributed to the persistence of conflict in the area because they reduce the transaction costs of engaging in war. Some countries have been hostile to their neighbors by sponsoring rebel movements to destabilize enemy nations or supporting national armies to quell the rebellion. External financing has also facilitated rebellions and the persistence of conflicts in the region. Examples include French troops assisting the Rwandan Armed Forces against the uprising by the Rwandan Patriotic Front, and the US sponsoring the training of 6,000 members of the Uganda People's Defense Forces (UPDF), which motivated the Government of Uganda to conduct an offensive attack, Operation Iron Fist, against the LRA in 2002. Non-monetary support by the local population also explains prolonged armed conflicts in the region. For example, the rebellion led by Laurent Kabila of the

ADFL relied on the support of ethnic groups opposed to Mobutu's regime (such as the Banyamulenge) to wage a rebellion against Mobutu's government (Kisangani 2003).

Positive externalities from neighboring countries related to a successful armed conflict elsewhere served as a motivating factor for other individuals and communities, particularly due to the transnational ethnic identities and refugee flows in the GLR. In 1959, the Rwandan Hutus succeeded in a bloody revolution that shifted political power from the Tutsi monarchy to the Hutu. This revolution motivated Hutus in Burundi to rebel against the power-holding Tutsi. Aware of this motive, the Tutsi held on to political power and increased their dominance to prevent a similar revolution in Burundi (Nkurunziza 2022).

2.5.2 Disincentives for Engaging in Armed Conflicts

Despite prolonged and ongoing conflicts, some positive and negative factors have been critical in quelling rebellion or preventing the onset of a battle. The threat of punishment through prosecution, litigation, or disciplinary actions and penalties for those involved in armed rebellion can potentially change behavior. Stigmatizing and isolating leaders through apprehension and persecution using existing laws and norms makes engaging in armed conflict unattractive. Also, taking action against leaders who engage in armed conflicts serves as a moral example to existing and aspiring leaders. It also increases the potential cost of war against the benefits, thus discouraging would-be participants. The Rome Statute of the International Criminal Court, a treaty that brought into use the International Criminal Court (ICC), is an example of international litigation used to prosecute genocide crimes, crimes against humanity, and war crimes at the global level. It came into force on 1 July 2002. As of November 2019, 27 African countries were signatories to the Rome Statute; DRC and Uganda are parties to the treaty. Burundi withdrew in 2017, while South Sudan and Rwanda are not parties. The International Tribunal[4] for Rwanda was set up to prosecute persons responsible for crimes such as murder and persecution. Its existence has been crucial in quieting down the likelihood of recurrences of the genocide in Rwanda. For its part, Uganda self-referred the atrocities committed by the LRA to the ICC in December 2003. Subsequently, the ICC issued a warrant for the arrest of five prominent leaders of the LRA. The ICC's involvement perhaps explains the LRA's later reduced attacks on civilians and participation at the Juba peace talks in 2006.

Disciplinary actions have taken the form of legal frameworks that hinder the exploitation of minerals such as tin and tantalum from conflict-affected countries like

[4] International Criminal Tribunals and International Criminal Courts act as forces to provide prosecution measures against those intending to commit crimes against humanity.

DRC. Examples include the Organization for Economic Cooperation and Development (OECD) Due Diligence Guideline[5] and the US Dodd-Frank Wall Street Reform and Consumer Act. The Dodd-Frank Wall Street Reform and Consumer Act instituted in 2010 requires all countries listed on the US stock exchange to provide specific assurance that any product manufactured or contracted does not contain minerals that finance or benefit armed groups in DRC and its neighbors (Bloem 2019; Cuvelier et al. 2014). Such a measure requiring transparency and strict reporting has led several companies to shun minerals from DRC and seek supply chains elsewhere. DRC, for its part, self-imposed the ban on the export of such metals for some period immediately after the passing of the Dodd-Frank Wall Street Reform and Consumer Act.

Impunity and security guarantees through amnesties have helped to quell rebellions in the region by motivating those intending to continue to fight for an unknown cause to stop and come forward. Uganda passed the Amnesty Act on 21 January 2000 to encourage LRA combatants, particularly those forcefully abducted, to renounce war and return to their communities. Following this, over 13,000 LRA former rebels returned home. Other armed groups, such as the Allied Democratic Forces, West Nile Bank Front, and Ugandan National Rescue Front, also benefited from the Amnesty.

2.6 Conclusion

Using a case study review of public documents from five countries of the GLR, namely Uganda, DRC, South Sudan, Burundi, and Rwanda, this chapter examined the factors that drive the onset and persistence of armed conflicts in the GLR. It relied on economic and noneconomic theoretical explanations relating to opportunism and grievance to describe factors driving conflict. Many economic, political, social, and cultural explanations explain the likely motives, and existing theories relate them to opportunistic or grievance (social-cultural and political) reasons.

Factors that explain the onset and persistence of wars in the region include (1) availability and access to cheap conflict capital such as military equipment, (2) support from internal and external sources, (3) a positive externality from neighboring countries, (4) grievances from high inequality and lack of political rights, (5) the moral agency to revenge or reciprocate ill-treatment, anarchy or the lack of institutions, and (6) supernatural beliefs and religiosity. Prosecution, litigation, disciplinary actions, and penalties have quelled some armed conflicts, examples being Uganda's self-referral to the ICC to defeating the LRA rebellion, the International Tribunal for Rwanda, which was essential for silencing any attempts similar to the genocide, and the Dodd-Frank Wall Street Reform and Consumer Act in the US, which is a check to prevent the sourcing of mineral wealth from conflict-affected DRC.

---

[5] The OECD Due Diligence Guideline provides recommendations that companies can voluntarily adhere to, including the policy of not purchasing conflict-related minerals as a way of not supporting conflict-related activities that don't respect human life.

For the GLR, opportunistic factors cannot be distinctly isolated from noneconomic factors when explaining armed conflicts in the region. While the desire to control or access natural resources, including land and the economic benefits associated with rebellion, explains conflicts in the area, grievances stemming from ethnic isolation due to the divisive legacies of colonialism and the governance systems in place also partly explain the conflicts in the region. In fact, all three factors explain some of the prominent conflicts in the region, including the ongoing conflict in South Sudan. Within all the five countries, the emergence of internal armed conflicts has an ethnic dimension linked to colonial times and autocratic leadership. Ethnic dominance, rather than ethnic diversity or fractionalization, seems to be the root cause of several armed conflicts. The Bush War in Uganda, the RPF rebellion in Rwanda, the LRA rebellion in Uganda, the Mayi-Mayi revolt in DRC, the several conflicts that have marred Burundi's small nation, and the current active conflict in South Sudan are motivated by discrimination and marginalization. Discrimination and marginalization along the lines of ethnicity emanate from the largely autocratic political system in the region that supports the enrichment of elites or a dominant ethnic. Despite this, it is challenging to separate ethnic arguments from greed or opportunistic incentives by rebel leaders to acquire mineral wealth, gain positions of power, or loot. The timing and geographical placement of conflicts in all countries in the GLR, including South Sudan, closely follow changes in regimes or leadership, highlighting the importance of political leadership in initiating disputes in the region. The conflicts in the area also have a historical colonial dimension and an international dimension. Past colonial masters continuously have a direct hand in quelling rebellions or providing foreign aid assistance to former colonies. Some conflicts in the DRC started because of the refugee influx from Rwanda into DRC, and their subsequent antagonization of the local communities around the Kivu region also tends to disregard the notion that natural resources cause armed conflict. Instead, natural resources are more likely to sustain or increase the battle's duration as rebels loot minerals.

Economic theoretical models also limit understanding of the motives for conflict, with no explanations provided for factors such as the historical path dependence of armed conflicts in the region and the neighboring effect (to protect territory). Importantly, the incentives that motivated individuals and communities to engage in armed conflict in the past still persist and remain the primary motives behind current active armed conflicts. Countries also continue to meddle in other countries' armed conflicts, creating an environment of suspicion and untrustworthiness. Governments need to pay closer attention to these incentives to stop repeating historical armed conflicts in the region.

Appendix

See Fig. 2.6.

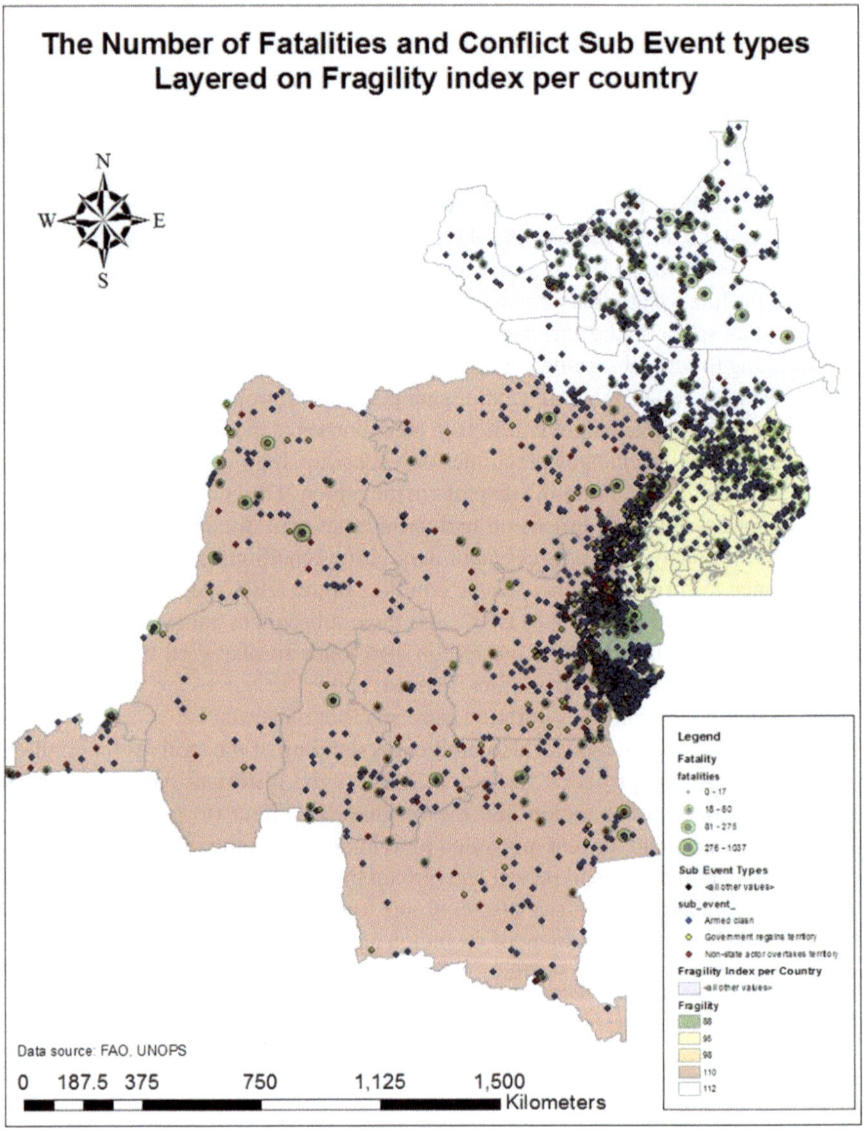

Fig. 2.6 Armed Conflicts in the Great Lake Region. *Source* Author's construction based on ACLED from 1997–2019

References

Acemoglu, D., Vindigni, A., & Ticchi, D. (2010). Persistence of Civil Wars. *European Economic Association*, *8*(May), 664–676.

Adelman, S., & Peterman, A. (2014). Resettlement and gender dimensions of land rights in post-conflict Northern Uganda. *World Development*, *64*, 583–596. https://doi.org/10.1016/j.worlddev.2014.06.031

Ager, A., & Strang, A. (2008). Understanding Integration: A Conceptual Framework. *Journal of Refugee Studies*, *21*(2), 166–191. https://doi.org/10.1093/jrs/fen016

Ahabwe, G., & Depio, S. (2019). *How Effective is the Self-Reliance Agenda in Uganda's* (Issue 107).

Akerlof, G. A., & Kranton, R. E. (2000). Economics and Identity. *Economics and Identity*, *CXV*(3), 715–753.

Akresh, R., Lucchetti, L., & Thirumurthy, H. (2012). Wars and child health: Evidence from the Eritrean – Ethiopian conflict. *Journal of Development Economics*, *99*(2), 330–340. https://doi.org/10.1016/j.jdeveco.2012.04.001

Allen, D., & Lueck, D. (1992). Contract Choice in Modern Agriculture: Cash Rent versus Cropshare. *The Journal of Law and Economics*, *35*(2), 397–426. http://www.jstor.com/stable/725546

Allen, T. (1991). Understanding Alice: Uganda's Holy spirit Movement in Context. *Journal of the International African Institute*, *61*(3), 370–399. https://www.jstor.org/stable/1160031?seq=1#metadata_info_tab_contents

Allen, T., & Koen, V. (2010). *The Lord's Resistance Army: Myth and Reality* (T. Allen & K. Vlassenroot (eds.); Issue November). Zed Books Ltd. http://www.zedbooks.co.uk/

Andreoni, J., & Bernheim, D. (2009). Social image and the 50–50 norm: a theoretical and experimental analysis of audience effects. *Econometrica*, *77*(5), 1607–1636. https://doi.org/10.3982/ECTA7384

Andreoni, J., & Miller, J. (2002). Giving According to GARP: An Experimental Test of the Consistency of Preferences for Altruism. *Econometrica*, *70*(2), 737–753.

Annan, J., Blattman, C., Mazurana, D., & Carlson, K. (2011). Civil war, reintegration, and gender in northern Uganda. *Journal of Conflict Resolution*, *55*(6), 877–908. https://doi.org/10.1177/0022002711408013

Ashraf, N., Bohnet, I., & Piankov, N. (2006). Decomposing trust and trustworthiness. *Experimental Economics*, *9*(3), 193–208. https://doi.org/10.1007/s10683-006-9122-4

Ashraf, N., Gine, X., & Karlan, D. (2009). Finding missing markets (and a disturbing epilogue): Evidence from an export crop adoption and marketing intervention in Kenya. *American Journal of Agricultural Economics*, *91*(November), 973–990. https://doi.org/10.1111/j.1467-8276.2009.01319.x

Bakwesegha, C., Brubaker, R., Connor, W., Ellis, A., Esman, M., Hannan, H., Hechter, M., Kalin, W., Lemarchand, R., Lund, Michaels, S., van der Stoel, M., Miall, H., Zartmann, William, I., Ropers, N., Rothchild, D., Tishkov, Valery, A., Vinas, A., & Waldman, P. (2004). Facing Ethnic Conflicts: Toward a New Realism. In G. Wimmer (Ed.), *Toward a new realism*. Rowman & Littlefield Publishers, 2004. https://books.google.de/books?id=DdtOAQAAQBAJ&dq=conrad+schetter+conflict&lr=&source=gbs_navlinks_s

Barr, A. (2003). Trust and expected trustworthiness: Experimental evidence from Zimbabwean villages. *Economic Journal*, *113*(489), 614–630. https://doi.org/10.1111/1468-0297.t01-1-00150

Bauer, M., Blattman, C., Chytilová, J., Henrich, J., Miguel, E., & Mitts, T. (2016). Can War Foster Cooperation? *Journal of Economic Perspectives*, *30*(3), 249–274. https://doi.org/10.1257/jep.30.3.249

Bauer, M., Fiala, N., & Levely, I. (2018). Trusting Former Rebels: An Experimental Approach to Understanding Reintegration after Civil War. *Economic Journal*, *128*(613), 1786–1819. https://doi.org/10.1111/ecoj.12503

Baumgartner, T., Götte, L., Gügler, R., & Fehr, E. (2012). The mentalizing network orchestrates the impact of parochial altruism on social norm enforcement. *Human Brain Mapping*, *33*(6), 1452–1469. https://doi.org/10.1002/hbm.21298

Bellemare, C., & Kröger, S. (2007). On representative social capital. *European Economic Review*, *51*(1), 183–202. https://doi.org/10.1016/j.euroecorev.2006.03.006

Bellows, J., & Miguel, E. (2006). War and institutions: New evidence from Sierra Leone. *American Economic Review*, *96*(2), 394–399. https://doi.org/10.1257/000282806777212323

Bellows, J., & Miguel, E. (2009). War and local collective action in Sierra Leone. *Journal of Public Economics*, *93*(11–12), 1144–1157. https://doi.org/10.1016/j.jpubeco.2009.07.012

Bennett, D. S., & Stam, A. C. (2016). The Duration of Interstate Wars, 1816–1985 Author(s): D. Scott Bennett and Allan C. Stam III Source: The American Political Science Review, Vol. 90, No. 2 (Jun., 1996), pp. 239–257 Published by: American Political Science Association Stabl. *The American Political Science Review*, *90*(2), 239–257.

Berg, J., Dickhaut, J., & McCabe, K. (1995). Trust, reciprocity, and social history. *Games and Economic Behavior*, *10*(1), 122–142. https://doi.org/10.1006/game.1995.1027

Bernhard, H., Fischbacher, U., & Fehr, E. (2006). Parochial altruism in humans. *Nature*, *442*(7105), 912–915. https://doi.org/10.1038/nature04981

Besley, T., & Persson, T. (2008a). The Incidence of Civil War: Theory and Evidence. In Intergovernmental Panel on Climate Change (Ed.), *NBER Working paper series* (Vol. 14585). Cambridge University Press. https://doi.org/10.3386/w14585

Besley, T., & Persson, T. (2008b). The Incidence of Civil War: Theory and Evidence. In Intergovernmental Panel on Climate Change (Ed.), *NBER Working paper series* (Vol. 14585). Cambridge University Press. https://doi.org/10.3386/w14585

Binswanger, H. P., & Rosenzweig, M. R. (1981). Contractual arrangements, Employment and wages in rural labor markets: A critical review. In *Studies in employment & rural development series* (Issue SER 67). http://documents.worldbank.org/curated/en/412971467997610342/Contractual-arrangements-employment-and-wages-in-rural-labor-markets-a-critical-review

Blattman, C., & Annan, J. (2010). The Consequences of Child Soldiering. *Review of Economics and Statistics*, *92*(4), 882. https://doi.org/10.1162/REST_a_00036

Blattman, C., & Miguel, E. (2010). Civil War. *Journal of Economic Literature*, *48*(1), 3–57. https://doi.org/10.1257/jel.48.1.3

Bloem, J. (2019). Good Intentions Gone Bad? The Dodd-Frank Act and Conflict in Africa's Great Lakes Region. In *HiCN*.

Bohnet, H., & Schmitz, C. P. (2019). *Uganda: A role model for refugee integration?* (No. 2; 2019).

Brosché, J., & Höglund, K. (2016). Crisis of governance in South Sudan: Electoral politics and violence in the world's newest nation. *Journal of Modern African Studies*, *54*(1), 67–90. https://doi.org/10.1017/S0022278X15000828

Brück, T., D'Errico, M., & Pietrelli, R. (2018). The effects of violent conflict on household resilience and food security: Evidence from the 2014 Gaza conflict. *World Development*, *2018*. https://doi.org/10.1016/j.worlddev.2018.05.008

Bundervoet, T., Verwimp, P., & Akresh, R. (2009). Health and civil war in rural Burundi. *Journal of Human Resources*, *44*(2), 536–563. https://doi.org/10.3368/jhr.44.2.536

Burke, M., & Young, P. (2009). Social Norms. In A. Bisin, J. Benhabib, & M. Jackson (Eds.), *The Handbook of Social Economics* (pp. 1–51).

Burks, S. V., Carpenter, J. P., & Verhoogen, E. (2003). Playing both roles in the trust game.pdf. *Journal of Economic Behaviour and Organisation*, *51*, 195–216. https://doi.org/10.1016/S0167-2681(02)00093-8

Cameron, A. C., Gelbach, J. B., & Miller, D. L. (2007). *Nber Technical Working Paper Series*. *90*(August), 414–427. https://pdfs.semanticscholar.org/df0a/ff0cb4db55166abbf5e33696d67698f81d3d.pdf%5Cnhttp://www.mitpressjournals.org/doi/pdf/10.1162/rest.90.3.414

Cesarini, D., Dawes, C. T., Fowler, J. H., Johannesson, M., & Lichtenstein, P. (2008). Heritability of cooperative behaviour in the trust game. *PNAS*, *105*(10), 3721–3726. https://doi.org/10.1073/pnas.0710069105

Charness, G., & Rabin, M. (2002). Understanding Social Preferences with Simple Tests. *The Quarterly Journal of Economics*, *117*(3), 817–869. http://www.jstor.org/
Chaudhuri, A., Paichayontvijit, T., & Shen, L. (2013a). Gender differences in trust and trustworthiness: Individuals, single sex and mixed sex groups. *Journal of Economic Psychology*, *34*, 181–194. https://doi.org/10.1016/j.joep.2012.09.013
Chaudhuri, A., Paichayontvijit, T., & Shen, L. (2013b). Gender differences in trust and trustworthiness: Individuals, single sex and mixed sex groups. *Journal of Economic Psychology*, *34*, 181–194. https://doi.org/10.1016/j.joep.2012.09.013
Chen, Y., & Li, S. X. (2009). Group identity and social preferences. *American Economic Review*, *99*(1), 431–457. https://doi.org/10.1257/aer.99.1.431
Coggio, T. (2019). Can Uganda's Breakthrough Refugee-Hosting Model Be Sustained? *Migration Policy Institute*, 1–11. https://www.migrationpolicy.org
Collier, P. (1999). On the Economic Consequences of Civil War. *Oxford Economic Papers*, *51*(January 1999), 168–183.
Collier, P., & Hoeffler, A. (2004). Greed and grievance in civil war. *Oxford Economic Papers*, *56*(2004), 563–595. https://doi.org/10.1093/oep/gpf064
Collier, P., Hoeffler, A., & Söderbom, M. (2004). Collier 2004 – Duration of civil wars. *Journal of Peace Research*, *41*(3), 253–273.
Cox, J. C. (2004a). How to identify trust and reciprocity. *Games and Economic Behavior*, *46*(2), 260–281. https://doi.org/10.1016/S0899-8256(03)00119-2
Cox, J. C. (2004b). How to identify trust and reciprocity. *Games and Economic Behavior*, *8256*(03), 260–281. https://doi.org/10.1016/S0899-8256(03)00119-2
Cramer, C. (2002). Homo Economicus Goes to War: Methodological Individualism, Rational Choice and the Political Economy of War. *World Development*, *30*(11), 1845–1864. https://doi.org/10.1016/S0305-750X(02)00120-1
Cunningham, D. E., Gleditsch, K. S., & Salehyan, I. (2009). It Takes Two: A Dyadic Analysis of Civil War Duration and Outcome. *Journal of Conflict Resolution*, *53*(4), 570–597. https://www.jstor.org/stable/20684603?seq=1#metadata_info_tab_contents
Cuvelier, J., Van Bockstaal, S., Vlassenroot, K., & Iguma, C. (2014). Analyzing the Impact of the Dodd-Frank Act on Congolese Livelihoods. In *Conflict Prevention and Peace Forum* (Vol. 1, Issue November). https://doi.org/10.1017/CBO9781107415324.004
d'Errico, M., Winters, P., & Romano, D. (2024). Assessing Uganda's Progressive Refugee Policy in the Era of COVID-19: Introduction to the Special Issue. *Journal of Development Studies*, *60*(3), 351–359. https://doi.org/10.1080/00220388.2023.2282364
Deininger, K., & Feder, G. (2001). Chapter 6 Land institutions and land markets. In B. Gardner & G. Rausser (Eds.), *Handbook of Agricultural Economics* (2001st ed., Vol. 1, Issue PART A, pp. 287–331). Elsevier Science B.V. https://doi.org/10.1016/S1574-0072(01)10009-5
Denison, R. F., & Muller, K. (2016). The evolution of cooperation. *Scientist*, *30*(1). https://doi.org/10.5840/tpm201467114
Dessalegn, A. G. (2017). The Cause and Consequence of Conflict in South Sudan. *International Journal of Political Science and Development*, *5*(1), 15–21. https://doi.org/10.14662/IJPSD2016.063
Development Pathways. (2018). *Analysis of Refugee Vulnerability in Uganda and Recommendations for Improved Targeting of Food Assistance* (Issue April 2018).
di Montenegro, T. X. (2017). *China's Interest in Africa: Conflict or Stability?* [Florida International University]. https://doi.org/10.25148/etd.FIDC001790
Elwert, G. (2018). Intervention in markets of violence. In *Potentials of disorder* (Issue September 2001, pp. 219–242). Manchester University Press. https://doi.org/10.7765/9781526137586.00017
Eswaran, M., & Kotwal, A. (1985). A Theory of Contractual Structure in Agriculture. *The American Economic Review*, *75*(3), 352–367.
Everett, J. A. C., Faber, N. S., & Crockett, M. (2015). Preferences and beliefs in ingroup favoritism. *Frontiers in Behavioral Neuroscience*, *9*(FEB), 1–21. https://doi.org/10.3389/fnbeh.2015.00015

Everts, E. (2003). Identifying a particular family humor style: A sociolinguistic discourse analysis. *Humor – International Journal of Humor Research, 16*(4), 752. https://doi.org/10.1515/humr.2003.021

FAO. (2018). *Food Security, Resilience and Well-Being Analysis of Refugees and Host Communities in Northern Uganda.* https://doi.org/10.11975/j.issn.1002-6819.2015.24.025

FAO, & World Food Program. (2018). *Monitoring food security in countries with conflict situations: A joint FAO/WFP update for the United Nations Security Council* (Issue 3).

Fearon, J. D. (1995). Rationalist Explanations for War Author. *International Organization, 49*(3), 379–414.

Fehr, E. (2009). On the Economics and Biology of Trust. *European Economic Association, 7*(2–3), 235–266.

Fehr, E., Fischbacher, U., & Gächter, S. (2002). Strong reciprocity, human cooperation, and the enforcement of social norms. *Human Nature, 13*(1), 1–25. https://doi.org/10.1007/s12110-002-1012-7

Fehr, E., & Schmidt, K. M. (1999). A Theory of Fairness, Competition, and Cooperation. *The Quarterly Journal of Economics, 114*(3), 817–868. https://doi.org/10.1162/003355399556151

Fershtman, C., & Gneezy, U. (2001a). Discrimination in a Segmented Society: An Experimental Approach. *The Quarterly Journal of Economics.* https://rady.ucsd.edu/faculty/directory/gneezy/pub/docs/discrimination-society.pdf

Fershtman, C., & Gneezy, U. (2001b). Discrimination in a Segmented Society: An Experimental Approach. *The Quarterly Journal of Economics.*

Fisman, B. R., Kariv, S., & Markovits, D. (2007). Individual Preferences for Giving. *The American Economic Review, 97*(5).

Fisman, R., Jakiela, P., & Kariv, S. (2017). Distributional preferences and political behavior. *Journal of Public Economics, 155*, 1–10. https://doi.org/10.1016/j.jpubeco.2017.08.010

García, A. D. (2020). Armed groups, IHL and the invisible world: How spiritual beliefs shape warfare. *International Review of the Red Cross, 102*(915), 1179–1199. https://doi.org/10.1017/S1816383121000229

Gates, S. (2015). Recruitment , Retention , and Religion in Rebel Groups. In *"Peace, Conflict, and Development", ESOP,* (Issue March 2015).

Geanakoplosand, J., Pearce, D., & Ennio, S. (1989). Psychological Games and Sequential Rationality. *Games and Economic Behaviour, 1*(1989), 60–79.

Gebregziabher, G., & Holden, S. T. (2011). Distress rentals and the land rental market as a safety net: Contract choice evidence from Tigray, Ethiopia. *Agricultural Economics, 42*(SUPPL. 1), 45–60. https://doi.org/10.1111/j.1574-0862.2011.00551.x

Ghatak, M., & Karaivanov, A. (2014). Contractual structure in agriculture with endogenous matching. *Journal of Development Economics, 110*, 239–249. https://doi.org/10.1016/j.jdeveco.2013.05.005

Ghobarah, H. A., Huth, P., & Russett, B. (2003). and Maim the Shooting Wars Kill Civil People-Long After Stops. *The American Political Science Review, 97*(2), 189–202. http://www.jstor.org/stable/3118203

Glaeser, E. L., Laibson, D. I., Scheinkman, J. A., & Soutter, C. L. (2000). Glaeser et al 2000_article.pdf. *Quarterly Journal of Economics, 115*(3), 811–846.

Grossman, H. (1991). A General Equilibrium Model of Insurrections. In *American Economic Review* (Vol. 81, Issue 4, pp. 912–921). https://doi.org/10.2307/2006650

Guerrero, S. (2009). The Effects of the War in Iraq on Nutrition and Health: An Analysis Using Anthropometric Outcomes of Children. *SSRN Electronic Journal, 14056.* https://doi.org/10.2139/ssrn.1359161

Guerrero Serdan, G. (2009). The Effects of the War in Iraq on Nutrition and Health: An Analysis Using Anthropometric Outcomes of Children. *SSRN Electronic Journal, 14056.* https://doi.org/10.2139/ssrn.1359161

Harris, C., Jenkins, M., & Glaser, D. (2006). Gender Differences in Risk Assessment: Why do women take fewer risks than men? *Judgement and Decision Making, 1*(1), 48–63. http://journal.sjdm.org/jdm06016.pdf

Hartman, A. C., & Morse, B. S. (2018). Violence, Empathy and Altruism: Evidence from the Ivorian Refugee Crisis in Liberia. *British Journal of Political Science*, 1–25. https://doi.org/10.1017/S0007123417000655

Haselhuhn, M. P., Kennedy, J. A., Kray, L. J., Van Zant, A. B., & Schweitzer, M. E. (2015). Gender differences in trust dynamics: Women trust more than men following a trust violation. *Journal of Experimental Social Psychology, 56*, 104–109. https://doi.org/10.1016/j.jesp.2014.09.007

Henrich, J., Boyd, R., & Bowles, S. (2005). "Economic Man" in Cross-Cultural Perspective: Ethnography and Experiments from 15 Small-Scale Societies. *Behavioral and Brain Sciences, 28*(2005), 795–855.

Henrich, J., Ensminger, J., Mcelreath, R., Barr, A., Barrett, C., Bolyanatz, A., Cardenas, J. C., Gurven, M., Gwako, E., Henrich, N., Lesorogol, C., Marlowe, F., Tracer, D., & Ziker, J. (2010). Markets, Religion, Community size, and the Evolution of Fairness and Punishment. *Science, 327*(March 2010), 1480–1484. https://doi.org/10.1126/science.1182238

Henrich, J., McElreath, R., Barr, A., Ensminger, J., Barrett, C., Bolyanatz, A., Cardaroas, J. C., Gurven, M., Gwako, E., Henrich, N., Lesoronol, C., Marlowe, F., Tracer, D., & Ziker, J. (2006a). Costly punishment across human societies. *Science, 312*(5781), 1767–1770. https://doi.org/10.1126/science.1127333

Henrich, J., McElreath, R., Barr, A., Ensminger, J., Barrett, C., Bolyanatz, A., Cardenas, J. C., Gurven, M., Gwako, E., Henrich, N., Lesorogol, C., Marlowe, F., Tracer, D., & Ziker, J. (2006b). Costly punishment across human societies. MATERIAL RESPALDO. *Science (New York, N.Y.), 312*(5781), 1767–1770. https://doi.org/10.1126/science.1127333

Hirshleifer, J. (1995). Theorizing about conflict. In K. Hartley & T. Sandler (Eds.), *Handbook of Defense Economics* (Vol. 1, pp. 165–189). Elsevier. https://doi.org/10.1016/S1574-0013(05)80009-2

Hoeffler, A. (2012). On the Causes of Civil War. In *Oxford Economic Papers* (Vol. 50). Oxford University Press. https://doi.org/10.1093/oxfordhb/9780195392777.013.0009

Holden, S. T., & Otsuka, K. (2014). The roles of land tenure reforms and land markets in the context of population growth and land use intensification in Africa. *Food Policy, 48*, 88–97. https://doi.org/10.1016/j.foodpol.2014.03.005

Hovil, L. (2001). *Refuges and the Security Situation in Adjumani District* (Refugee Law Project, Issue 2).

Jakiela, P. (2011). Using economic experiments to measure informal institutions. In W. University (Ed.), *The Legacy and Work of Douglass C. North: Understanding Institutions and Development Economics* (pp. 248–265). Department of Economics, Washington University. https://doi.org/10.1017/CBO9781107300361.013

Johnson, N. D., & Mislin, A. A. (2011). Trust games: A meta-analysis. *Journal of Economic Psychology, 32*(5), 865–889. https://doi.org/10.1016/j.joep.2011.05.007

Joras, U., & Schetter, C. (2004). Hidden ties: Similarities between Research and Policy Approaches to Ethnic Conflicts. In G. Wimmer & U. D. Howowitz (Eds.), *Facing Ethnic Conflicts. Towards a New Realism* (pp. 315–332). Lanham, Rowman & Littlefield.

Jourdan, L. (2011). Mayi-Mayi: Young rebels in Kivu, DRC. *Africa Development, 36*(3–4), 89–111.

Karlan, D. S. (2005). Using Experimental Economics to Measure Social Capital and Predict Financial Decisions. *American Economic Review, 95*(5 (Dec., 2005)), 1688–1699. https://www.jstor.org/stable/4132772

Keswell, M., & Carter, M. R. (2014). Poverty and land redistribution. *Journal of Development Economics, 110*, 250–261. https://doi.org/10.1016/j.jdeveco.2013.10.003

Kimbrough, E. O., & Vostroknutov, A. (2016). Norms Make Preferences Social. *Journal of the European Economic Association, 14*(3), 608–638. https://doi.org/10.1111/jeea.12152

Kisangani, E. (2003). Conflict in the Democratic Republic of Congo: A mosaic of insurgent groups. *International Journal of World Peace, 20*(3), 51–80. www.jstor.org/stable/20753410

Kosfeld, M., Heinrichs, M., Zak, P. J., Fischbacher, U., & Fehr, E. (2005). Oxytocin increases trust in humans. *Nature, 435*(7042), 673–676. https://doi.org/10.1038/nature03701
Kosfeld, M., & Rustagi, D. (2015). Leader punishment and cooperation in groups: Experimental field evidence from commons management in Ethiopia. *American Economic Review, 105*(2), 747–783. https://doi.org/10.1257/aer.20120700
Kreibaum, M. (2016). Their Suffering, Our Burden? How Congolese Refugees Affect the Ugandan Population. *World Development, 78*, 262–287. https://doi.org/10.1016/j.worlddev.2015.10.019
Lemarchand, R. (2008). The Burundi Killings of 1972. In *Online Encyclopedia of Mass Violence* (Issue June). https://www.sciencespo.fr/mass-violence-war-massacre-resistance/en/document/burundi-killings-1972.html
Loewenstein, G., & Thompson, L. (1989). Social utility and Decision making in interpersonal contexts. *Journal of Personality and Social Psychology, 57*(3), 426–441.
Ma, T. (2009). China and Congo's coltan connection. In *Project 2049 Institute.*
Martiniello, G. (2010). African land questions, agrarian transitions and the state: the contradictions of neo-liberal land reforms. *Review of African Political Economy, 37*(125), 387–389. https://doi.org/10.1080/03056244.2010.511784
Maystadt, J.-F., & Verwimp, P. (2014). Winners and Losers among a Refugee-Hosting Population. *Economic Development and Cultural Change, 62*(4), 769–809. https://doi.org/10.1086/676458
Melander, E., Pettersson, T., & Themnér, L. (2016). Organized violence, 1989–2015. *Journal of Peace Research, 53*(5), 727–742. https://doi.org/10.1177/0022343316663032
Merkx, J. (2000). Document. Refugee identities and relief in an African borderland: a study of northern Uganda and southern Sudan. In *New issues in Refugee Research* (Vol. 21, Issue 19). https://doi.org/10.1093/rsq/21.1_and_2.113
Mkandawire, T. (2002). The terrible toll of post-colonial "rebel movements" in Africa: Towards an explanation of the violence against the peasantry. *Journal of Modern African Studies, 40*(2), 181–215. https://doi.org/10.1017/S0022278X02003889
Mkandawire, T. (2015). Neopatrimonialism and the Political Economy of Economic Performance in Africa: Critical Reflections. *World Politics, 67*(3), 563–612. https://doi.org/10.1017/S0043887115000009X
Ngaruko, F., & Nkirunziza, J. (2000). An economic interpretation of conflict in Burundi. *Journal of African Economies, 9*(3), 370–409. https://doi.org/10.1093/jae/9.3.370
Nindorera, W. (2012). *The CNDD-FDD in Burundi: The path from armed to political struggle* (Issue 10).
Nkurunziza, J. D. (2015). Timing and Sequencing of Post-Conflict Reconstruction and Peace-building in Burundi. In *CRPD Working Paper* (Issue 34). https://doi.org/10.1093/acprof:oso/9780198757276.003.0013
Nkurunziza, J. D. (2022). The origin and persistence of state fragility in Burundi. In *State Fragility, Growth and Development* (Issue April). https://doi.org/10.4324/9781003297697-4
Nshimirimana, F. (2024). *Exclusionary Governance in Burundi:Implications for Democracy and Consolidating Peace.*
Nyadera, I. N. (2018). South Sudan conflict from 2013 to 2018: Rethinking the causes, situation and solutions. *African Journal on Conflict Resolution, 18*(2), 59–86.
O'Brien, A. (2009). Shots in the Dark: The 2008 South Sudan Civilian Disarmament Campaign. In *HSBA Working Paper*.
Odera, L. C. (2013). The Role of Trust as an Informal Institution in the Informal Sector in Africa. *Africa Development, 38*(3–4), 121 – 146.
Peterson, R. (2001). Resistance and Rebellion; Lessons from Eastern Europe. In *Cambrige University Press*. https://doi.org/10.1007/BF02430448
Pham, P. N., Vinck, P., & Stover, E. (2008). The Lord's Resistance Army and Forced Conscription in Northern Uganda. *Human Rights Quarterly, 30*(2008), 404–411.
Poole, L. (2019). *The refugee response in northern Uganda: Resources beyond international humanitarian assistance* (No. 2019; HPG Working Paper, Issue February). www.odi.org/hpg

Powell, R. (2006). War as a commitment problem. *International Organization, 60*(1), 169–203. https://doi.org/10.1017/S0020818306060061

Rabbie, J. M., Schot, J. C., & Visser, L. (1989). Social identity theory: A conceptual and empirical critique from the perspective of a behavioural interaction model. *European Journal of Social Psychology, 19*(3), 171–202. https://doi.org/10.1002/ejsp.2420190302

Rabellino, D., Morese, R., Ciaramidaro, A., Bara, B. G., & Bosco, F. M. (2016). Third-party punishment: altruistic and anti-social behaviours in in-group and out-group settings. *Journal of Cognitive Psychology, 28*(4), 486–495. https://doi.org/10.1080/20445911.2016.1138961

Rabin, M. (1993). Incorporating fairness into game theory and economics. *The American Economic Review, 83*(5), 1281–1302. http://www.jstor.org/stable/2117561

Raleigh, C., Linke, A., Hegre, H., & Karlsen, J. (2010). Introducing ACLED-Armed Conflict Location and Event Data. *Journal of Peace Research, 47*(5), 651–660.

Refugee law project. (2022). Negotiating peace: Resolution of Conflicts in Uganda's West Nile Region. In *Refugee Law Project Working Paper* (Issue 12). https://doi.org/10.4324/9781003317487-18

Relief web. (2002). *Rwanda-Uganda: Interahamwe reported present in Uganda.* https://reliefweb.int/report/democratic-republic-congo/rwanda-uganda-interahamwe-reported-present-uganda

Rockmore, M. (2017). The cost of fear: The welfare effect of the risk of violence in Northern Uganda. *World Bank Economic Review, 31*(3), 650–669. https://doi.org/10.1093/wber/lhw025

Rockmore, M. (2020). Conflict-Risk and Agricultural Portfolios: Evidence from Northern Uganda. *The Journal of Development Studies, 2016*, 1–21. https://doi.org/10.1080/00220388.2019.1703953

Rufanges, C. J., & Aspa, J. M. R. (2016). *Democratic Republic of Congo: A Review of 20 years of war* (Issue April). https://escolapau.uab.cat/img/programas/alerta/alerta/RDCongo_20AnosGuerra_I.pdf

Saferworld. (2010). Karamoja conflict and security assessment. In *Report* (Issue September).

Shemyakina, O. (2011). The effect of armed conflict on accumulation of schooling: Results from Tajikistan. *Journal of Development Economics, 95*(2), 186–200. https://doi.org/10.1016/j.jdeveco.2010.05.002

Sigman, R., & Lindberg, S. I. (2017). Neopatrimonialism and Democracy: An Empirical Investigation of Africa's Political Regimes. *SSRN Electronic Journal, January.* https://doi.org/10.2139/ssrn.3066654

Skaperdas, S. (2008). An economic approach to analyzing civil wars. *Economics of Governance, 9*(1), 25–44. https://doi.org/10.1007/s10101-007-0043-2

State Parties to the 1951 Convention relating to the Status of Refugees and the 1967 Protocol, (2011). https://doi.org/10.1093/rsq/hdn023

Tajfel, H., Billig, M. G., & Bundy, R. (1971). Social categorization and intergroup behaviour. *European Journal of Social Pszchology, 1*(2), 149–178. https://doi.org/10.1002/ejsp.2420010202

The Fund For Peace. (2019). *Fragile States Index Annual Report 2019.* www.fundforpeace.org

Titeca, K. (2024). Uganda and the DRC conflict: the interests driving Kampala's involvement. *The Conversation*, 23–26.

Uganda Bureau of Statistics. (2024a). National Population and Housing Census 2024: Preliminary Results. In *National Population and Household Census* (Vol. 256, Issue June).

Uganda Bureau of Statistics. (2024b). National Population and Housing Census 2024. In *Census 2024.* http://libdcms.nida.ac.th/thesis6/2010/b166706.pdf

UN, & African Union. (2011). *Fifth Anniversary of the signing of the Peace, Security and Cooperation Framework (PSCF)* (Vol. 16, Issue 0).

UNDP. (2017). *Summary of Study Uganda's Contribution To.* https://data2.unhcr.org/en/documents/download/64687

UNECA. (2015). *Conflicts in the Democratic Republic of Congo: Causes, impact and implications for the Great Lakes region.* Routledge. https://www.uneca.org/sites/default/files/PublicationFiles/conflits_in_drc_eng_25sept_rev1.pdf

UNECA. (2016). Conflict in the democratic Republic of Congo: Causes, impact and implications for the Great Lakes region. In *Routledge Handbook of Security Studies: Second Edition*. https://doi.org/10.4324/9781315753393

UNHCR. (2018). *South Sudan Regional Refugee Response Plan* (Issue December). http://reporting.unhcr.org/sites/default/files/2018SouthSudanRegionalRefugeeResponsePlan-Jan-Dec 2018%28January2018%29_0.pdf

UNHCR. (2019a). *Global Trends Forced Displacemnet in 2018*. www.unhcr.org/5c6fb2d04

UNHCR. (2019b). Uganda Country Refugee Response Plan. *The UN Refugee Agency, Jan 2019–Dec 2020*, 72. http://reporting.unhcr.org/sites/default/files/UgandaCountryRRP2019-20%28January2019%29.pdf

United Nations Development Programme. (2018). *Understanding land dynamics and livelihood in refugee hosting districts of northern Uganda.*

United Nations High Commision for Refugees (UNHCR), & Government of Uganda (GoU). (2019). *Refugee and Host Population by District*. Uganda Comprehensive Refugee Response Portal. https://data2.unhcr.org/en/country/uga

Venugopalan, H. (2016). Understanding the Conflict in Congo. In *ORF ISSUE BRIEF* (Issue May). https://www.orfonline.org/wp-content/uploads/2016/05/ORF_IssueBrief_139_Venugopalan_Final.pdf

Vlassenroot, K., & Van Acker, F. (2001). War as Exit from Exclusion? The Formation of Mayi-Mayi Militias in Eastern Congo. *Afrika Focus, 17*(1–2), 51–77. https://doi.org/10.21825/af.v17i1-2.5426

von Braun, J., Teklu, T., & Webb, P. (1998). *Famine in Africa. Causes, Response and Prevention.* The John Hopkins Univerisity Press.

Voors, M. J., Nillesen, E. E. M., Verwimp, P., Bulte, E. H., Lensink, R., & Soest, D. P. Van. (2012a). Violent Conflict and Behavior: A field experiment in Burundi. *American Economic Review, 102*(2), 941–964.

Voors, M. J., Nillesen, E. E. M., Verwimp, P., Bulte, E. H., Lensink, R., & Van Soest, D. P. (2012b). Violent Conflict and Behaviour: a field experiment in Burundi. *Source: The American Economic Review, 102*(2), 941–964. https://doi.org/10.1257/aer.102.2.941

Wallensteen, P., & Axell, K. (1993). Armed Conflict at the End of the Cold War , 1989–92. *Journal of Peace Research, 30*(3), 331–346.

Werner, K., & Lambsdorff, J. G. (2019). Emotional Numbing and Lessons Learned after a Violent Conflict – Experimental Evidence from Ambon, Indonesia. *The Journal of Development Studies*, 1–15. https://doi.org/10.1080/00220388.2019.1590550

Whyte, S. R., & Acio, E. (2017). Generations and Access to Land in Postconflict Northern Uganda: Youth Have No Voice in Land Matters. *African Studies Review, 60*(3), 17–36. https://doi.org/10.1017/asr.2017.120

World Bank. (2015). *Forced Displacement in the Great Lakes Region*. http://hdl.handle.net/10986/21708

World Bank. (2016). *The Uganda Poverty Assessment Report 2016. Farms, cities and good fortune: assessing poverty reduction in Uganda from 2006 to 2013*. http://pubdocs.worldbank.org/en/890971474327477241/Uganda-Poverty-Assessment-Report-2016-Overview.pdf

WorldBank. (2016). *The Uganda Poverty Assessment Report, 2016: Farms, Cities and good fortune: assessing poverty reduction in Uganda from 2006 to 2013.*

Yami, M., & van Asten, P. (2018). Relevance of informal institutions for achieving sustainable crop intensification in Uganda. *Food Security, 10*(1), 141–150. https://doi.org/10.1007/s12571-017-0754-3

Young, J. (2016). Popular struggles and elite co-optation: the Nuer White Army in South Sudan's Civil War. In E. LeBrun (Ed.), *Small Arms Survey*. Graduate Institute of International and Development studies.
Zhu, H., Filipski, M., Valli, J., Gonzalez, E., Gupta, A., & Taylor, J. E. (2016a). *Economic Impact of Refugee Settlements in Uganda* (Issue November).
Zhu, H., Taylor, J. E., Gupta, A., Filipski, M., Valli, J., & Gonzalez, E. E. (2016b). Economic Impacts of Giving Land to Refugees. In *Agricultural and Applied Economics Association 2018 Annual Meeting*. Agricultural and Applied Economics Association. https://doi.org/10.22004/ag.econ.274212

Chapter 3
Prosocial Attitudes in Forced Displacement: Evidence from Northern Uganda

3.1 Introduction

Armed conflicts are associated with the displacement of multitudes of people forced to flee from the comfort of their homes to other countries as refugees. The countries or communities to which they flee have their own identities characterized by similar norms, ethnicity, religion, and taboos. Hosting refugees who differ in social identity creates a social characterization of 'us' (hosting communities) and 'them' (refugees), which is likely to affect social behavior between the two groups (Tajfel et al. 1971). External organizations and government agencies offering support to displaced persons often distinguish between refugees and host communities when providing services. Refugees are likely to have correlated preferences stemming from shared norms, taboos, and kinship (Bénabou/Tirole 2011; Denison/Müller 2016), and uncorrelated choices regarding hosting communities.

Nevertheless, the categorization of social identity evolves (Akerlof/Kranton 2000), and with repeated social interactions, some preferences might change (Fehr et al. 2002). Discrimination against out-groups or favoritism to in-group members may be ambiguous, as evidenced in several studies (Baumgartner et al. 2012; Bernhard et al. 2006; Chen/Li 2009; Tajfel et al. 1971). It is even more ambiguous for social groups exposed to war, such as refugees and host communities, according to literature that shows that war experiences increase prosocial behavior (Bauer et al. 2016; Voors et al. 2012a, b).

This chapter contributes to this puzzle by examining the prosocial behavior of two social groups: refugees fleeing armed conflict, and hosting communities that have previously experienced armed conflict. The context studied here is unique because communities currently hosting refugees from South Sudan were refugees in the past. The primary goal is to investigate forms of discrimination in trust, reciprocity of trust, and altruism among refugees and hosts.

A. Adong, *Armed Conflicts and Forced Displacements in the Anthropocene*,
The Anthropocene: Politik—Economics—Society—Science 41,
https://doi.org/10.1007/978-3-032-04820-2_3

The theory of social identity in psychology literature postulates altruistic behavior towards in-group members, and mistrust, hostility, or indifference towards out-groups (Baumgartner et al. 2012; Tajfel et al. 1971). In economics, the concept of social identity is extended to include gender discrimination, household division of labor, and social exclusion based on ethnicity or religion (Akerlof/Kranton 2000). Fershtman/Gneezy (2001a, b) distinguish between discrimination arising from a taste for discrimination and discrimination arising from ethnic stereotypes. The former reflects prejudice, already embedded in one's utility function, and can reflect dislike, anger, or similar emotions. The latter on stereotypes reflects perceptions held towards a group and is not necessarily standardized. In the trust game, it is not possible to distinguish between the two forms of discrimination. Comparing results from the trust and the dictator game, it is possible to distinguish between trust emanating from prejudice and that originating from stereotypes or beliefs about a given social identity (Fershtman/Gneezy 2001b). This chapter provides information on one's partner's social orientation, specifically whether they are refugees or hosts, and therefore cannot distinguish between discrimination arising from prejudice (prejudicial attitudes) and discrimination arising from stereotypes.

It was hypothesized that individuals from the same social identity will tend to favor those from their own social group. In this case, refugees tend to show preferences for trustworthiness and altruism among fellow refugees, while discriminating against hosts. Hosts will have preferences in trust and generosity for hosts and discriminate against refugees (out of taste for discrimination or ethnic stereotypes). Secondly, it was hypothesized that these preferences for one's social group will change with remoteness from urban areas, such as district headquarters. The assumption was that repeated social interaction leads to a change in attitudes toward discrimination against out-groups (Fehr et al. 2002). The treatment involved the random assignment of information about whether one was playing with a refugee or a member of the host community. The above hypothesis was tested by conducting trust and dictator games with refugees and the host community members in the Adjumani district in Uganda. The tests employed a within-subject design in which all players participated in both the trust and dictator games in an unexpected order. The context provided a unique setting for understanding the role of social identity in the integration of refugees. The refugee settlements are located near host communities with no restrictions on interactions. Also, both refugees and hosts have experienced war and have some shared norms and cultures.

The most closely related paper to this study in literature is by Hartman/Morse (2018), who studied violence, empathy, and altruism during the Ivorian refugee crisis in Liberia. Hartman/Morse (2018) explore how past exposure to violence affects altruism towards members of a different ethnic or religious group in the Liberian context. They fail to rule out omitted factors by using survey data, conjoint experiments, and observational approaches to measure altruism.[1] Their findings are corroborated by the research undertaken for this book, which involved conducting

[1] In conjoint experiments, players are presented with a hypothetical condition and told to make a choice based on several factors, such as gender, ethnicity, religion, food security and other factors

lab experiments in the field, using trust and dictator games with refugees and host community members to address the endogeneity of preferences. Hartman/Morse (2018) also rely on host communities' self-reported behavior, which may not accurately reflect the households' actual reality. In a controlled experimental environment, such biases from self-reporting are limited. Additionally, the study presented in this book focused on a different behavioral puzzle of understanding trust, trustworthiness, and altruism, which influence many informal social and economic interactions that remain largely informal (Bauer et al. 2018; Berg et al. 1995). Limited studies focus on this puzzle or have a similar context. Bauer et al. (2018) use trust and dictator games to investigate whether the experience of being abducted to fight for a rebel group affects individual trustworthiness. Werner/Lambsdorff (2019) investigate the impact of activation of memories of conflict on prosociality and find no evidence for discrimination of out-groups. Other studies artificially create social groups in the lab (Chen/Li 2009; Everett et al. 2015), which might not depict real-life categorization of individual social group identities based on regular interactions, emotional ties, or prevailing norms (Everett et al. 2015).

Lastly, unlike many studies centered on refugee livelihoods, this chapter contributes to the limited research focusing on refugees and their hosts' behavioral aspects. The results are crucial to the policy arena in many humanitarian contexts where concern for the vulnerable displaced people's assistance is the prime agenda. Recent policy discussions on refugee settlement have centered on whether refugees should be integrated with local communities and allowed some degree of work and freedom of movement or be secluded in designated camps and settlements (Bohnet/Schmitz 2019). Uganda is heralded for its move towards reintegrating refugees into host communities (refugees live with host communities rather than in secluded camps) with no restrictions on work, access to land, and movement.

The lab experiments conducted in the field indicate that refugees showed preferences for reciprocating trust and altruism towards hosts with increasing remoteness from district headquarters. Hosts showed preferences for trust towards fellow hosts, although this changed with increasing remoteness from the urban areas, particularly from the district headquarters. Hosts nevertheless showed no preferences for altruistic behavior toward fellow hosts, even with increasing remoteness. The results can be attributed to increased interaction opportunities between the two groups arising from greater remoteness from the district headquarters due to high transaction costs that limit travel, and interactions in closer confines. Other factors may be a higher population density in remote settlements, a high ratio of refugees to hosts, or being nearer the South Sudan border, thus creating a higher likelihood of shared language and cultural identity between hosts and refugees. The distribution of settlements and the fact that the experiments incorporated controls for settlement-fixed effects may rule out these inferences. There is limited self selection and screening of refugees into particular localities, thus limiting the possibility of bias. Refugee settlements are established as needed; once the existing cluster has reached its capacity, another

that the players consider prime and that are likely to affect the choices made. Hartman/Morse (2018) use conjoint experiments to elicit respondents' preferences over attributes of refugees.

settlement is established. There is also limited migration of refugees from one settlement to another. Lastly, the results may be influenced by the fact that only trustworthy and altruistic refugees move into Uganda following forced displacement. Nevertheless, this is less likely to be the case, given the history and nature of the conflict in South Sudan that drives refugees to Uganda.

To ensure the findings' robustness, socioeconomic information about the players from household surveys was used to check for randomization success. The players' socioeconomic characteristics were controlled in the regression and the findings were corroborated by survey responses and focus group discussions. The findings rule out the possibility that, when remoteness increases, refugees reciprocate trust more with hosts than with fellow refugees in order to gain favor from them. Focus group discussions also showed that refugees perceive hosts as being the same with shared cultures and tribes. Less trust by hosts towards refugees does not stem from their anticipation of less reciprocity from the latter. In focus group discussions, hosts indicated that refugees were thieves and a danger to collective resources.

The rest of this chapter is structured as follows: the next section reviews the extent of forced displacements and hosting in the Great Lakes Region. Section 3.2 reviews the literature on social preferences. Section 3.3 then discusses the methods, including experimental design, sampling, and procedures for the game. Section 3.4 presents the main results from the experiment, and Sect. 3.5 offers conclusions and policy recommendations.

3.1.1 Review of the Extent of Forced Displacements and Hosting in the Great Lakes Region

The Great Lakes Region (GLR) has a high number of forced displaced persons, with many refugees coming from within the region due to conflict. Following the definition by the World Bank (2015), forced displacement is the experience of being forced or obliged to flee a country of nationality or a place of habitual residence in order to avoid the risk of persecution, armed conflict, or situations of generalized violence. Forced displacement within the GLR follows a series of armed conflicts within the area, with the possibility of current Internally Displaced Persons (IDPs) ending up as refugees. Displacements in the region have been a source of instability and continue to be a threat. For example, displaced Rwandan refugees in eastern DRC were known to cause tension and were a focus of subsequent conflict events (World Bank 2015). Most of the forced displacements within the region tend to occur within a short period. Displaced persons are settled in rural areas and their stays are usually protracted (World Bank 2015). Table 3.1 shows the number of displaced persons in GLR as of 2024, with DRC having the highest number of forced displacements, most of them involving people internally displaced because of ongoing conflicts in the eastern part of the country.

Table 3.1 The number of forced displaced persons in GLR

Country	Number of displaced persons
Uganda	1,700,000
Tanzania	224,056
South Sudan	1,500,000
Rwanda	127,885
Burundi	96,715
DRC	8,000,000
Total	11,648,656

Source UNHCR data base 2024

Forced displaced persons, including refugees, Internally Displaced Persons, returnees, and the host communities, are a vulnerable group whose rights need to be protected. Table 3.1 is a detail of the refugee flows that resulted from the different armed conflicts. In Tanzania for example, refugee flows follow the different armed conflicts that took place in DRC and the 1970 refugee flows from Burundi due to interethnic fighting in Burundi.

All the countries within the GLR have signed and ratified the UN Refugee Convention (State Parties to the 1951 Convention relating to the Status of Refugees and the 1967 Protocol 2011). GLR countries have also signed up to the African Union Convention for the Protection and Assistance of IDPs in Africa. In 2013, the countries signed the African Union's Peace, Security, and Cooperation Framework for the Democratic Republic of the Congo and the Region (PSCF) in Addis Ababa to cooperate on durable solutions to the armed conflicts in DRC and the region. Although modest progress in the implementation of PSCF has been recorded, armed conflicts continue in the area, particularly in DRC and South Sudan (UN/African Union 2011).

Existing national laws, regulations, and policies that uphold the integrity and rights of displaced persons vary between countries, with some being very restrictive regarding the activities of refugees. Uganda's Refugee Act, for example, is heralded for its progressive refugee policy that allows for the freedom of refugees to work (d'Errico et al. 2024), while countries such as Kenya have more restrictive policies (Table 3.2).

3.2 Review of Literature on Social Preferences

3.2.1 Trust, Reciprocity, and Altruism

Social preference models incorporate fairness concerns such as difference aversion and reciprocity when individuals care for their pay-offs and pay-offs received by others (Fehr/Schmidt 1999). Social preferences include distributional preferences and concerns for reciprocity. Distributional concerns like difference aversion are

Table 3.2 Refugee flows from conflicts and forced displacement situations in the Great Lakes Region

Refugee flows	Origin of forced displacements
• 1950s Rwandan refugee flows to Uganda and the DRC from interethnic fighting in Rwanda • 1970s Burundian refugee flows, mainly to Tanzania, from interethnic fighting in Burundi • 1994 post-genocide flows of Rwandan refugees to DRC and Tanzania, and to Burundi and Uganda • 1994 post-genocide return of Rwandan refugees from Uganda to Rwanda • 1996–present return of Rwandan refugees from the DRC to Rwanda • 2000–2008 return of Burundian refugees to Burundi • 1992–1996, 1996–2007, 1998–2003, and 2003–present conflict in DRC, resulting in refugee flows to Rwanda, Uganda, and internal displacement • 2011 South Sudanese conflict resulting in refugee influx to Uganda, Kenya, Tanzania etc. • Horn of Africa conflicts in Ethiopia, Somalia and Sudan, resulting in the flow of refugees to East African countries *Source* World Bank (2015)	• In Burundi: internal displacement, refugees from the DRC and Rwanda and returned refugees from the DRC and Tanzania • In the DRC: internal displacement, refugees from Burundi and Rwanda, returned refugees from Burundi, Rwanda, Tanzania, Uganda, South Sudan, Burundi, Congo, Somalia, Angola, Sudan • In Rwanda: refugees from DRC and Burundi, returned refugees from Sudan, Eritrea, Ethiopia, Somalia, South Sudan, Afghanistan, Cameroon • In Tanzania: refugees from Burundi and the DRC • In Uganda: refugees from Burundi, the DRC, South Sudan, Eritrea, Somalia, Burundi, Sudan, Ethiopia and Rwanda (refugees are mainly from Southern and Eastern Africa) • South Sudan: South Sudan and Sudan *Source* UNHCR Population Statistics Database 2024

motivated by the desire to reduce differences in pay-offs (Fisman et al. 2007). Reciprocity is driven by the desire to raise or lower pay-offs depending on how fairly others behave (Rabin 1993).

To understand social preferences using two-person games, consider two players, A and B, in a non-strategic setting. If π_i represents monetary pay-offs for person i and π is a set of possible pay-offs for a game, to maximize utility, A chooses pay-offs $(\pi_A, \pi_B) \in \pi$ in which case $U_A = \pi_A$. Nevertheless, with concerns for altruism, a more general form of utility suffices in which player A's utility is a weighted sum of her material pay-off and partner's (B) material pay-off and can be represented by Eqs. 3.1 and 3.2 (adopted from Charness/Rabin 2002) below

In this case, if $\pi_B \geq \pi_A$, then

$$U_B(\pi_A, \pi_B) \equiv (1 - p - \theta q)\pi_B + (p + \theta q)\pi_A \tag{3.1}$$

and when $\pi_B \leq \pi_A$ then

$$U_B(\pi_A, \pi_B) \equiv (1 - \delta - \theta q)\pi_B + (\delta + \theta q)\pi_A \tag{3.2}$$

The weight B places on A's pay-off depends on: (1) equity concerns (whether A is getting a higher or lower pay-off than B) (Fehr/Schmidt 1999; Loewenstein/Thompson 1989), (2) reciprocity behavior (whether A has behaved unfairly or not), (3) warm-glow giving and (4) simply altruistic concerns (Rabin 1993). Parameter θ allows for incorporating preferences due to reciprocity behavior, while p and δ allows for distributional outcomes other than reciprocity (Charness/Rabin 2002), such as competitive preferences and difference aversion. Other factors likely to affect how much B gives to A include the level of anonymity, gender of A or the framing of the game (Andreoni/Miller 2002), and psychological emotions like anger and surprise (Geanakoplosand et al. 1989). These also enter the utility function of A represented as

$$U_A = u_A(\pi_{A,}\pi_B; \gamma)$$

where γ is a vector of all these attributes.

The assumption $\delta \leq p \leq 0$ holds if player B always prefers to have a competitive advantage (higher pay-off than others) but maintains fairness concerns. $\delta < 0 < p < 1$ holds if B's interests lie in minimizing disparities in monetary pay-off, the case for difference aversion (Loewenstein/Thompson 1989). For reciprocal behavior, B's value for p and δ vary with B's perception of player A's intentions depending on whether A is fair or not in behavior. If A is not fair in behavior, then $\theta > 0$; when $= -1$.

3.2.1.1 Trust and Dictator Games

To measure trust and trustworthiness, Berg et al. (1995) proposed a two-player sequential game of trust with no contract to enforce agreement (Johnson/Mislin 2011). It involves two players – the sender/trustor/investor and receiver/trustee anonymously paired and endowed with an initial amount, say X_0. In the first stage, the sender decides how much to send to the receiver. He can send nothing, in which case he remains with all the endowment of X_0, or send a proportion X_a of the endowment which lies in the range $0 \leq X_a \leq X_0$ in the hope that he will get some of it back if the trustee reciprocates. In this case, he remains with $X_0 - X_a$. The amount sent by the trustor is tripled by the experimenter $3X_a$ and passed to the receiver (trustee) who decides how much to send back to the trustor, denoted as $Kb(3X_a)$. Subsequently, the amount the trustor sends in the hope that the other party will reciprocate measures trust while the amount sent back by the receiver or trustee measures trustworthiness (Berg et al. 1995; Johnson/Mislin 2011).

If the initial endowment was 10 units, for example, the trustor's strategy X_a is given by $(0, 1, 2\ldots\ldots.10)$, while the trustee's strategy is such that K_b : $(0, 3, \ldots\ldots\ldots 30)$, which should satisfy $0 \leq K_b(3X_a) \leq 3X_a$. The pay-offs will be such that trustors get $P_a(X_0, K_b) = X_0 - X_a + K_b(3X_0)$ while trustees get $P_b(X_a, K_b) = 3X_a - K_b(3X_a)$. If the subjects have a strictly increasing direct utility function for wealth given by $V_i(W_i + P_i(X_a - K_b))$, where V_i is the utility function and W represents welfare for $i = a, b$, and want to maximize their welfare, then the dominant trustee's strategy will be to keep all the money, in which case $K_b(3X_a) = 0$. In anticipation of this behavior, trustors send nothing, such that $X_a = 0$. The subgame-perfect equilibrium is such that if subjects have selfish interests and only care about their monetary pay-offs, the trustee will never send anything back because returning money reduces one's pay-off (Burks et al. 2003).

The dictator game shows that people still make some transfers even when they expect nothing and are not sure of the partner's status (Andreoni/Miller 2002). The dictator game distinguishes expectations of reciprocity from preferences not conditioned on others' behaviors (Ashraf et al. 2006; Bauer et al. 2018). In the dictator game, two players – a dictator (D) and receiver (R) – split a prize normalized to have a unit value. If $X \epsilon (0, 1)$ denotes what the receiver gets, then D is left with $(1 - X)$. D chooses what to transfer with probability $(1 - p)$ and nature sets this equal to some fixed value X_0 with probability of p (Andreoni/Bernheim 2009). In a standard dictator game, p is 0. The difference between what is sent in the dictator and trust game constitutes the portion of trust attributed to the other party's expectations of reciprocity (Ashraf et al. 2006).

Evidence also shows that people playing either role (trustor or trustee) do make some transfers (Berg et al. 1995; Burks et al. 2003; Cesarini et al. 2008; Kosfeld et al. 2005) in the trust game, showing trust and trustworthiness. For every definite amount sent by the trustor, the trustee's average net return is positive (Rabin 1993). Returning positive amounts by senders in the trust game is attributed to unconditional altruism, inequality aversion, and reciprocity (Andreoni/Miller 2002; Bauer et al. 2018). Dictator games are used for measuring unconditional selflessness, not directly linked to kinship, reciprocity, or the immediate threat of punishment (Andreoni/Bernheim 2009; Cox 2004a). Cameron et al. (2007) and Fehr/Schmidt (1999) attribute positive transfers, especially equal splits, to inequity aversion – the resistance to inequitable outcomes. Other factors to explain the puzzle of positive giving are attributed to genetics (Kosfeld/Rustagi 2015), environment (Cesarini et al. 2008), gender (Haselhuhn et al. 2015), social preferences and internalized norms (Andreoni/Bernheim 2009; Ashraf et al. 2006; Burks et al. 2003; Kimbrough/Vostroknutov 2016), audience effects or social image (Andreoni/Bernheim 2009), fairness and reciprocity (Charness/Rabin 2002). Ashraf et al. (2006) find that expectations of return and unconditional kindness account for the variance in trust. Andreoni et al. (2002) agree that people behave with kindness to others, and when rephrased in the language of prices and income, can be shown to be rational.

Investigating whether trust and trustworthiness are gender-sensitive, Chaudhuri et al. (2013a, b) find that female individuals are most reciprocal, although such gender differences dissipate over time. Haselhuhn et al. (2015) find that women are both less likely to lose trust and more likely to restore trust than men. Several studies find a positive relationship (Bauer et al. 2018; Bellows/Miguel 2009; Hartman/Morse 2018; Voors et al. 2012a, b) between social preferences and cooperative behavior. Voors et al. (2012a, b) find that individuals exposed to violence display more altruistic behavior towards their neighbors, are more risk-seeking, and have higher discount rates. Bellows/Miguel (2006) find that households affected by war are more likely to attend community meetings and join political and community groups. Hartman/Morse (2018) study how regions plagued by recurring periods of war and displacement are altruistic towards members of different ethnic or religious groups and find that violence promotes intergroup cooperation. Lastly, Bauer et al. (2018) explore the effects of forced military services on trust and trustworthiness and find that soldiering experience increases individual reliability and community engagement.

3.2.2 *Social Identity and Discrimination*

Favoring members of one's ethnic, racial, or language in-group is referred to as parochialism (Bernhard et al. 2006), even with no expected gains (Rabellino et al. 2016). In the psychology literature, parochial altruism theory is associated with altruistic behavior towards in-group members (one's ethnic, racial, or any other social group) and mistrust, indifference, or hostility towards out-groups (Baumgartner et al. 2012; Tajfel et al. 1971). In neoclassical utility functions, a proxy for forms of exclusion and discrimination based on gender, ethnicity, and religion is used to understand gender discrimination, labor division, and many others (Akerlof/Kranton 2000). Social identity is synonymous with a norm of groupings associated with parochial social instincts (Bernhard et al. 2006), and members within the social cluster benefit from altruistic behavior amongst members. When there is a categorization of 'us' and 'them' (Tajfel et al. 1971), then social identity creates social bridges and affects the integration of refugees with hosts (Ager/Strang 2008). Discrimination based on social status influences the social connection between groups and their interactions.

Several studies reveal how prosocial behavior favors in-groups compared to out-groups (Baumgartner et al. 2012; Bernhard et al. 2006; Chen/Li 2009; Rabellino et al. 2016; Tajfel et al. 1971). Bernhard et al. (2006), using "punishment experiments" in Papua New Guinea, found that punishers protect in-group victims much more than out-group victims. On their part, the norm violators have higher expectations of lenience by punishers from their social group. Similarly, Baumgartner et al. (2012) find that more reliable in-group networks lead to more severe punishment of out-groups for norm violation than of in-groups.

Empirical findings show evidence of in-group favoritism (Chen/Li 2009; Rabellino et al. 2016). Chen/Li (2009) find that 19 and 13% of the study sample are more likely to reward an in-group member for good behavior and punish them for misbehavior, respectively. They also find that participants are significantly more likely to choose social-welfare-maximizing actions when matched with an in-group member than an out-group member. Rabellino et al. (2016) find that punishers tend to punish those who exhibit unfair play towards their group members.

Several factors may explain social preferences for in-groups. First, higher expectations of reciprocity (Bernhard et al. 2006) from in-group members compared to out-group members minimize differences within the group (inequity aversion within the group likely to be higher). Second, the desire to maximize in-group pay-offs relative to out-group pay-offs increases inequity feelings to out-groups (Everett et al. 2015). Third, maximizing utility is selfish behavior because of the perceived higher reciprocity from in-group rather than out-group (Rabbie et al. 1989). Fourth, observed immoral acts of out-groups, which threaten resources (Everett et al. 2015), might explain one's group preferences.

Like other preferences, favoring one's group can be shaped by economic and social conditions such as market integration (Fehr et al. 2002). Markets allow for repeated interactions between non-kin, and, commonly, non-cooperative actions such as cheating get punished such that in the long run, cooperations develop (Denison/Muller 2016). Market integration is also associated with greater prosociality (Henrich et al. 2005). Prosocial attitudes towards individuals with similar life experiences, such as war, might also outride discrimination from differences in social identity (Hartman/Morse 2018). Shared ethnic backgrounds between refugees and hosts may also invoke hosts' altruism or sympathetic feelings (Kreibaum 2016).

3.3 Methods

3.3.1 Empirical Strategy

The experiment investigated whether refugees favored fellow refugees when reciprocating trust and altruism based on whether they had been informed that they would be playing the trust and dictator games with a refugee or with a host. All refugees were receivers and were randomly assigned information that their sender was either a host or a fellow refugee. Similarly, the experiment explored whether hosts favored fellow hosts in trust and altruism based on whether they had been told they would be playing the trust and dictator games with fellow hosts or with refugees. All hosts were senders and were randomly assigned information that their receiver was a refugee or a fellow host.

Equations 3.3 and 3.4 were used for refugees and hosts, respectively.

$$D_{ir} = \alpha + \beta_1 P_r + \beta_2 T_r + \beta_3 P_r T_r + \delta controls + \epsilon_r \tag{3.3}$$

$$D_{ih} = \alpha + \beta_1 P_h + \beta_2 T_h + \beta_3 P_h T_h + \delta controls + \epsilon_h \tag{3.4}$$

where D_{ir} is the outcome for individual i in the refugee household r and can be trustworthiness or altruism. To measure trustworthiness, responses were solicited using the strategic method on how much one would send back if the trustor sent UGX 1,000 and if the trustor sent back UGX 2,000, respectively. P_r is the treatment dummy variable equal to one if the subject is randomly assigned to the information they play with a refugee or equal to zero if they are randomly assigned to the information they play with a host. The coefficient β_1 in Eq. 3.3 measures the average treatment effect and is a measure of the difference in the level of trustworthiness towards refugees and the host community. T_r measures the distance of the player's home from district headquarters. Distance is captured as a dummy equal to one for players located 10 km or more from the district headquarters and equal to zero if located less than 10 km. It was hypothesized that remoteness from the district increases prosocial attitudes of trust, reciprocating trust, and altruism towards out-groups because of increased opportunities for interaction due to closer confines resulting from limited movement due to the high transaction costs of travel.

The coefficient β_1 in Eq. 3.4 measures the difference in the level of trust towards refugees and the host community members. In Eq. 3.4, D_{ih} is the outcome for individual i in the host community household h and can be either trust or altruism of host communities. Trust is the measure of the amount sent in the trust game, while altruism is the amount of money sent in the dictator games. The description of other variables used in the model is in Appendix, Table 3.10. For both Eqs. 3.3 and 3.4, *controls* is an individual vector for characteristics of the player, such as age, gender, level of education, and household characteristics, such as household size and wealth, that affect behavior (Henrich et al. 2006a, b), and ϵ_r and ϵ_h are the error terms with standard errors clustered at the settlement level.

3.3.2 *The Experiment*

3.3.2.1 Experimental Design

The experiment used a within-subject design whereby a participant played both the trust game and the dictator game in random order and followed the gold standard trust game discussed previously. Trustors were given an endowment (UGX 2000) and had the opportunity to send money to another participant after being told whether their partner was a member of the host community or a refugee. Treatment was the information given to players regarding whether their playing partner was a refugee or a member of the host community. Refugees and hosts were randomly assigned to treatment arm one (playing with refugees) or treatment arm two (playing with hosts). Players were assigned to the same treatment in both the dictator and the trust games. Other details of the matched partner, such as names and the location from which they came, remained anonymous. Subsequently, each trustee chose how much of the tripled amount to send back to the trustor. The hosts played as senders (trustors).

In contrast, refugees played as receivers (trustees) to measure the degree of trust by hosts, who were the owners of most of the resources, and the degree of trustworthiness of resource-constrained refugees. In the dictator game, participants were asked to decide what amount they would want to send to an anonymous partner after being informed that the amount sent would be tripled and the receiver would not have to return any of that amount. The receiver, on the other hand, did not send back any money to the sender.

3.3.2.2 Study Area: Northern Uganda

Uganda is a landlocked country situated in East Africa, with about 45.9 million people, according to the 2024 population census (Uganda Bureau of Statistics 2024b). Between 2006 and 2013, poverty reduced from 31.2% of the population living below the poverty line to 19.7% (World Bank 2016). Nevertheless, poverty remains concentrated in the Northern and Eastern parts, with 84% of the poor living in these regions.

The Northern region has experienced several armed conflicts over the decades since independence in 1962. The downfall of President Idi Amin in 1979 led to ethnic clashes (Merkx 2000). Many people of Alur, Lugbara, Kakwa, and Madi descent were harassed and had to flee to Southern Sudan, where similar tribes exist. In 1986, the National Resistance Movement (NRM) led by Yoweri Museveni took over political leadership, and several uprisings such as the Holy Spirit Movement of Alice Lakwena and the Lord's Resistance Army (LRA) under the supervision of Joseph Kony emerged. The armed conflict between the LRA and the Government of Uganda lasted for two decades, and several people were displaced and relocated to internal displacement camps.

Despite a history of displacement of its people due to armed conflicts, Uganda currently has one of the most significant refugee influxes globally. It is third (after Turkey and Pakistan) as a "refugee go-to host country", hosting about 1.4 million refugees fleeing from the ethnic armed conflict in South Sudan, DRC, and Somalia. It has a generous refugee policy that allows refugees free movement, work, engagement in business opportunities, and access to services such as health care and education. This model contrasts with the reluctance shown by several countries whose policies on refugees confine refugees to camps with no freedom of movement or right to work.

The study described here was conducted in Adjumani district located in the West Nile region of northern Uganda (Fig. 3.1). Adjumani has been plagued by several civil tensions arising internally within Uganda but also from neighboring Sudan. For example, in 1979, the overthrow of President Idi Amin was accompanied by public pressure forcing communities from Adjumani to flee to South Sudan. In 1986, displaced populations returned home due to escalating conflict in South Sudan (Hovil 2001). Adjumani was also affected by the two decades of the LRA war, which traumatized many communities in Northern Uganda. Currently, Adjumani has the highest refugee ratio to host population (43:57) communities in Uganda. As of 2016, it also has one of the largest refugee settlements in Uganda, with about 185,000 inhabitants (United Nations High Commision for Refugees (UNHCR)/Government of Uganda (GoU) 2019).

3.3.2.3 Sampling and Sample Selection

A multistage sampling technique was used. Refugee settlements were randomly selected from 'new' and 'old' settlements in the first stage. New settlements had

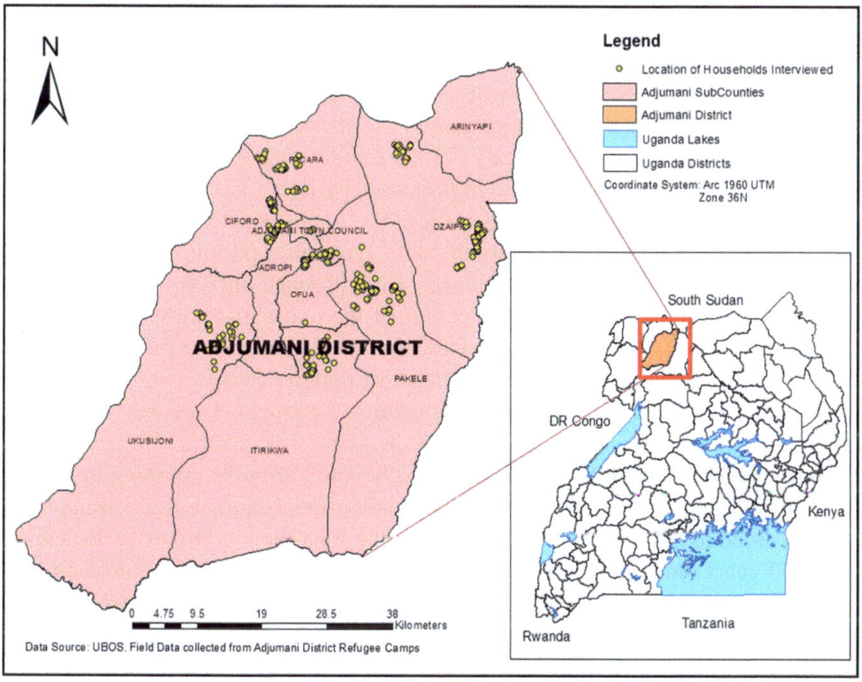

Fig. 3.1 A map of Adjumani district showing the distribution of the households in the study. *Source* Author's construction

been established in 2016, while old ones had been in existence for more than three years in 2018. The study covered Elema, Boroli, Mugula, Oliji, Alere, Agojo, Maji, Merieyi, Ayilo, and Pagirinya settlements in Adjumani district. In the second stage, households were randomly selected from a list of refugee households. 288 refugee households were randomly selected from 10 refugee settlements using probability proportional to size sampling. Two of the five host community local councils within a 15 km radius[2] of each refugee settlement were also randomly chosen. 331 host households were randomly selected from the eligible local councils using probability proportional to size sampling. In total, we surveyed 619 households from localities, as shown in Fig. 3.1, between April and May 2018 and conducted experiments in June 2018. The corresponding number of refugee and host community households surveyed in each settlement is in the Appendix, Table 3.11.

[2] Zhu et al. (2016a, b) established that the majority of refugee activities and transactions took place within a 15 km radius of the settlements.

3.3.2.4 Experimental Procedure and Instructions

The experimental procedures and instructions closely followed Bauer et al. (2018), who conducted trust and dictator games in Northern Uganda, Gulu and Kitgum districts, which are about 157 km and 115 km from Adjumani district, respectively. Bauer et al. (2018) adapted the written protocols by Barr (2003) and Henrich et al. (2006a, b). In order to conduct the study described in this chapter, research assistants were intensively trained for two months with sequential piloting of the games in Kampala. The household head – or, in his or her absence, the spouse – played the games, and in a few cases an adult member of the household above 18 years was allowed to take part. A short exit interview was conducted to ascertain the player's demographic characteristics and solicit their risk preferences.

Hosts and refugees were randomly assigned to treatment (knowing whether the anonymous person with whom they played the game was either a refugee or host). To minimize any possibility of creating antagonism within the communities, hosts and refugees played in separate places close to their local council. A uniform profile was read aloud to the players, for example, that their partner was between the ages of 18 and 60 years old, and that they were refugees (assuming this was the treatment) registered and staying in one of the refugee camps demarcated by the Government of Uganda in Adjumani district. The enumerators made no mention of the village or refugee settlement to avoid biasing the results. Both parties were told what information was shared with the other party depending on the treatment. For example, members of the host community given the information that their anonymous partner was a refugee were aware that their partner knew that they were from the host community. Similarly, refugees were informed that the senders knew that they were refugees living in nearby settlements.

Playing games in a specific order is likely to bring about order effects due to learning. To address order effects, we allowed for alterations in the order in which the games were played. To further understand the role of risk in making decisions in the games, we solicited risk preferences by asking players to choose between four gambles with different pay-offs, although no actual pay-offs were made.

We conducted the experiments in the local languages; instructions were given first at the group level and then individually to ensure that participants understood everything well. We also tested the player's comprehension of the game. Only three players could not comprehend the game and were replaced. In the end, the total pay was a sum of the show-up fee plus the payment for correct predictions and the amount from the outcome of either the dictator or trust game determined by tossing a coin. The challenge with this design is that half of the respondents did not have an actual match (hosts that send to fellow hosts or refugees that send to fellow refugees); in such a case, payment was based on solicited responses of their expectations in the trust and dictator games.

3.4 Results and Discussions

3.4.1 Descriptive Statistics

Descriptive statistics for refugees and the host community are in Table 3.3: Characteristics of refugees and members of the host community. On average, refugee players were 39 years old, and hosts were, on average, 38 years old. 80 and 47% of all refugees and host players respectively were female. On average, refugee household heads were younger and widowed, while the hosts' household heads tended to be older and married. A significant proportion of refugees had hardly any education; 39% of the refugees had not attended any formal school, whereas only 12% of hosts had not been to school. Refugees also had more household members than hosts. The average refugee household size was 6.5 compared to an average household size of 5.4 for hosts. As expected, refugees were more impoverished (less likely to be in the highest wealth quintile). Refugees were also, on average, closer to the district headquarters. Lastly, 73% of refugees, unlike 45% of hosts, had experienced war in the past.

3.4.2 Randomization Check

There were no significant differences in several of the characteristics, such as age, marital status, household size, and wealth (Appendix, Table 3.12) by treatment assignment for refugees and hosts players of the game. Nevertheless, there were significant differences in average years of schooling and level of risk preferences.

Equation 3.5 tested for the significance of the covariates on the likelihood of being treated.

y_i is the dependent variable of the kind of treatment respondent i received. β is the coefficient for other control variables like gender of the player, gender of the household head, education of the player, level of risk aversion, wealth, household size, and if a household had been affected by war or not.

$$y_i = \beta Covariate + \varepsilon_i \tag{3.5}$$

Overall, there was a balance on both refugees' treatment and hosts on several variables (Appendix, Table 3.13). Also, analysis failed to reject the likelihood ratio chi square test that all of the coefficients in the logistic model were zero, showing that the randomization was successful for both groups, suggesting that treatment was successfully randomized. Therefore, any observed outcomes, such as parochialism, can only be attributed to the treatment and not other factors. As a robustness check, alternative probit models were used, which produced similar non-significance of the model variables. The Kolmogorov Smirnov, a non-parametric test that does not take into account the underlying cumulative distribution function being tested, also

Table 3.3 Characteristics of refugees and members of the host community

Characteristics of the player	Refugees	Hosts	t-statistics
Age	38.66(14.61)	37.66 (14.33)	0.83
Gender (1 = female)	0.8(0.39)	0.47(0.50)	−8.6
Education			
No formal education	0.39(0.49)	0.12(0.32)	**8.16**
Primary	0.41(0.49)	0.63(0.48)	5.4
Secondary and above	0.19(0.40)	0.25(0.43)	1.66
Characteristics of households			
Years of schooling of the household head	4.02(4.40)	5.54(3.69)	**4.51**
Gender of household head (1 = male)	0.25(0.44)	0.63(0.48)	**9.86**
Marital status (1 = married, 0 = single, separated, not married)	0.49(0.50)	0.73(0.45)	6
Experienced death in the household (1 = yes)	0.28(0.44)	0.24(0.42)	1.07
Experienced war (1 = yes)	0.73(0.44)	0.43(0.49)	**7.62**
Household size	6.37(3.33)	5.49(2.98)	**3.31**
Household is risk-lover (1 = yes, 0 = no)	0.5(0.50)	0.4(0.49)	**2.65**
Lowest wealth quintile	0.29(0.45)	0.28(0.45)	0.39
Second lowest wealth quintile	0.27(0.44)	0.17(0.38)	**2.78**
Third lowest wealth quintile	0.28(0.45)	0.23(0.42)	**1.72**
Highest wealth quintile	0.15(0.36)	0.32(0.46)	**4.87**
Distance to district headquarters	6.73(3.70)	9.96(5.10)	**8.611**
Distance to tarmac	9.33(6.72)	10.16(8.18)	1.33

Source Author's construction

showed no statistical difference by treatment received for both refugees and hosts for a number of the variables (Appendix, Table 3.14).

3.4.3 Experimental Outcomes for Refugees

This section presents the differences in trustworthiness/reciprocity and altruism of refugees towards fellow refugees and hosts. It was hypothesized that refugees are more likely to be trustworthy and generous to fellow refugees than to hosts due to in-group preferences, but this changes with increasing remoteness from district headquarters.

Table 3.4 Experimental outcomes for refugees: trust and dictator games

Experimental outcomes	Receivers (refugees)			
Treatment+	Refugees	Host community	All	t value
Trustworthiness: average percentage returned	36.36(18.30)	38.62(18.90)	37.25(18.47)	0.9505
Beliefs of expected trustworthiness: perception of what others think they send back (average percentage)	43.14(17.82)	41.99(17.89)	42.66(17.81)	−0.5
Expected trust: beliefs of sender's transfer in the trust game (UGX)	1115.65(530.15)	1048.54(530.97)	1088(530.45)	0.984
Altruism: transfer in the dictator game (UGX)	785.71(604.60)	839.62(649.34)	807.69(622.56)	−0.685
Expected altruism: expectation of sender's transfer in dictator game (UGX)	980.51(491.37)	1084.90(619.03)	1000 (547.38)	−1.512

Source Author's construction
+ Treatment is the knowledge of whether one plays with a refugee or host. Numbers in parentheses are standard errors

3.4.3.1 The Trustworthiness of Refugees Towards Fellow Refugees and Towards Hosts

Using the strategy method, we asked refugees (receivers) to transfer the tripled amount when the trustor sent them UGX 1000 and UGX 2000.[3] The percentage amount returned in both decisions is a measure of the level of trustworthiness. Refugees sent back almost equal amounts to fellow refugees and hosts irrespective of treatment. The average percentage returned to fellow refugees was 36.36% compared to 38.6% returned to hosts (Table 3.4: Experimental outcomes for refugees: trust and dictator games), which is in line with proportions sent in similar studies using trust games.

For example, Johnson/Mislin (2011) found that players send an average of 31.9% in a meta-analysis of trust games conducted across Africa while Bauer et al. (2018), in a study amongst former rebels in northern Uganda, found that the average percentage returned ranges from 34 to 35%. Figure 3.2 suggests that refugees seem to reciprocate

[3] With an exchange rate of 1 USD = UGX 3685, UGX 1,000 is approx. USD 0.27 and UGX 2,000 is approx. USD 0.54 cents. More than 25% of refugees live on less than UGX 1,000 per day and 69% on less than UGX 2,000 per day (Development Pathways 2018).

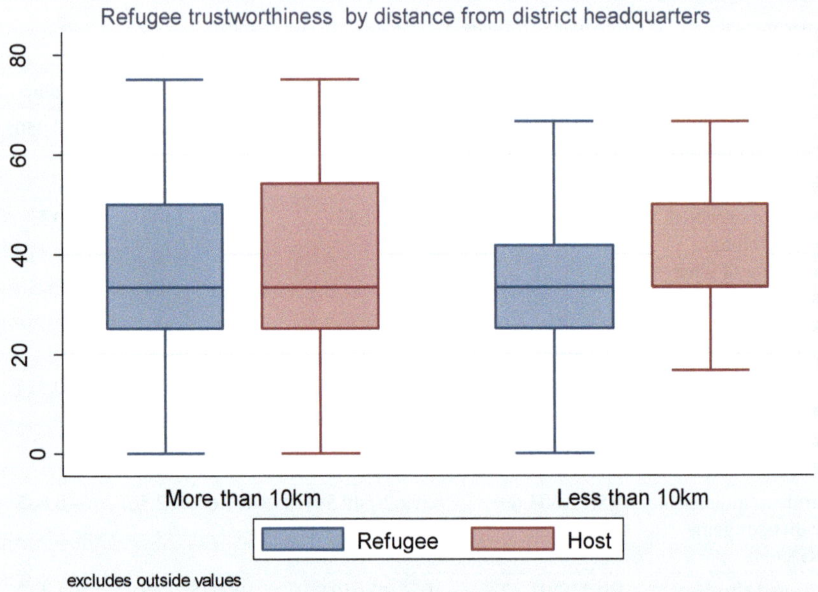

Fig. 3.2 Variation in the trustworthiness of refugees by remoteness from district headquarters

more to hosts than to fellow refugees irrespective of the remoteness from district headquarters. This was further examined by investigating whether discrimination in reciprocating trust differs from refugee remoteness in regression analysis.

In Table 3.5, the first column is the parsimonious regression of treatment's effect on the amount reciprocated. The second column includes distance to the district headquarters as a dummy variable and other control variables.

The fourth column consists of the distance expressed as a continuous variable, and the last column includes an interaction term between distance and treatment. Panel A is the level of trustworthiness measured by the average percentage of the tripled amount sent back when one receives UGX 1,000 and UGX 2,000. Panel B (Table 3.5) is the proportion of the tripled amount of money refugees return on receiving UGX 1,000, and Panel C is the proportion of the tripled amount of money refugees return when they receive UGX 2,000. The results show that the average treatment effect is negative but non-significant on the average amount returned by refugees. Analysis of the average treatment effects on trustworthiness when refugees received the tripled amount UGX 1,000 and UGX 2,000 sent by trustors in Panels B and C of Table 3.5, respectively, found that refugees transfer less to fellow refugees than to hosts by 5 percentage points ($p = 0.10$) of the tripled UGX 1,000 that trustors send. Nevertheless, the treatment effect is statistically insignificant for a more considerable amount of UGX 2,000 in panel c of Table 3.5.

Table 3.5 Refugees and trustworthiness

	(1)	(2)	(3)	(4)	(5)
Panel A					
Dependent variable	Average percentage returned in the trust game				
Treatment (1 = partner is refugee, 0 = partner is host)	−2.438 (1.98)	−2.835 (2.19)	−1.679 (3.28)	−3.012 (2.23)	−0.248 (4.67)
Distance to district (≥10 km) (d)		2.276 (3.89)	3.806 (4.93)		
Treatment * Distance (d)			−2.679 (4.23)		
Distance (km)				−0.0231 (0.41)	0.165 (0.48)
Distance * Treatment					−0.314 (0.40)
Constant	38.70*** (2.45)	45.39*** (6.40)	44.86*** (6.71)	47.27*** (7.69)	45.67*** (8.31)
Observations	249	234	234	234	234
R-squared	0.004	0.066	0.068	0.063	0.064
Panel B					
Dependent variable	Percentage of the amount returned when trustor sends UGX 1000				
Treatment (1 = partner is refugee, 0 = partner is host)	−4.202* (2.41)	−4.662* (2.55)	−5.78 (3.74)	−4.991* (2.63)	−8.087 (5.73)
Distance to district (≥10 km) (d)		0.712 (4.50)	−0.768 (5.45)		
Treatment * Distance (d)			2.591 (4.84)		
Distance (km)				−0.281 (0.44)	−0.491 (0.51)
Distance * Treatment					0.351 (0.49)
Constant	40.06*** (2.83)	51.42*** (6.61)	54.94*** (7.03)	58.00*** (7.58)	59.79*** (8.40)
Observations	249	234	234	234	234
R-squared	0.01	0.055	0.056	0.058	0.059
Panel C					
Dependent variable	Percentage of the amount sent back when trustor sends UGX 2000				
Treatment (1 = partner is refugee, 0 = partner is host)	−0.673 (2.10)	−1.008 (2.44)	2.421 (3.50)	−1.034 (2.44)	7.591 (4.62)
Distance to district (≥10 km) (d)		3.839 (3.71)	8.38 (4.97)		

(continued)

Table 3.5 (continued)

	(1)	(2)	(3)	(4)	(5)
Treatment * Distance (d)			−7.948* (4.31)		
Distance (km)				0.234 (0.42)	0.82 (0.49)
Distance * Treatment					−0.979** (0.40)
Constant	37.34*** (2.43)	36.37*** (7.40)	34.77*** (7.56)	36.54*** (8.73)	31.55*** (9.14)
Observations	249	234	234	234	234
R-squared	0	0.077	0.085	0.071	0.081

Notes ** $p < 0.05$, * $p < 0.1$. Numbers in parentheses are standard errors, and the analysis is clustered at the village level with settlement fixed effects. Treatment is a dummy for 1= knowledge that one plays the trust game with a refugee and 0 = knowledge that one plays with hosts. In all the columns except (1), factors controlled for include age, marital status, risk levels, gender, and education level of the player and household size, wealth of the household (based on principal component analysis of total household assets, such as the value of livestock, possession of charcoal stove, radio, bicycle, and phone), and order of the games

The third column consists of an interaction term between the dummy variable for distance to the center and the treatment to predict the effect of remoteness and knowledge of one's social orientation.

When analyzing the impact of remoteness on the level of reciprocity with knowledge of one's social identity (interaction of distance with treatment), no statistically significant effects of the interaction were found (column 3 and 5, Panel C). Refugees located more than 10 km from district headquarters reciprocate trust more to hosts than to refugees by 8 percentage points at the extensive margin. The results suggest that remoteness increases refugees' preferences to reciprocate trust at the intensive margin, perhaps from more interaction opportunities in remote areas than in areas close to the district.

Refugee's beliefs of partner's expected trustworthiness: are there prior beliefs of partner's expectations in discrimination? Examining refugees' impressions of the partner's loyalty expectations helps to explain any preconceived notions or stereotypes that refugees may have of their partner. For this reason, refugees were asked how much they thought their partners in the trust game expected from them (tripled amount) in return if they were sent UGX 1,000 and sent UGX 2,000. Results in Table 3.15. in the Appendix for both panels A and B (intensive and extensive amounts) show that treatment had no significant effect on refugees' beliefs of their partners' expected reciprocity. Similarly, knowledge of whether one played with hosts or refugees did not affect refugees' opinions about the partners' expectations with increasing remoteness. The results suggest that refugees have no prior expectations of discrimination by either fellow refugees or by hosts.

Do refugees have some preferences for being kind (altruistic) to fellow refugees rather than to fellow hosts? The dictator game in which treatment is the random assignment to information on whether one plays with a fellow refugee or host helps to ascertain whether refugees may have some preferences for being generous to fellow refugees rather than hosts. On average, refugees transferred more money to hosts (UGX 839.62) than to fellow refugees (UGX 785.71) in the dictator game; the difference nevertheless is statistically insignificant (Table 3.6). Treatment did not affect the amount transferred in the dictator game (Table 3.6, panel A) or in the amounts expected to be received (Table 3.6, panel B) when controls were in place for other variables likely to affect altruistic behavior. Nevertheless, the interaction between treatment and distance (measured as a dummy) is negative and significant, suggesting that refugees are less likely to be generous to fellow refugees with increasing remoteness from district headquarters. Specifically, refugees further than 10 km from district headquarters transferred more to hosts than to refugees by 15 percentage points. The results defy the hypothesis and theory of parochial altruism between people of the same social identity (Chen/Li 2009; Tajfel et al. 1971) and emphasize the role of remoteness from commercial places such as the district headquarters.

Refugees' altruistic preferences for another social identity rather than their own in remote areas can be attributed to increased opportunities for interaction and prospects for integration. Expected altruism by refugees was also investigated (Panel B) and yielded results that mirror those of altruism in Panel A. Nevertheless, the interaction between treatment and distance is not significant. The results also show no significant effect of treatment by remoteness on refugees' expectations of discrimination in trust (Appendix, Table 3.16).

3.4.4 Experimental Outcomes for Hosts

This section explores trust, beliefs of expected trust, expected trustworthiness, and the hosts' altruism towards fellow hosts and refugees. Under examination were hosts' differences in trust and altruism towards refugees and hosts given the treatment. A regression controlling for all variables in the Appendix shows that the randomization of treatment within-host was balanced.

3.4.4.1 Trust of Hosts Towards Refugees and Fellow Hosts

Table 3.7 provides the results of experimental outcomes for the hosts. On average, hosts transferred slightly more money to fellow hosts than to refugees, although the difference is not statistically different ($p = 0.313$). Of the UGX 2,000 endowment, hosts sent, on average, 47.7% of this endowment to refugees and 48.7% of this endowment to fellow hosts. Johnson/Mislin (2011) found that trustors sent, on average, 50% of their donation in the trust game, while another study amongst former rebels in Northern Uganda found that subjects transferred, on average, 55.7%

Table 3.6 Altruism and expected altruism by refugees

Sample	Refugees		
	(1)	(2)	(3)
Panel (a)			
Dependent variable	Altruism: transfer in the dictator game		
Treatment (1 = partner is refugee, 0 = partner is host)	−2.446 (3.62)	−1.795 (3.23)	1.682 (3.15)
Distance to district (≥10 km) (d)		14.00*** (3.39)	22.94*** (3.1)
Treatment * Distance (d)			−15.43*** (5.12)
Constant	41.26*** (4.04)	28.00** (11.56)	26.28** (11.52)
Observations	255	242	242
R-squared	0.002	0.092	0.102
Panel (b)			
Dependent variable	Expected Altruism: elicited expectations of partner's transfer in the dictator game		
Treatment (1 = partner is refugee, 0 = partner is host)	−5.685* (3.18)	−5.422 (3.38)	−2.832 (3.18)
Distance to district (≥10 km) (d)		8.763** (3.74)	15.43** (6.37)
Treatment * Distance (d)			−11.49 (11.67)
Constant	54.37*** (3.12)	52.80*** (4.76)	51.52*** (5.43)
Observations	255	242	242
R-squared	0.011	0.041	0.048

Source Author's construction.
Notes are the same as for Table 3.5

of their endowment of UGX 2,000 (Bauer et al. 2018). Hosts' expected trustworthiness – defined as the tripled amount (percentage) that hosts expected receivers to return in the trust – was higher from fellow hosts, although the result is also not statistically different.

Similarly, altruism measured by the amounts transferred in the dictator game was higher towards hosts than towards refugees, but the difference is not statistically different. Hosts' expected altruism (beliefs of what senders would transfer in the dictator game) was higher from refugees than from fellow hosts, although the difference is not statistically significant. Those who had experienced war sent on average 48.9% of their UGX 2,000 endowment in the trust game, while those who had not experienced any war forwarded 49.7% of their UGX 2,000 endowment. To confirm

Table 3.7 Experimental outcomes (trust and dictator games) for the host (UGX)

Experimental outcomes	Senders			
Treatment+	Refugees	Host	All	t-test of difference
Trust: transfer in the trust game	953.48 (600.33)	973.45 (589.49)	961.4 (595.1)	−0.277
Expected trustworthiness: expectations of average amount to be returned (%)	49.95 (20.38)	51.33 (18.81)	50.5 (19.8)	−0.575
Altruism: transfer in the dictator game	719.51 (602.13)	810.81 (667.60)	756.4 (629.8)	−1.18
Expected altruism: belief of sender's transfer in dictator game	993.90 (536.94)	954.95 (562.25)	978.2 (546.6)	0.579

+Treatment is knowing whether your partner in the game is a refugee or member of the host community. The numbers in parentheses are standard errors

the results, other variables, such as the player's risk attitude, age, education level and marital status, were controlled in a regression.

3.4.4.2 Trust and Investments: Do Hosts Show More Preferences in Trust and Investments Towards Fellow Hosts than Towards Refugees?

Table 3.8 shows the trust (Panel A) and investment behavior (Panel B) of hosts. Trust is the percentage amount transferred by the trustor in the trust game, while investment is the percentage difference between the amounts transferred in the trust game and the amounts transferred in the dictator game. Treatment is a random assignment to information on whether one plays with hosts or refugees. Column (1) in Table 3.8 is a regression of the dependent variable on treatment while in column (2) and column (4), controls were used for all variables likely to explain trust, including distance as a dummy variable of less than 10 km (column 2) or as a continuous variable (columns 4 and 5). To examine whether increasing remoteness caused hosts to trust their fellow hosts more than refugees, treatment was correlated with distance both as a dummy (column 3) and as a continuous variable (column 5).

The average treatment effect was negatively affected after controlling for distance and its interaction with the treatment in columns 3 and 5 in Table 3.8. Hosts transferred less to refugees than to hosts by 10 percentage points, suggesting that they showed a preference for trusting fellow hosts more than refugees. Nevertheless, interacting treatment with distance (dummy and continuous variable) had a significant positive effect. Hosts located 10 km or more from the district headquarters transferred more of the share of their endowment to refugees than hosts by 22 percentage points. In other words, hosts trusted refugees more than fellow hosts with increasing remoteness from the district, suggesting that remoteness reduces discrimination of trust and overturns the theory of biases in social preferences towards one's social identity.

Table 3.8 Trust and investment behavior by hosts

Sample	Hosts as senders				
	(1)	(2)	(3)	(4)	(5)
Panel A					
Dependent variable	Trust – percentage amount sent in the trust game				
Treatment (1 = partner is refugee, 0 = partner is host)	−1.48 (5.29)	−2.536 (5.18)	−10.07** (4.81)	−2.583 (5.23)	−19.48** (8.54)
Distance to district (≥10 km) (d)		−3.933 (5.48)	−17.50** (7.78)		
Treatment * Distance (d)			22.23*** (6.54)		
Distance (km)				−0.461 (0.52)	−1.886** (0.70)
Distance * Treatment					2.217*** (0.73)
Constant	49.10*** (4.40)	43.19*** (12.44)	46.86*** (12.34)	45.94*** (12.82)	55.32*** (13.22)
Observations	279	262	262	262	262
R-squared	0.001	0.034	0.064	0.035	0.063
Panel B					
Dependent variable	Investment: percentage difference between trust and dictator allocations				
Treatment (1 = partner is refugee, 0 = partner is host)	0.997 (7.34)	0.839 (7.60)	−10.29 (6.42)	0.736 (7.74)	−22.47* (10.96)
Distance to district (≥10 km) (d)		−9.110** (4.00)	−29.16*** (8.83)		
Treatment * Distance (d)			32.85*** (9.20)		
Distance (km)				−0.912** (0.39)	−2.868*** (0.81)
Distance * Treatment					3.043*** (0.87)
Constant	4.955 (5.76)	4.747 (11.41)	10.17 (11.56)	9.745 (11.18)	22.63* (13.03)
Observations	279	262	262	262	262
R-squared	0	0.035	0.072	0.034	0.064

Source Author's construction
Notes are the same as for Table 3.5

There are likely to be increased opportunities for repeated interaction between host community members and refugees in places far away from district headquarters in remote areas.

Based on Cox (2004a, b), pure behavioral trust was identified by taking the difference between the amount of money sent in the trust game and the dictator game. This difference is the 'investment portion' of the trust game allocation or the strategic element of the trusting behavior (Bauer et al. 2018; Cox 2004a; Fehr 2009). Controlling for all factors likely to affect investment (Table 3.8; panel b), hosts invested in refugees more than fellow hosts in remote areas. Specifically, hosts who were more than 10 km from district headquarters invested 32 percentage points more to refugees than to other hosts, suggesting that remoteness increases hosts' investments towards refugees more than towards fellow hosts.

3.4.4.3 Hosts' Beliefs About Partners' Expectations of Trust and Trustworthiness: Are There Prior Beliefs and Expectations in Discrimination?

In order to measure beliefs about their partners' trust expectations, hosts were asked what they believed their partners would expect from them as senders in the trust game. Results in Appendix Table 3.17, columns 3 and 5 (Panel A) indicate that, after controlling for distance and its interaction with treatment, the effect of treatment on beliefs about a partner's expected trust was negative and statistically significant. They reveal that hosts believe that their fellow hosts expected more trust from them than refugees do. Also, hosts' beliefs about the confidence expectations of fellow hosts decreased with increasing remoteness, and remoteness had no effect on preferences of trust towards one's social identity. Despite these beliefs, hosts' perceived expectations of trust by their partners do not reflect their actual behavior measured in the trust game.

Theory suggests that the amount sent by the trustor reflects both expectations of trustworthiness as well as social preferences towards the receiver (Ashraf et al. 2006; Fehr 2009), such that the combined effect might produce a non-result in the trust game (Bauer et al. 2018). Similarly, hosts might think of refugees as untrustworthy because of differences in ethnicity or the likelihood of returning to South Sudan. On the other hand, it is also likely that hosts may not discriminate against refugees for altruistic reasons. In such circumstances, host communities' negative and positive considerations about refugees may cancel out in the trust game and produce a non-result.

These considerations are explored more in Table 3.17, Panels B and C in the Appendix, where expectations of reciprocity are assessed when hosts sent UGX 1,000 and UGX 2,000, respectively. The results show that treatment and remoteness had no significant effect on reciprocity expectations at the intensive and extensive margins. This suggests that hosts had no prior beliefs of expected discrimination in reciprocity by either refugees or fellow hosts, but believed that fellow hosts expect more from them in trust.

3.4.4.4 Are Hosts Parochial Altruistic?

We investigated whether hosts have parochial altruistic behavior or have a prior expectation of parochial altruism. On average, hosts sent 40.5% and 36% of their UGX 2,000 endowment to fellow hosts and refugees, respectively, in the dictator game (Table 3.9). Using a statistical t-test, the difference in the amount sent by treatment is nevertheless statistically insignificant ($p = 0.228$). The Kolmogorov–Smirnov test indicates no statistical difference in distributing the amount posted in the dictator game by hosts to either refugees or fellow hosts. Those who had experienced war sent on average 33.33% of their UGX 2,000 compared to 42.1% posted by those who had not experienced war. Results in Table 3.9, Panel A, confirm and show that treatment had no significant effect on the proportion of the endowment transferred by the host in the dictator game, suggesting no discrimination in altruism by the hosts. Remoteness did not seem to influence altruistic parochial behavior either.

3.4.5 Discussion of the Experimental Results

The results show that refugees discriminated against fellow refugees in reciprocating trust at the intensive margin and were more generous to hosts than to fellow refugees in more remote areas. This suggests that refugees don't have any prejudices against hosts and are biased against fellow refugees in rural areas. Similarly, refugees had no prior beliefs that their partners expected them to discriminate based on whether they were refugees or hosts. In the focus group discussions, refugees considered themselves no different in identity from hosts, given similar languages in some instances. This corresponds to results in other studies conducted in the refugee settlements in northern Uganda (FAO 2018). This finding suggests that refugees feel integrated with their hosts. One's identity within a particular group provides a sense of belonging (Ager/Strang 2008). The results also revealed that hosts were more likely to trust fellow hosts than refugees and thought that their partners expected them to discriminate by social identity.

Nevertheless, with increasing remoteness from district headquarters, hosts were more likely to trust and invest in refugees than in fellow hosts. In the focus group discussions, hosts had mixed responses with regard to trusting refugees. Some empathized with the refugees' situation; others did not trust refugees because they considered them thieves. 61% thought that refugees were thieves (Appendix, Table 3.18). Generally, many hosts associated refugee influx more with positive outcomes, such as improved health and education, than with negative issues, such as increased inequality.

It is also likely that with greater remoteness, the refugees' propensity to favor hosts over fellow refugees when reciprocating trust and playing fair may be due to their perception that hosts were of higher economic and social status than refugees. Indeed, the refugees regarded their hosts highly both socially and economically. Refugees were asked to place neighbors who were fellow refugees and hosts on

Table 3.9 Altruistic behavior and expectations of altruism by hosts

Sample	Host (senders)				
	(1)	(2)	(3)	(4)	(5)
Panel A					
Dependent variable	Host's altruism				
Treatment (1 = partner is refugee, 0 = partner is host)	−4.6 (3.87)	−6.36 (4.23)	−1.026 (5.43)	−6.55 (4.20)	1.437 (8.97)
Distance to district (<10 km) (d)		−6.835* (3.60)	−0.923 (6.42)		
Treatment * Distance (d)			−10.09 (7.14)		
Distance (km)				−0.706** −0.328	−0.175 −0.691
Distance (km) * Treatment					−0.853 −0.827
Constant	40.63*** (3.06)	54.64*** (8.78)	52.14*** (9.48)	57.19*** (8.75)	52.81*** (10.87)
Observations	273	254	254	254	254
R-squared	0.005	0.032	0.038	0.033	0.037
Panel B					
Dependent variable	Host's expectations of altruism				
Treatment (1 = partner is refugee, 0 = partner is host)	−5.685* (3.18)	2.128 (2.08)	−2.832 (3.18)	1.984 (2.04)	1.305 (5.45)
Distance to the district (≥10 km) (d)		−8.805* (4.52)	15.43** (6.37)		
Treatment * Distance (d)			−11.49 (11.67)		
Distance (km)				−0.747 (0.44)	−0.793 (0.51)
Distance (km) * Treatment					0.0725 (0.46)
Constant	54.37*** (3.12)	67.92*** (5.63)	51.52*** (5.43)	69.74*** (5.84)	70.11*** (5.61)
Observations	255	254	242	254	254
R-squared	0.011	0.067	0.048	0.059	0.059

Source Author's construction
Notes are the same as for Table 3.5

a ten-step socioeconomic status ladder. In this paradigm, people who are entirely without free choice and control over the way their lives turn out stand on the bottom rung, while those with the highest degree of free will over their lives stand on the highest rung. On average, refugees placed themselves at 3.5, their neighbors who were fellow refugees at 3.7 and hosts at a higher average of 5.9, suggesting that refugees perceived fellow refugees to be of a slightly lower economic and social status than hosts.

Refugees' high regard for hosts relative to fellow refugees was highly correlated to distance from district headquarters. However, it is appropriate to rule out the possibility that the higher perceived social and economic status of hosts relative to refugees might explain refugees' positive attitudes towards hosts compared to fellow refugees. If this were the case, differences in refugees' beliefs of their partners' expected reciprocity should have been significantly different when the partner was a host and when the partner was a refugee. Similarly, suppose hosts' perceived socioeconomic status of hosts relative to refugees mattered in their social attitudes towards refugees or hosts. In that case, their prior beliefs in expectations of trust should have been significantly different. However, this was not the case.

The fact that trustworthiness, trust, and altruism towards partners of another social identity increases with remoteness reveals the possibility of more significant and meaningful interactions between hosts and refugees in remote areas than in urban areas. First, settlements in remote areas with high transportation costs confine both parties to a smaller radius, increasing interaction (Kreibaum 2016). Business opportunities such as home-owned shops in rural areas are avenues for close interactions, unlike in the urban areas, where communication is with a diverse population. Indeed our data shows that more home-owned shops exist in rural areas. There is a 30% correlation between distance from district headquarters and the number of shops available within the community. Increased prosociality towards outgroups might be explained by the higher density of refugees in remote settlements. For example, Ayilo, Mungula and Pagirinya have the highest refugee population. To minimize these effects, controls were in place for settlement fixed effects, and analysis was focused at the village level. Lastly, increased prosociality towards outgroups might have been attributable to settlements in the remote areas being closer to the South Sudan border and therefore sharing similar languages and culture. However, this was not the case, as Adjumani town has a central location. Some settlements are far away from the South Sudan border and Adjumani town, but closer to other Ugandan districts.

3.4.5.1 Concerns for Self-selection

Remoteness seems to increase the likelihood of trust or reciprocating trust to a partner who does not share their social identity. Suppose refugee placement in different settlements involves self-selection and systematic screening and is thus non-random. In that case, there are likely to be correlations between refugees and hosts' behavior to remoteness. The research presented here indicates that the placement of refugees in settlements in Uganda has been random. Refugee settlements have been established sequentially as per the influx of refugees into the country. Any batch of refugees fleeing from war at a given point in time gets settled in a particular locality until it can no longer take in any more refugees, at which point a new settlement is established. In this case, refugees cannot choose which areas to live in, thus eliminating the possibilities of self-selection and screening to a given location. It can also be argued that the refugee influx into Uganda has been non-random, given the possibility that only refugees who are trustworthy, empathetic, and generous decide to move into Uganda following a conflict. Nevertheless, this is unlikely, given the nature of war and displacements from South Sudan, which are numerous, spontaneous, and randomly displace households, irrespective of social status and behavior.

3.5 Conclusion

This chapter examined trust, trustworthiness, and altruism between hosting communities and refugees who had been exposed to armed conflicts. It was hypothesized that there was likely to be favoritism in trust, trustworthiness, and altruism towards people from the same social identity arising from discrimination or ethnic stereotypes and that such social preferences would change with remoteness from urban areas such as district headquarters. This corresponds to the assumption that remoteness from urban areas allows for meaningful and repeated interactions between refugees and hosts. To examine these theories, trust and dictator games were conducted in eleven refugee settlements in Adjumani district and randomly selected host community villages close to the settlements. Host communities and refugees were randomly assigned to treatment, which was the knowledge of whether the partner with whom the games were played was either a refugee or a host. Other characteristics of the partner remained anonymous for all the players.

The study found that refugees were more likely to reciprocate trust and show altruism towards hosts with increasing remoteness from urban areas, specifically district headquarters. Refugees located more than 10 km from district headquarters transferred more of their endowment (as a measure of trust and generosity) to hosts than to fellow refugees by 8 and 15 percentage points, respectively.

The possibility that refugees' behavior might be due to their partner's beliefs ceases to apply, as no prior convictions of the partners' expectations of discrimination were found, even with increasing remoteness. On the other hand, host communities were likely to trust hosts when they knew who they were playing with, but their preferences changed with increasing remoteness from urban areas. The results show that hosts transferred less of their endowment in trust to refugees than to hosts by 10 percentage points; nevertheless, hosts located 10 km or more from the district headquarters trusted refugees more than hosts by 22 percentage points' difference. Unlike refugees, hosts were not altruistic towards either fellow hosts or refugees, even with increasing remoteness. Hosts also anticipated that their partners would expect them to favor fellow hosts in trust but were indifferent about whether their partners would expect them to be more altruistic. The mistrust by hosts shows that existing stereotypes or beliefs about refugees that hosts hold onto are likely to create social divides and affect refugee integration. For example, about 61% of hosts believed that refugees were thieves. Such stereotypes might, for instance, lead hosts to exclude refugees in their social and economic interactions. The fact that remoteness from urban areas increased trust, altruism, and reciprocity suggests that refugees and hosts had closer social ties and were therefore more integrated in remote areas. The findings can mainly be attributed to increased opportunities for interaction from small business opportunities like shops and to narrower confines of interaction in rural areas due to the high transaction costs of travel.

From the policy perspective, there is a need to make investments in social development interventions to create and foster social cohesion dimensions such as trust, feelings of shared identity and sense of social belonging, tolerance, compromise, and integration, which reduce any prejudices. Activities that allow for interaction – such as sports, religious worship, and community groups – can also build bridges and break any social divides.

Appendix

See Tables 3.10, 3.11, 3.12, 3.13, 3.14, 3.15, 3.16, 3.17 and 3.18.

Table 3.10 Variable description

Concept	Variable name	Description
Trust behavior		Amount trustors send in the trust game
Trustworthy		The average amount trustees would send back if they were sent UGX 1,000 and UGX 2,000
Altruism		Amount dictator sends in the dictator game
Beliefs about expected trust		What trustees believe trustors will send in the trust game
Beliefs about expected trustworthiness		What trustors expect trustees to return measured as the average amount expected to be returned when the trustors send UGX 1,000 and UGX 2,000
Beliefs about partner's expected trustworthiness		What trustees believe trustors expect in return measured as an average

(continued)

Table 3.10 (continued)

Concept	Variable name	Description
Treatment	Treatment	Having information on whether one's partner is a host or is a refugee
Risk	Risk level	Measured as a dummy variable of risk lover or risk-averse
Total assets	Total assets	Assets is a measured as an index from principal component analysis of total productive household assets (agriculture and non-agriculture assets), the value of livestock, and possession of charcoal stove, radio, bicycle, and phone following principal component analysis
Marital status	Marital status	Dummy variable of whether the household head was married or not (separated, widowed or single)

Table 3.11 Number of refugees and hosts interviewed from each of the settlements

	Number of refugees	Number of hosts	Distance from settlement to Adjumani town (km)	The population of refugees as of December 31, 2017
Pagirinya	55	48	17	32,055
Agojo	41	51	9	3,026
Alere 1	31	24	7	5,986 (whole of Alere)
Ayilo	9	37	21	34,470
Merieyi	35	70	3	3,509
Boroli	41	35	15	12,415
Olijo	16	12	17	1,342
Elema	12	17	12	4,834
Mungula	35	28	21	5,972
Alere 2	13	9	7	Same as Alere above

Table 3.12 Differences in characteristics by treatment received

	Receivers (refugees)				Senders (host community)			
Variable	Refugees (N = 104)	Host community (N = 154)	All (N = 257)	t	Refugees (N = 112)	Host community (N = 159)	All (N = 271)	t
Treatment (Information on who you play with)								
Characteristic of players								
Age	38.17(13.86)	38.61(14.53)	38.35(14.11)	0.241	37.92(14.52)	36.60(14.25)	37.38(14.40)	−0.74
Player is female	0.77 (0.41)	0.85(0.35)	0.80(.39)	1.588	0.51(0.50)	0.43(0.49)	0.48(0.50)	−1.4
Education								
None	0.37 (0.48)	0.46 (0.50)	0.4(0.49)	1.515	0.11(0.32)	0.1(0.30)	0.10(0.31)	−0.41
Primary	0.38(0.49)	0.41(0.49)	0.38(0.49)	0.484	0.67(0.03)	0.57(0.50)	0.63(0.48)	−1.65
Secondary and above	0.25 (0.43)	0.12(0.33)	0.12(0.33)	−2.47	0.21(0.41)	0.32(0.47)	0.25(0.43)	2.11
Average years of schooling	**4.53(4.70)**	**3.26(4.02)**	**4.01(0.28)**	**−2.241**	**5.16(3.68)**	**6.17(3.57)**	**5.57(3.66)**	**2.25**
Characteristics of households								
Age of the household head	40.86(14.62)	43.3(16.03)	41.84(4.47)	1.25	55.00(12.06)	41.75(13.07)	49.56(18.03)	−0.91
Household head is single or separated	0.15(0.35)	0.17(0.38)	0.16(0.36)	0.49	0.09(0.30)	0.1(0.31)	0.1(0.30)	0.207
Household head is widowed	0.34(0.47)	0.35(0.47)	0.34(0.02)	0.121	0.18(0.38)	0.13(0.34)	0.16(0.36)	−1.01
Household head is married	0.50(0.50)	0.47(0.50)	0.49(0.50)	−0.48	0.72(0.45)	0.75(0.42)	0.73(0.44)	0.7

(continued)

Table 3.12 (continued)

	Receivers (refugees)				Senders (host community)			
Household size	6.6(3.62)	5.22(2.86)	6.45(3.33)	−0.88	5.45(2.85)	5.33(2.81)	5.4(2.83)	−0.33
Wealth	−0.12(0.88)	−0.23(0.74)	−0.17(0.82)	−1.028	0.19(1.13)	0.01(1.08)	0.12(1.11)	−1.30
Risk preference	**2.66(1.14)**	**2.38(1.17)**	**2.55(1.16)**	**−1.859**	**3.03(1.12)**	**2.72(1.03)**	**2.90(1.09)**	**−2.27**
Household had a death or accident shock	0.29(0.45)	0.23(0.42)	0.27(0.44)	−1.11	0.19(0.40)	0.26(0.44)	0.22(0.41)	1.33
Household has experienced war	0.76(0.42)	0.56(0.47)	0.72(0.44)	−1.63	0.49(0.50)	0.40(0.49)	0.45(0.49)	−1.45
Household's perception of refugee influx (Index)					0.002(1.00)	0.07(0.96)	0.03(0.986)	0.589
Characteristics by community								
Presence of shops	0.973(0.160)	0.990(0.098)	0.98(0.14)	0.936	0.763(0.425)	0.75(0.434)	0.76(0.43)	0.264
Distance to the district (km)	6.69(3.67)	6.98(3.62)	6.8(3.64)	0.62	8.98(5.17)	9.74(4.72)	9.29(5.0)	1.23
Distance to the nearest tarmac (km)	8.98(6.44)	9.41(6.91)	9.15(6.63)	0.52	8.37(7.39)	10.03(7.77)	9.06(7.58)	1.78
Distance to SACCO (km)	1.42(0.45)	1.33(0.47)	1.39(0.48)	1.33	1.55(0.49)	1.54(0.50)	1.54(0.49)	−0.09

The wealth of households is an index from principal component analysis of total productive household assets, livestock value, and possession of charcoal stove, radio, bicycle, and phone. The numbers in parentheses are standard deviations

Table 3.13 Randomization balance of treatment within refugees and members of the host community

Dependent variable (treatment is whether one has information that they play with refugees or host community)	Refugees	Host community
Death/accident of household member^{+}	0.062 (0.07)	−0.086 (0.07)
Affected by war^{++}	0.146* (0.07)	0.104 (0.06)
Gender of household head^{+++}	−0.098 (0.09)	0.049 (0.07)
Gender of player^{+++}	−0.038 (0.09)	−0.021 (0.07)
Age of player	0.001 (0.00)	0.00 (0.00)
Age of household head	−0.001 (0.00)	0.001 (0.00)
Household size	0.006 (0.01)	−0.001 (0.01)
Primary education (Cf: no education)	0.07 (0.08)	−0.004 (0.11)
Secondary education and above (Cf: no education)	0.228* (0.11)	−0.119 (0.12)
Medium risklover (Cf: high risklover)	0.153 (0.08)	−0.144 (0.10)
Medium risk averse (Cf: high risk lover)	−0.018 (0.09)	−0.079 (0.11)
Highly risk averse (Cf: high risk lover)	0.175* (0.08)	0.081 (0.10)
Wealth	0.02 (0.04)	0.042 (0.03)
Duration of refugee status	−0.001* 0.00	
No. observations	235	253
Wald chi2	23.8	21.56
Pseudo R2	0.085	0.068

+ Dummy, 1 = yes, 0 = no; ++ dummy 1 = yes, 0 = no; +++ dummy 1 = female, 0 = male

Table 3.14 Kolmogorov-Smirnov test for equality of distribution functions

Characteristics	Refugees		Hosts	
	Kolmogorov-Smirnov value	*p* value	Kolmogorov-Smirnov value	*p* value
Gender of player	0.0795	0.83	0.089	0.658
Age of the player	0.095	0.636	0.0838	0.738
Have no formal education	0.0698	0.924	0.0168	1
Have a primary education	0.0303	1	0.094	0.6
Have a secondary education and above	0.1254	0.29	0.111	0.389
Household size	0.08	0.84	0.0603	0.975
Refugee duration	0.1474	0.137	0.148	0.14
Lowest wealth quintile	0.0587	0.985	0.0705	0.898
Second lowest wealth quintile	0.06	0.981	0.0232	1
Third lowest wealth quintile	0.0386	1	0.0437	1
Highest wealth quintile	0.0372	1	0.0911	0.645

Table 3.15 Refugees' beliefs of partners' expected reciprocity

Sample	Refugees				
	(1)	(2)	(3)	(4)	(5)
Panel A					
Dependent variable	Refugees' beliefs of partners' expected reciprocity when they receive UGX 1,000 in trust game (percentages)				
Treatment	1.915 (3.78)	1.622 (4.05)	−2.483 (4.48)	1.792 (4.06)	−2.063 (6.75)
Distance to district (<10 km) (d)		−1.529 (3.85)	−6.982 (6.05)		
Treatment * Distance (d)			9.485 −7.563		
Distance (km)				0.0534 (0.46)	−0.208 (0.65)
Distance * Treatment					0.437 (0.78)

(continued)

Table 3.15 (continued)

Sample	Refugees				
	(1)	(2)	(3)	(4)	(5)
Constant	44.66*** (3.36)	37.98*** (11.18)	39.87*** (10.75)	36.30*** (11.34)	38.53*** (10.52)
Observations	249	234	234	234	234
R-squared	0.002	0.04	0.05	0.039	0.041
Panel B					
Dependent variable	Refugees' beliefs of partners' expected reciprocity when they receive UGX 2,000 in trust game (percentage)				
Treatment	0.291 (2.60)	−0.371 (2.58)	0.48 (2.72)	−0.233 (2.52)	3.538 (3.85)
Distance to district (<10 km) (d)		1.432 (2.71)	2.562 (4.68)		
Treatment * Distance (d)			−1.965 (5.58)		
Distance (km)				0.243 (0.35)	0.499 (0.50)
Distance * Treatment					−0.427 (0.53)
Constant	39.32*** (2.43)	44.70*** (7.05)	44.31*** (7.25)	43.08*** (7.65)	40.89*** (7.69)
Observations	249	234	234	234	234
R-squared	0	0.077	0.077	0.079	0.081

Notes Same notes as for Table 3.12

Table 3.16 Refugees' anticipation of trust from partners

	(1)	(2)	(3)	(4)	(5)
Dependent variable	Refugees' elicited beliefs of expected transfers from senders in the trust game				
Treatment	3.395 (3.95)	2.28 (3.92)	−4.494 (4.58)	2.135 (3.98)	−6.686 (6.94)
Distance to district (<10 km) (d)		−0.0585 (5.57)	−9.057 (6.76)		
Treatment * Distance (d)			15.65** (7.44)		
Distance (km)				−0.148 (0.60)	−0.748 (0.84)
Distance * Treatment					1 (0.79)

(continued)

Table 3.16 (continued)

	(1)	(2)	(3)	(4)	(5)
Dependent variable	Refugees' elicited beliefs of expected transfers from senders in the trust game				
Constant	52.43*** (3.16)	56.15*** (8.96)	59.27*** (9.11)	57.72*** (10.32)	62.83*** (12.28)
Observations	249	234	234	234	234
R-squared	0.004	0.037	0.057	0.038	0.044

Notes for the above table are the same as for Table 3.12

Table 3.17 Hosts' beliefs of expected trust and their expectations of trustworthiness

Sample	Hosts				
	(1)	(2)	(3)	(4)	(5)
Panel A					
Dependent variable	Elicited beliefs of partner's expected trust				
Treatment	−2.897 (1.79)	−3.532 (2.41)	−4.409*** (1.15)	−3.631 (2.36)	−8.442*** (2.86)
Distance to district (<10 km) (d)		−10.29** (3.69)	−11.87*** (2.20)		
Treatment * Distance (d)			2.599 (7.00)		
Distance (km)				−0.852** (0.35)	−1.256*** (0.26)
Distance * Treatment					0.632 (0.57)
Constant	55.86*** (1.97)	59.30*** (6.37)	59.72*** (6.06)	63.31*** (7.91)	66.03*** (6.89)
Observations	280	263	263	263	263
R-squared	0.003	0.07	0.071	0.057	0.061
Panel B					
Dependent variable	Elicited beliefs of expected trustworthiness when sent UGX 1,000				
Treatment	1.715 (3.20)	−0.175 (3.48)	−2.283 (3.27)	−0.182 (3.45)	−5.661 (5.93)
Distance to district (<10 km) (d)		−2.419 (2.28)	−6.223 (5.05)		
Distance * Treatment			6.25 (7.54)		
Distance (km)				0.044 (0.20)	−0.418 (0.59)

(continued)

Table 3.17 (continued)

Sample	Hosts				
	(1)	(2)	(3)	(4)	(5)
Distance * Treatment					0.719 (0.82)
Constant	50.75*** (2.84)	43.34*** (10.31)	44.37*** (10.67)	42.21*** (10.44)	45.23*** (11.27)
Observations	280	263	263	263	263
R-squared	0.001	0.037	0.041	0.035	0.04
Panel C					
Dependent variable	Elicited beliefs of expected trustworthiness when sent UGX 2,000				
Treatment	−2.831 (3.16)	−3.471 (3.46)	−3.21 (2.71)	−3.441 (3.33)	−4.196 (5.24)
Distance to district (<10 km) (d)		0.615 (3.08)	1.086 (5.68)		
Treatment * Distance (d)			−0.774 (9.26)		
Distance (km)				0.44 (0.26)	0.376 (0.56)
Distance * Treatment					0.0991 (0.84)
Constant	51.35*** (2.58)	41.58*** (6.82)	41.45*** (6.61)	37.99*** (7.16)	38.41*** (7.49)
Observations	280	263	263	263	263
R-squared	0.005	0.043	0.043	0.052	0.052

Notes are the same as for Table 3.12

Table 3.18 Perception of the host community on the influx of refugees

Impact of the refugee influx	Proportion saying yes
Land wrangles increased	39.27
Health services have improved	90.63
Education	91.24
Inequality increased	36.86
Business opportunities have improved	82.18
Livelihood loss	38.67
Access to improved water	80.66
Increased theft impact	61.63
Increased prostitution	39.88
Increased opportunities for NGO	51.96

References

Acemoglu, D., Vindigni, A., & Ticchi, D. (2010). Persistence of Civil Wars. *European Economic Association*, *8*(May), 664–676.

Adelman, S., & Peterman, A. (2014). Resettlement and gender dimensions of land rights in post-conflict Northern Uganda. *World Development*, *64*, 583–596. https://doi.org/10.1016/j.worlddev.2014.06.031

Ager, A., & Strang, A. (2008). Understanding Integration: A Conceptual Framework. *Journal of Refugee Studies*, *21*(2), 166–191. https://doi.org/10.1093/jrs/fen016

Ahabwe, G., & Depio, S. (2019). *How Effective is the Self-Reliance Agenda in Uganda's* (Issue 107).

Akerlof, G. A., & Kranton, R. E. (2000). Economics and Identity. *Economics and Identity*, *CXV*(3), 715–753.

Akresh, R., Lucchetti, L., & Thirumurthy, H. (2012). Wars and child health: Evidence from the Eritrean – Ethiopian conflict. *Journal of Development Economics*, *99*(2), 330–340. https://doi.org/10.1016/j.jdeveco.2012.04.001

Allen, D., & Lueck, D. (1992). Contract Choice in Modern Agriculture: Cash Rent versus Cropshare. *The Journal of Law and Economics*, *35*(2), 397–426. http://www.jstor.com/stable/725546

Allen, T. (1991). Understanding Alice: Uganda's Holy spirit Movement in Context. *Journal of the International African Institute*, *61*(3), 370–399. https://www.jstor.org/stable/1160031?seq=1#metadata_info_tab_contents

Allen, T., & Koen, V. (2010). *The Lord's Resistance Army: Myth and Reality* (T. Allen & K. Vlassenroot (eds.); Issue November). Zed Books Ltd. http://www.zedbooks.co.uk/

Andreoni, J., & Bernheim, D. (2009). Social image and the 50–50 norm: a theoretical and experimental analysis of audience effects. *Econometrica*, *77*(5), 1607–1636. https://doi.org/10.3982/ECTA7384

Andreoni, J., & Miller, J. (2002). Giving According to GARP: An Experimental Test of the Consistency of Preferences for Altruism. *Econometrica*, *70*(2), 737–753.

Annan, J., Blattman, C., Mazurana, D., & Carlson, K. (2011). Civil war, reintegration, and gender in northern Uganda. *Journal of Conflict Resolution*, *55*(6), 877–908. https://doi.org/10.1177/0022002711408013

Ashraf, N., Bohnet, I., & Piankov, N. (2006). Decomposing trust and trustworthiness. *Experimental Economics*, *9*(3), 193–208. https://doi.org/10.1007/s10683-006-9122-4

Ashraf, N., Gine, X., & Karlan, D. (2009). Finding missing markets (and a disturbing epilogue): Evidence from an export crop adoption and marketing intervention in Kenya. *American Journal of Agricultural Economics*, *91*(November), 973–990. https://doi.org/10.1111/j.1467-8276.2009.01319.x

Bakwesegha, C., Brubaker, R., Connor, W., Ellis, A., Esman, M., Hannan, H., Hechter, M., Kalin, W., Lemarchand, R., Lund, Michaels, S., van der Stoel, M., Miall, H., Zartmann, William, I., Ropers, N., Rothchild, D., Tishkov, Valery, A., Vinas, A., & Waldman, P. (2004). Facing Ethnic Conflicts: Toward a New Realism. In G. Wimmer (Ed.), *Toward a new realism*. Rowman & Littlefield Publishers, 2004. https://books.google.de/books?id=DdtOAQAAQBAJ&dq=conrad+schetter+conflict&lr=&source=gbs_navlinks_s

Barr, A. (2003). Trust and expected trustworthiness: Experimental evidence from Zimbabwean villages. *Economic Journal*, *113*(489), 614–630. https://doi.org/10.1111/1468-0297.t01-1-00150

Bauer, M., Blattman, C., Chytilová, J., Henrich, J., Miguel, E., & Mitts, T. (2016). Can War Foster Cooperation? *Journal of Economic Perspectives*, *30*(3), 249–274. https://doi.org/10.1257/jep.30.3.249

Bauer, M., Fiala, N., & Levely, I. (2018). Trusting Former Rebels: An Experimental Approach to Understanding Reintegration after Civil War. *Economic Journal*, *128*(613), 1786–1819. https://doi.org/10.1111/ecoj.12503

Baumgartner, T., Götte, L., Gügler, R., & Fehr, E. (2012). The mentalizing network orchestrates the impact of parochial altruism on social norm enforcement. *Human Brain Mapping*, *33*(6), 1452–1469. https://doi.org/10.1002/hbm.21298

Bellemare, C., & Kröger, S. (2007). On representative social capital. *European Economic Review*, *51*(1), 183–202. https://doi.org/10.1016/j.euroecorev.2006.03.006

Bellows, J., & Miguel, E. (2006). War and institutions: New evidence from Sierra Leone. *American Economic Review*, *96*(2), 394–399. https://doi.org/10.1257/000282806777212323

Bellows, J., & Miguel, E. (2009). War and local collective action in Sierra Leone. *Journal of Public Economics*, *93*(11–12), 1144–1157. https://doi.org/10.1016/j.jpubeco.2009.07.012

Bennett, D. S., & Stam, A. C. (2016). The Duration of Interstate Wars, 1816–1985 Author (s): D. Scott Bennett and Allan C. Stam III Source: The American Political Science Review, Vol. 90, No. 2 (Jun., 1996), pp. 239–257 Published by: American Political Science Association Stabl. *The American Political Science Review*, *90*(2), 239–257.

Berg, J., Dickhaut, J., & McCabe, K. (1995). Trust, reciprocity, and social history. *Games and Economic Behavior*, *10*(1), 122–142. https://doi.org/10.1006/game.1995.1027

Bernhard, H., Fischbacher, U., & Fehr, E. (2006). Parochial altruism in humans. *Nature*, *442*(7105), 912–915. https://doi.org/10.1038/nature04981

Besley, T., & Persson, T. (2008a). The Incidence of Civil War: Theory and Evidence. In Intergovernmental Panel on Climate Change (Ed.), *NBER Working paper series* (Vol. 14585). Cambridge University Press. https://doi.org/10.3386/w14585

Besley, T., & Persson, T. (2008b). The Incidence of Civil War: Theory and Evidence. In Intergovernmental Panel on Climate Change (Ed.), *NBER Working paper series* (Vol. 14585). Cambridge University Press. https://doi.org/10.3386/w14585

Binswanger, H. P., & Rosenzweig, M. R. (1981). Contractual arrangements, Employment and wages in rural labor markets: A critical review. In *Studies in employment & rural development series* (Issue SER 67). http://documents.worldbank.org/curated/en/412971467997610342/Contractual-arrangements-employment-and-wages-in-rural-labor-markets-a-critical-review

Blattman, C., & Annan, J. (2010). The Consequences of Child Soldiering. *Review of Economics and Statistics*, *92*(4), 882. https://doi.org/10.1162/REST_a_00036

Blattman, C., & Miguel, E. (2010). Civil War. *Journal of Economic Literature*, *48*(1), 3–57. https://doi.org/10.1257/jel.48.1.3

Bloem, J. (2019). Good Intentions Gone Bad? The Dodd-Frank Act and Conflict in Africa's Great Lakes Region. In *HiCN*.

Bohnet, H., & Schmitz, C. P. (2019). *Uganda: A role model for refugee integration?* (No. 2; 2019).

Brosché, J., & Höglund, K. (2016). Crisis of governance in South Sudan: Electoral politics and violence in the world's newest nation. *Journal of Modern African Studies*, *54*(1), 67–90. https://doi.org/10.1017/S0022278X15000828

Brück, T., D'Errico, M., & Pietrelli, R. (2018). The effects of violent conflict on household resilience and food security: Evidence from the 2014 Gaza conflict. *World Development*, *2018*. https://doi.org/10.1016/j.worlddev.2018.05.008

Bundervoet, T., Verwimp, P., & Akresh, R. (2009). Health and civil war in rural Burundi. *Journal of Human Resources*, *44*(2), 536–563. https://doi.org/10.3368/jhr.44.2.536

Burke, M., & Young, P. (2009). Social Norms. In A. Bisin, J. Benhabib, & M. Jackson (Eds.), *The Handbook of Social Economics* (pp. 1–51).

Burks, S. V., Carpenter, J. P., & Verhoogen, E. (2003). Playing both roles in the trust game.pdf. *Journal of Economic Behaviour and Organisation*, *51*, 195–216. https://doi.org/10.1016/S0167-2681(02)00093-8

Cameron, A. C., Gelbach, J. B., & Miller, D. L. (2007). *Nber Technical Working Paper Series*. *90*(August), 414–427. https://pdfs.semanticscholar.org/df0a/ff0cb4db55166abbf5e33696d67698f81d3d.pdf%5Cnhttp://www.mitpressjournals.org/doi/pdf/10.1162/rest.90.3.414

Cesarini, D., Dawes, C. T., Fowler, J. H., Johannesson, M., & Lichtenstein, P. (2008). Heritability of cooperative behaviour in the trust game. *PNAS*, *105*(10), 3721–3726. https://doi.org/10.1073/pnas.0710069105

Charness, G., & Rabin, M. (2002). Understanding Social Preferences with Simple Tests. *The Quarterly Journal of Economics*, *117*(3), 817–869. http://www.jstor.org/
Chaudhuri, A., Paichayontvijit, T., & Shen, L. (2013a). Gender differences in trust and trustworthiness: Individuals, single sex and mixed sex groups. *Journal of Economic Psychology*, *34*, 181–194. https://doi.org/10.1016/j.joep.2012.09.013
Chaudhuri, A., Paichayontvijit, T., & Shen, L. (2013b). Gender differences in trust and trustworthiness: Individuals, single sex and mixed sex groups. *Journal of Economic Psychology*, *34*, 181–194. https://doi.org/10.1016/j.joep.2012.09.013
Chen, Y., & Li, S. X. (2009). Group identity and social preferences. *American Economic Review*, *99*(1), 431–457. https://doi.org/10.1257/aer.99.1.431
Coggio, T. (2019). Can Uganda's Breakthrough Refugee-Hosting Model Be Sustained? *Migration Policy Institute*, 1–11. https://www.migrationpolicy.org
Collier, P. (1999). On the Economic Consequences of Civil War. *Oxford Economic Papers*, *51*(January 1999), 168–183.
Collier, P., & Hoeffler, A. (2004). Greed and grievance in civil war. *Oxford Economic Papers*, *56*(2004), 563–595. https://doi.org/10.1093/oep/gpf064
Collier, P., Hoeffler, A., & Soderbom, M. (2004). Collier 2004 – Duration of civil wars. *Journal of Peace Research*, *41*(3), 253–273.
Cox, J. C. (2004a). How to identify trust and reciprocity. *Games and Economic Behavior*, *46*(2), 260–281. https://doi.org/10.1016/S0899-8256(03)00119-2
Cox, J. C. (2004b). How to identify trust and reciprocity. *Games and Economic Behavior*, *8256*(03), 260–281. https://doi.org/10.1016/S0899-8256(03)00119-2
Cramer, C. (2002). Homo Economicus Goes to War: Methodological Individualism, Rational Choice and the Political Economy of War. *World Development*, *30*(11), 1845–1864. https://doi.org/10.1016/S0305-750X(02)00120-1
Cunningham, D. E., Gleditsch, K. S., & Salehyan, I. (2009). It Takes Two: A Dyadic Analysis of Civil War Duration and Outcome. *Journal of Conflict Resolution*, *53*(4), 570–597. https://www.jstor.org/stable/20684603?seq=1#metadata_info_tab_contents
Cuvelier, J., Van Bockstaal, S., Vlassenroot, K., & Iguma, C. (2014). Analyzing the Impact of the Dodd-Frank Act on Congolese Livelihoods. In *Conflict Prevention and Peace Forum* (Vol. 1, Issue November). https://doi.org/10.1017/CBO9781107415324.004
d'Errico, M., Winters, P., & Romano, D. (2024). Assessing Uganda's Progressive Refugee Policy in the Era of COVID-19: Introduction to the Special Issue. *Journal of Development Studies*, *60*(3), 351–359. https://doi.org/10.1080/00220388.2023.2282364
Deininger, K., & Feder, G. (2001). Chapter 6 Land institutions and land markets. In B. Gardner & G. Rausser (Eds.), *Handbook of Agricultural Economics* (2001st ed., Vol. 1, Issue PART A, pp. 287–331). Elsevier Science B.V. https://doi.org/10.1016/S1574-0072(01)10009-5
Denison, R. F., & Muller, K. (2016). The evolution of cooperation. *Scientist*, *30*(1). https://doi.org/10.5840/tpm201467114
Dessalegn, A. G. (2017). The Cause and Consequence of Conflict in South Sudan. *International Journal of Political Science and Development*, *5*(1), 15–21. https://doi.org/10.14662/IJPSD2016.063
Development Pathways. (2018). *Analysis of Refugee Vulnerability in Uganda and Recommendations for Improved Targeting of Food Assistance* (Issue April 2018).
di Montenegro, T. X. (2017). *China's Interest in Africa: Conflict or Stability?* [Florida International University]. https://doi.org/10.25148/etd.FIDC001790
Elwert, G. (2018). Intervention in markets of violence. In *Potentials of disorder* (Issue September 2001, pp. 219–242). Manchester University Press. https://doi.org/10.7765/9781526137586.00017
Eswaran, M., & Kotwal, A. (1985). A Theory of Contractual Structure in Agriculture. *The American Economic Review*, *75*(3), 352–367.
Everett, J. A. C., Faber, N. S., & Crockett, M. (2015). Preferences and beliefs in ingroup favoritism. *Frontiers in Behavioral Neuroscience*, *9*(FEB), 1–21. https://doi.org/10.3389/fnbeh.2015.00015

Everts, E. (2003). Identifying a particular family humor style: A sociolinguistic discourse analysis. *Humor – International Journal of Humor Research*, *16*(4), 752. https://doi.org/10.1515/humr.2003.021

FAO. (2018). *Food Security, Resilience and Well-Being Analysis of Refugees and Host Communities in Northern Uganda.* https://doi.org/10.11975/j.issn.1002-6819.2015.24.025

FAO, & World Food Program. (2018). *Monitoring food security in countries with conflict situations: A joint FAO/WFP update for the United Nations Security Council* (Issue 3).

Fearon, J. D. (1995). Rationalist Explanations for War Author. *International Organization*, *49*(3), 379–414.

Fehr, E. (2009). On the Economics and Biology of Trust. *European Economic Association*, *7*(2–3), 235–266.

Fehr, E., Fischbacher, U., & Gächter, S. (2002). Strong reciprocity, human cooperation, and the enforcement of social norms. *Human Nature*, *13*(1), 1–25. https://doi.org/10.1007/s12110-002-1012-7

Fehr, E., & Schmidt, K. M. (1999). A Theory of Fairness, Competition, and Cooperation. *The Quarterly Journal of Economics*, *114*(3), 817–868. https://doi.org/10.1162/003355399556151

Fershtman, C., & Gneezy, U. (2001a). Discrimination in a Segmented Society: An Experimental Approach. *The Quarterly Journal of Economics*. https://rady.ucsd.edu/faculty/directory/gneezy/pub/docs/discrimination-society.pdf

Fershtman, C., & Gneezy, U. (2001b). Discrimination in a Segmented Society: An Experimental Approach. *The Quarterly Journal of Economics*.

Fisman, B. R., Kariv, S., & Markovits, D. (2007). Individual Preferences for Giving. *The American Economic Review*, *97*(5).

Fisman, R., Jakiela, P., & Kariv, S. (2017). Distributional preferences and political behavior. *Journal of Public Economics*, *155*, 1–10. https://doi.org/10.1016/j.jpubeco.2017.08.010

García, A. D. (2020). Armed groups, IHL and the invisible world: How spiritual beliefs shape warfare. *International Review of the Red Cross*, *102*(915), 1179–1199. https://doi.org/10.1017/S1816383121000229

Gates, S. (2015). Recruitment, Retention, and Religion in Rebel Groups. In *"Peace, Conflict, and Development", ESOP*, (Issue March 2015).

Geanakoplosand, J., Pearce, D., & Ennio, S. (1989). Psychological Games and Sequential Rationality. *Games and Economic Behaviour*, *1*(1989), 60–79.

Gebregziabher, G., & Holden, S. T. (2011). Distress rentals and the land rental market as a safety net: Contract choice evidence from Tigray, Ethiopia. *Agricultural Economics*, *42*(SUPPL. 1), 45–60. https://doi.org/10.1111/j.1574-0862.2011.00551.x

Ghatak, M., & Karaivanov, A. (2014). Contractual structure in agriculture with endogenous matching. *Journal of Development Economics*, *110*, 239–249. https://doi.org/10.1016/j.jdeveco.2013.05.005

Ghobarah, H. A., Huth, P., & Russett, B. (2003). and Maim the Shooting Wars Kill Civil People-Long After Stops. *The American Political Science Review*, *97*(2), 189–202. http://www.jstor.org/stable/3118203

Glaeser, E. L., Laibson, D. I., Scheinkman, J. A., & Soutter, C. L. (2000). Glaeser et al 2000_article.pdf. *Quarterly Journal of Economics*, *115*(3), 811–846.

Grossman, H. (1991). A General Equilibrium Model of Insurrections. In *American Economic Review* (Vol. 81, Issue 4, pp. 912–921). https://doi.org/10.2307/2006650

Guerrero, S. (2009). The Effects of the War in Iraq on Nutrition and Health: An Analysis Using Anthropometric Outcomes of Children. *SSRN Electronic Journal*, *14056*. https://doi.org/10.2139/ssrn.1359161

Guerrero Serdan, G. (2009). The Effects of the War in Iraq on Nutrition and Health: An Analysis Using Anthropometric Outcomes of Children. *SSRN Electronic Journal*, *14056*. https://doi.org/10.2139/ssrn.1359161

Harris, C., Jenkins, M., & Glaser, D. (2006). Gender Differences in Risk Assessment: Why do women take fewer risks than men? *Judgement and Decision Making, 1*(1), 48–63. http://journal.sjdm.org/jdm06016.pdf

Hartman, A. C., & Morse, B. S. (2018). Violence, Empathy and Altruism: Evidence from the Ivorian Refugee Crisis in Liberia. *British Journal of Political Science*, 1–25. https://doi.org/10.1017/S0007123417000655

Haselhuhn, M. P., Kennedy, J. A., Kray, L. J., Van Zant, A. B., & Schweitzer, M. E. (2015). Gender differences in trust dynamics: Women trust more than men following a trust violation. *Journal of Experimental Social Psychology, 56*, 104–109. https://doi.org/10.1016/j.jesp.2014.09.007

Henrich, J., Boyd, R., & Bowles, S. (2005). "Economic Man" in Cross-Cultural Perspective: Ethnography and Experiments from 15 Small-Scale Societies. *Behavioral and Brain Sciences, 28*(2005), 795–855.

Henrich, J., Ensminger, J., Mcelreath, R., Barr, A., Barrett, C., Bolyanatz, A., Cardenas, J. C., Gurven, M., Gwako, E., Henrich, N., Lesorogol, C., Marlowe, F., Tracer, D., & Ziker, J. (2010). Markets, Religion, Community size, and the Evolution of Fairness and Punishment. *Science, 327*(March 2010), 1480–1484. https://doi.org/10.1126/science.1182238

Henrich, J., McElreath, R., Barr, A., Ensminger, J., Barrett, C., Bolyanatz, A., Cardaroas, J. C., Gurven, M., Gwako, E., Henrich, N., Lesoronol, C., Marlowe, F., Tracer, D., & Ziker, J. (2006a). Costly punishment across human societies. *Science, 312*(5781), 1767–1770. https://doi.org/10.1126/science.1127333

Henrich, J., McElreath, R., Barr, A., Ensminger, J., Barrett, C., Bolyanatz, A., Cardenas, J. C., Gurven, M., Gwako, E., Henrich, N., Lesorogol, C., Marlowe, F., Tracer, D., & Ziker, J. (2006b). Costly punishment across human societies. MATERIAL RESPALDO. *Science (New York, N.Y.), 312*(5781), 1767–1770. https://doi.org/10.1126/science.1127333

Hirshleifer, J. (1995). Theorizing about conflict. In K. Hartley & T. Sandler (Eds.), *Handbook of Defense Economics* (Vol. 1, pp. 165–189). Elsevier. https://doi.org/10.1016/S1574-0013(05)80009-2

Hoeffler, A. (2012). On the Causes of Civil War. In *Oxford Economic Papers* (Vol. 50). Oxford University Press. https://doi.org/10.1093/oxfordhb/9780195392777.013.0009

Holden, S. T., & Otsuka, K. (2014). The roles of land tenure reforms and land markets in the context of population growth and land use intensification in Africa. *Food Policy, 48*, 88–97. https://doi.org/10.1016/j.foodpol.2014.03.005

Hovil, L. (2001). *Refuges and the Security Situation in Adjumani District* (Refugee Law Project, Issue 2).

Jakiela, P. (2011). Using economic experiments to measure informal institutions. In W. University (Ed.), *The Legacy and Work of Douglass C. North: Understanding Institutions and Development Economics* (pp. 248–265). Department of Economics, Washington University. https://doi.org/10.1017/CBO9781107300361.013

Johnson, N. D., & Mislin, A. A. (2011). Trust games: A meta-analysis. *Journal of Economic Psychology, 32*(5), 865–889. https://doi.org/10.1016/j.joep.2011.05.007

Joras, U., & Schetter, C. (2004). Hidden ties: Similarities between Research and Policy Approaches to Ethnic Conflicts. In G. Wimmer & U. D. Howowitz (Eds.), *Facing Ethnic Conflicts. Towards a New Realism* (pp. 315–332). Lanham, Rowman & Littlefield.

Jourdan, L. (2011). Mayi-Mayi: Young rebels in Kivu, DRC. *Africa Development, 36*(3–4), 89–111.

Karlan, D. S. (2005). Using Experimental Economics to Measure Social Capital and Predict Financial Decisions. *American Economic Review*, 95(5 (Dec., 2005)), 1688–1699. https://www.jstor.org/stable/4132772

Keswell, M., & Carter, M. R. (2014). Poverty and land redistribution. *Journal of Development Economics, 110*, 250–261. https://doi.org/10.1016/j.jdeveco.2013.10.003

Kimbrough, E. O., & Vostroknutov, A. (2016). Norms Make Preferences Social. *Journal of the European Economic Association, 14*(3), 608–638. https://doi.org/10.1111/jeea.12152

Kisangani, E. (2003). Conflict in the Democratic Republic of Congo: A mosaic of insurgent groups. *International Journal of World Peace, 20*(3), 51–80. www.jstor.org/stable/20753410

Kosfeld, M., Heinrichs, M., Zak, P. J., Fischbacher, U., & Fehr, E. (2005). Oxytocin increases trust in humans. *Nature, 435*(7042), 673–676. https://doi.org/10.1038/nature03701
Kosfeld, M., & Rustagi, D. (2015). Leader punishment and cooperation in groups: Experimental field evidence from commons management in Ethiopia. *American Economic Review, 105*(2), 747–783. https://doi.org/10.1257/aer.20120700
Kreibaum, M. (2016). Their Suffering, Our Burden? How Congolese Refugees Affect the Ugandan Population. *World Development, 78*, 262–287. https://doi.org/10.1016/j.worlddev.2015.10.019
Lemarchand, R. (2008). The Burundi Killings of 1972. In *Online Encyclopedia of Mass Violence* (Issue June). https://www.sciencespo.fr/mass-violence-war-massacre-resistance/en/document/burundi-killings-1972.html
Loewenstein, G., & Thompson, L. (1989). Social utility and Decision making in interpersonal contexts. *Journal of Personality and Social Psychology, 57*(3), 426–441.
Ma, T. (2009). China and Congo's coltan connection. In *Project 2049 Institute.*
Martiniello, G. (2010). African land questions, agrarian transitions and the state: the contradictions of neo-liberal land reforms. *Review of African Political Economy, 37*(125), 387–389. https://doi.org/10.1080/03056244.2010.511784
Maystadt, J.-F., & Verwimp, P. (2014). Winners and Losers among a Refugee-Hosting Population. *Economic Development and Cultural Change, 62*(4), 769–809. https://doi.org/10.1086/676458
Melander, E., Pettersson, T., & Themnér, L. (2016). Organized violence, 1989–2015. *Journal of Peace Research, 53*(5), 727–742. https://doi.org/10.1177/0022343316663032
Merkx, J. (2000). Document. Refugee identities and relief in an African borderland: a study of northern Uganda and southern Sudan. In *New issues in Refugee Research* (Vol. 21, Issue 19). https://doi.org/10.1093/rsq/21.1_and_2.113
Mkandawire, T. (2002). The terrible toll of post-colonial "rebel movements" in Africa: Towards an explanation of the violence against the peasantry. *Journal of Modern African Studies, 40*(2), 181–215. https://doi.org/10.1017/S0022278X02003889
Mkandawire, T. (2015). Neopatrimonialism and the Political Economy of Economic Performance in Africa: Critical Reflections. *World Politics, 67*(3), 563–612. https://doi.org/10.1017/S004388711500009X
Ngaruko, F., & Nkirunziza, J. (2000). An economic interpretation of conflict in Burundi. *Journal of African Economies, 9*(3), 370–409. https://doi.org/10.1093/jae/9.3.370
Nindorera, W. (2012). *The CNDD-FDD in Burundi: The path from armed to political struggle* (Issue 10).
Nkurunziza, J. D. (2015). Timing and Sequencing of Post-Conflict Reconstruction and Peacebuilding in Burundi. In *CRPD Working Paper* (Issue 34). https://doi.org/10.1093/acprof:oso/9780198757276.003.0013
Nkurunziza, J. D. (2022). The origin and persistence of state fragility in Burundi. In *State Fragility, Growth and Development* (Issue April). https://doi.org/10.4324/9781003297697-4
Nshimirimana, F. (2024). *Exclusionary Governance in Burundi:Implications for Democracy and Consolidating Peace.*
Nyadera, I. N. (2018). South Sudan conflict from 2013 to 2018: Rethinking the causes, situation and solutions. *African Journal on Conflict Resolution, 18*(2), 59–86.
O'Brien, A. (2009). Shots in the Dark: The 2008 South Sudan Civilian Disarmament Campaign. In *HSBA Working Paper*.
Odera, L. C. (2013). The Role of Trust as an Informal Institution in the Informal Sector in Africa. *Africa Development, 38*(3–4), 121–146.
Peterson, R. (2001). Resistance and Rebellion; Lessons from Eastern Europe. In *Cambrige University Press.* https://doi.org/10.1007/BF02430448
Pham, P. N., Vinck, P., & Stover, E. (2008). The Lord's Resistance Army and Forced Conscription in Northern Uganda. *Human Rights Quarterly, 30*(2008), 404–411.
Poole, L. (2019). *The refugee response in northern Uganda: Resources beyond international humanitarian assistance* (No. 2019; HPG Working Paper, Issue February). www.odi.org/hpg.

Powell, R. (2006). War as a commitment problem. *International Organization, 60*(1), 169–203. https://doi.org/10.1017/S0020818306060061

Rabbie, J. M., Schot, J. C., & Visser, L. (1989). Social identity theory: A conceptual and empirical critique from the perspective of a behavioural interaction model. *European Journal of Social Psychology, 19*(3), 171–202. https://doi.org/10.1002/ejsp.2420190302

Rabellino, D., Morese, R., Ciaramidaro, A., Bara, B. G., & Bosco, F. M. (2016). Third-party punishment: altruistic and anti-social behaviours in in-group and out-group settings. *Journal of Cognitive Psychology, 28*(4), 486–495. https://doi.org/10.1080/20445911.2016.1138961

Rabin, M. (1993). Incorporating fairness into game theory and economics. *The American Economic Review, 83*(5), 1281–1302. http://www.jstor.org/stable/2117561

Raleigh, C., Linke, A., Hegre, H., & Karlsen, J. (2010). Introducing ACLED-Armed Conflict Location and Event Data. *Journal of Peace Research, 47*(5), 651–660.

Refugee law project. (2022). Negotiating peace: Resolution of Conflicts in Uganda's West Nile Region. In *Refugee Law Project Working Paper* (Issue 12). https://doi.org/10.4324/978100331 7487-18

Relief web. (2002). *Rwanda-Uganda: Interahamwe reported present in Uganda.* https://reliefweb.int/report/democratic-republic-congo/rwanda-uganda-interahamwe-reported-present-uganda

Rockmore, M. (2017). The cost of fear: The welfare effect of the risk of violence in Northern Uganda. *World Bank Economic Review, 31*(3), 650–669. https://doi.org/10.1093/wber/lhw025

Rockmore, M. (2020). Conflict-Risk and Agricultural Portfolios: Evidence from Northern Uganda. *The Journal of Development Studies, 2016*, 1–21. https://doi.org/10.1080/00220388.2019.170 3953

Rufanges, C. J., & Aspa, J. M. R. (2016). *Democratic Republic of Congo: A Review of 20 years of war* (Issue April). https://escolapau.uab.cat/img/programas/alerta/alerta/RDCongo_20AnosGuerra_I.pdf

Saferworld. (2010). Karamoja conflict and security assessment. In *Report* (Issue September).

Shemyakina, O. (2011). The effect of armed conflict on accumulation of schooling: Results from Tajikistan. *Journal of Development Economics, 95*(2), 186–200. https://doi.org/10.1016/j.jdeveco.2010.05.002

Sigman, R., & Lindberg, S. I. (2017). Neopatrimonialism and Democracy: An Empirical Investigation of Africa's Political Regimes. *SSRN Electronic Journal, January*. https://doi.org/10.2139/ssrn.3066654

Skaperdas, S. (2008). An economic approach to analyzing civil wars. *Economics of Governance, 9*(1), 25–44. https://doi.org/10.1007/s10101-007-0043-2

State Parties to the 1951 Convention relating to the Status of Refugees and the 1967 Protocol. (2011). https://doi.org/10.1093/rsq/hdn023

Tajfel, H., Billig, M. G., & Bundy, R. (1971). Social categorization and intergroup behaviour. *European Journal of Social Pszchology, 1*(2), 149–178. https://doi.org/10.1002/ejsp.242001 0202

The Fund For Peace. (2019). *Fragile States Index Annual Report 2019*. www.fundforpeace.org

Titeca, K. (2024). Uganda and the DRC conflict: the interests driving Kampala's involvement. *The Conversation*, 23–26.

Uganda Bureau of Statistics. (2024a). National Population and Housing Census 2024: Preliminary Results. In *National Population and Household Census* (Vol. 256, Issue June).

Uganda Bureau of Statistics. (2024b). National Population and Housing Census 2024. In *Census 2024*. http://libdcms.nida.ac.th/thesis6/2010/b166706.pdf

UN, & African Union. (2011). *Fifth Anniversary of the signing of the Peace, Security and Cooperation Framework (PSCF)* (Vol. 46, Issue 0).

UNDP. (2017). *Summary of Study Uganda's' Contribution To.* https://data2.unhcr.org/en/documents/download/64687

UNECA. (2015). *Conflicts in the Democratic Republic of Congo: Causes, impact and implications for the Great Lakes region.* Routledge. https://www.uneca.org/sites/default/files/PublicationFiles/conflits_in_drc_eng_25sept_rev1.pdf

UNECA. (2016). Conflict in the democratic Republic of Congo: Causes, impact and implications for the Great Lakes region. In *Routledge Handbook of Security Studies: Second Edition*. https://doi.org/10.4324/9781315753393

UNHCR. (2018). *South Sudan Regional Refugee Response Plan* (Issue December). http://reporting.unhcr.org/sites/default/files/2018SouthSudanRegionalRefugeeResponsePlan-Jan-Dec2018%28January2018%29_0.pdf

UNHCR. (2019a). *Global Trends Forced Displacemnet in 2018*. www.unhcr.org/5c6fb2d04

UNHCR. (2019b). Uganda Country Refugee Response Plan. *The UN Refugee Agency, Jan 2019-Dec 2020*, 72. http://reporting.unhcr.org/sites/default/files/UgandaCountryRRP2019-20%28January2019%29.pdf

United Nations Development Programme. (2018). *Understanding land dynamics and livelihood in refugee hosting districts of northern Uganda*.

United Nations High Commision for Refugees (UNHCR), & Government of Uganda (GoU). (2019). *Refugee and Host Population by District*. Uganda Comprehensive Refugee Response Portal. https://data2.unhcr.org/en/country/uga

Venugopalan, H. (2016). Understanding the Conflict in Congo. In *ORF ISSUE BRIEF* (Issue May). https://www.orfonline.org/wp-content/uploads/2016/05/ORF_IssueBrief_139_Venugopalan_Final.pdf

Vlassenroot, K., & Van Acker, F. (2001). War as Exit from Exclusion? The Formation of Mayi-Mayi Militias in Eastern Congo. *Afrika Focus*, *17*(1–2), 51–77. https://doi.org/10.21825/af.v17i1-2.5426

von Braun, J., Teklu, T., & Webb, P. (1998). *Famine in Africa. Causes, Response and Prevention*. The John Hopkins Univerisity Press.

Voors, M. J., Nillesen, E. E. M., Verwimp, P., Bulte, E. H., Lensink, R., & Soest, D. P. Van. (2012a). Violent Conflict and Behavior: A field experiment in Burundi. *American Economic Review*, *102*(2), 941–964.

Voors, M. J., Nillesen, E. E. M., Verwimp, P., Bulte, E. H., Lensink, R., & Van Soest, D. P. (2012b). Violent Conflict and Behaviour: a field experiment in Burundi. *Source: The American Economic Review*, *102*(2), 941–964. https://doi.org/10.1257/aer.102.2.941

Wallensteen, P., & Axell, K. (1993). Armed Conflict at the End of the Cold War , 1989–92. *Journal of Peace Research*, *30*(3), 331–346.

Werner, K., & Lambsdorff, J. G. (2019). Emotional Numbing and Lessons Learned after a Violent Conflict – Experimental Evidence from Ambon, Indonesia. *The Journal of Development Studies*, 1–15. https://doi.org/10.1080/00220388.2019.1590550

Whyte, S. R., & Acio, E. (2017). Generations and Access to Land in Postconflict Northern Uganda: Youth Have No Voice in Land Matters. *African Studies Review*, *60*(3), 17–36. https://doi.org/10.1017/asr.2017.120

World Bank. (2015). *Forced Displacement in the Great Lakes Region*. http://hdl.handle.net/10986/21708

World Bank. (2016). *The Uganda Poverty Assessment Report 2016. Farms, cities and good fortune: assessing poverty reduction in Uganda from 2006 to 2013*. http://pubdocs.worldbank.org/en/890971474327477241/Uganda-Poverty-Assessment-Report-2016-Overview.pdf

WorldBank. (2016). *The Uganda Poverty Assessment Report, 2016: Farms, Cities and good fortune: assessing poverty reduction in Uganda from 2006 to 2013*.

Yami, M., & van Asten, P. (2018). Relevance of informal institutions for achieving sustainable crop intensification in Uganda. *Food Security*, *10*(1), 141–150. https://doi.org/10.1007/s12571-017-0754-3

Young, J. (2016). Popular struggles and elite co-optation: the Nuer White Army in South Sudan's Civil War. In E. LeBrun (Ed.), *Small Arms Survey*. Graduate Institute of International and Development studies.

Zhu, H., Filipski, M., Valli, J., Gonzalez, E., Gupta, A., & Taylor, J. E. (2016a). *Economic Impact of Refugee Settlements in Uganda* (Issue November).

Zhu, H., Taylor, J. E., Gupta, A., Filipski, M., Valli, J., & Gonzalez, E., E. (2016b). Economic Impacts of Giving Land to Refugees. In *Agricultural and Applied Economics Association 2018 Annual Meeting*. Agricultural and Applied Economics Association. https://doi.org/10.22004/ag.econ.274212

Chapter 4
Improving Refugee Self-reliance Through Access to Land: Do Social Preferences Matter?

4.1 Introduction

Land is a valuable resource for agrarian households displaced by conflict. It is crucial for boosting consumption and poverty reduction (Keswell/Carter 2014; Zhu et al. 2016a, b). With the proper support of land, refugees can contribute to their hosts' economic growth and development rather than being a burden (Kreibaum 2016) by improving their productive capacity (Zhu et al. 2016a, b). Land transfers to poor households boost their consumption by 25% (Keswell/Carter 2014). Zhu et al. (2016a, b) also show that the marginal benefit of providing refugees with land besides development aid significantly increases refugees' impacts on local incomes by a range of $92–$205. Despite the significant effect of land access, a substantial proportion of households emerging from conflict or displaced by conflict lack access and ownership rights to use land (Kreibaum 2016).

In many parts of the developing world, the structure of land ownership and land use is driven to a large extent by non-market informal land arrangements such as inheritance, allocation by village chiefs, friendly rental agreements among kin, access rights over a period, exchange of labor for land, sharecropping and fixed-wage contracts (Burke/Young 2009; Deininger/Feder 2001; Yami/van Asten 2018). Many households in such situations, particularly the land-poor, can only access land through informal land transactions, while it is also an income generating opportunity for landed families (Holden/Otsuka 2014). Such land arrangements usually respond to market imperfections such as risks and the absence of insurance markets (Binswanger/Rosenzweig 1981; Eswaran/Kotwal 1985). The informal land markets and partnerships do not depend on documentation or written contracts. Instead, they may rely on personal relationships of trust, altruism, and other informal institutions, such as existing cooperative norms, to settle for the best bargain, monitoring, enforcement, and verification (Holden/Otsuka 2014; Karlan 2005; Martiniello 2010), unlike formal contracts that rely on written rules that reinforce trust, certainty, and predictability (Odera 2013). For example, parties engaged in sharecropping may

A. Adong, *Armed Conflicts and Forced Displacements in the Anthropocene*,
The Anthropocene: Politik—Economics—Society—Science 41,
https://doi.org/10.1007/978-3-032-04820-2_4

depend on mutual trust that neither party reneges on the contractual arrangement through agency problems like moral hazard and shirking (Ghatak/Karaivanov 2014).

Similarly – due to altruistic or equity concerns – in sharecropping, the landowner might consider an equal share of the pie rather than competitive returns on labor and land or using the bargaining powers of an agent (Burke/Young 2009). It is also possible that the tenant/landowner might decide to bear all the costs of the inputs (perhaps due to altruism concerns) or share the expenses in the same proportion (fairness concerns) (Allen/Lueck 1992). In the context where contracting parties have experienced violence, empathy-driven altruism born out of previous exposure to violence (Hartman/Morse 2018) might explain contractual land arrangements like free land-giving between hosts and refugees.

This study explores whether refugees' and hosts' social preferences and trust behavior drive the willingness or previous engagement in land arrangements that improve refugees' access to land. Host communities' own productive inputs, such as land that refugees do not have, and private land transactions offer refugees an opportunity to acquire excess land from the hosts. Most of the research on social preferences is limited to just understanding individual attitudes and relations (Bauer et al. 2016, 2018), usually not the real outcomes but links to overcoming market failures and enforcing contracts (Bauer et al. 2018; Karlan 2005). This study explores whether social preferences of reciprocity, altruism, and trust predict previous engagement or the willingness to engage in different forms of land transactions between refugees and hosts. Examples of existing land arrangements between refugees and hosts include free land arrangements, exchange of labor for land, and land renting arrangements. It was hypothesized that more 'trusting' hosting communities and more trustworthy refugees are more likely and willing to engage in land transactions. It was also hypothesized that altruism and expectations of trustworthiness explain willingness or previous engagement in casual land arrangements.

The contribution of this chapter is threefold. First, it is of high policy relevance and aimed at addressing refugee integration into hosting communities and their self-reliance. Amid protracted refugee crises and unpredictable refugee inflows, humanitarian efforts are tailored toward ensuring refugee self-reliance and local integration (Hartman/Morse 2018). In Uganda, the government has embarked on free land distribution so that refugees can access and use land. However, this kind of gesture is costly and unsustainable in developing countries that are facing competing priorities and limited budgets (United Nations Development Programme 2018). Therefore, beyond direct government distribution of free land to refugees, it is crucial to explore alternative ways by which land can be made accessible to households displaced by armed conflicts. One likely avenue to achieve refugee land access and user rights is through their direct private engagement with local communities that own private or communal land. Refugee access to land through land transactions with hosts can potentially achieve the twin objectives of self-reliance and local integration. If trust and social preferences explain the willingness of hosts and refugees to engage in land transactions, then boosting these behavioral attributes amongst hosts and refugees offers alternative ways for refugees to acquire land. Also, if the community is willing to provide land to refugees through private land transactions, government land provision may erode this intrinsic motive (Frey/Jegen 2001). Land transactions between refugees and hosts are likely to lead to increased opportunities for interaction and social networking, which is helpful for the integration of refugees in the local communities.

Second, an experimental approach is used to measure trust, reciprocity, and altruism much more convincingly than other measures used in surveys (Glaeser et al. 2000) to show whether experimental games provide inferences to economic outcomes in institutional economics. Other studies have explored the linkages between behavioral attributes and informal insurance, market integration, and savings but not land transactions (Fisman et al. 2017; Jakiela 2011; Karlan 2005). For instance, Karlan (2005), using a similar empirical strategy, explores whether microfinance institutions' creditworthiness signals trustworthiness.

Lastly, this chapter contributes to the limited quantitative microeconomic literature focusing on refugees and their hosts' behavioral aspects. Most of the available research on forced displacements has been on the effect of refugee influx on the livelihoods of hosts (Kreibaum 2016; Maystadt/Verwimp 2014; Zhu et al. 2016a, b) with less focus on behavioral attitudes and their socioeconomic implications. Yet understanding attitudes and their implications is crucial to refugee management and local integration.

The main findings of the study indicate that high levels of trust and expectations of trustworthiness are significantly associated with the host's future willingness to engage in or previous engagement in land transactions. The results remain consistent, albeit of lower magnitude when excluding hosts with prior land engagement with refugees, which is a potential source of bias. The measures of trust identified in the experiments also corroborate survey measures of trust. In both trust measures, there is a statistical difference in the proportion of hosts who trust refugees and are willing to engage in land arrangements with them and those who trust refugees but are unwilling to engage in any land arrangements. Results also suggest that altruism by hosts does not signal their willingness to engage in land arrangements with refugees. However, this may not be causality but associations due to the possibility of reverse causality and endogeneity. Despite this, these findings are essential in verifying whether experimental games provide inferences for economic outcomes such as land transactions that may be largely informal. With humanitarian efforts leaning towards sustainable approaches that ensure refugees' self-reliance, fostering land transactions between hosts and refugees may provide an alternative approach to government land provision. Policies and interventions should be tailored towards building trust and social preferences amongst hosts and refugees.

The study focused on a population of Ugandan host communities and refugees from South Sudan who are quite similar in several aspects of their culture and ethnic backgrounds. The findings may therefore not be applicable in other contexts where the hosts and refugees may be very dissimilar in culture and customs, such as refugees from Sub-Saharan Africa fleeing to developed countries. Nevertheless, the findings may still be essential to host communities who have also been refugees in the past and are therefore, sympathetic towards refugees, a common phenomenon in refugee-hosting contexts in Sub-Saharan Africa.

The rest of this chapter is organized as follows. Section 4.1.1 reviews refugee hosting and land distribution in Uganda, comparing it with other regions in the GLR, and Sect. 4.1.2 briefly describes the study area. Section 4.2 is a review of the literature. Section 4.3 discusses the methodological approach, including a description of the experimental design and the empirical strategy. The results are presented and discussed in Sect. 4.4. Section 4.5 concludes the study with policy implications.

4.1.1 Refugee Hosting and Land Distribution in Uganda

Uganda is situated in central-eastern Africa with about 45.9 million people, and approximately 19.7% of its population is below the poverty line. Poverty is concentrated in its northern and eastern regions (World Bank 2016). Neighboring countries like the Democratic Republic of the Congo (DRC), South Sudan, and Rwanda have witnessed several internal and internationalized civil wars, leading to human suffering and displacements. Most of the displaced families have found their way into Uganda. Uganda hosts about 1.7 million refugees fleeing from South Sudan, DRC, Somalia, Rwanda, Eritrea, and Burundi, and the number has skyrocketed over the years (Fig. 4.1). Uganda is currently third after Turkey and Pakistan as a refugee-hosting country (UNDP 2017).

As enshrined in the 2006 Refugee Act and 2010 Refugee Regulations, Uganda's refugee policy allows refugees free movement, work, and access to services such as health and education in their host communities. The government of Uganda also gives refugees small plots of land (an average of 30 m by 30 m for residence) for

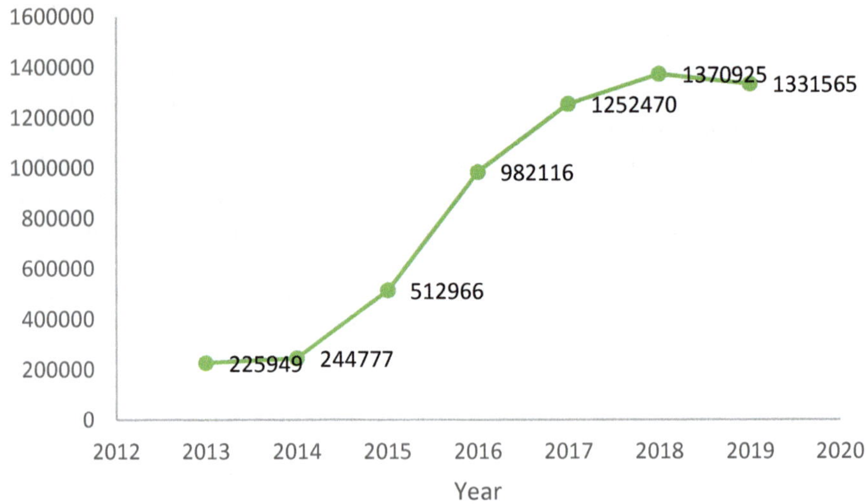

Fig. 4.1 Number of refugees fleeing into Uganda between 2012 and 2019. *Source* UNHCR (2019b)

residence and cultivation (Ahabwe/Depio 2019) and has generally been considered overly generous (UNHCR 2019b). Uganda's policy on refugees contrasts with the policies of other refugee-hosting countries within the region that are reluctant to use this approach of land distribution and instead confine refugees to camps (United Nations Development Programme 2018).

Currently, between 70 and 90% of refugees have officially received land from the government for cultivation (FAO 2018; Poole 2019; UNHCR 2018). Other avenues through which refugees acquire land include agreements with the land user, land purchases, and even incidences of walking in and cultivating without asking for permission (United Nations Development Programme 2018). Uganda's generous refugee policy of land distribution nevertheless constrains the government of Uganda and has proved unsustainable, given the protracted nature of refugee settlements and the unpredictable refugee influx. For example, in 2019/2020, 18% of the budget allocated to disaster preparedness and refugee management was used to resettle refugees, including land distribution. Free land distribution reduces government resources, which would otherwise be available for other competitive uses, for a poor-ranking nation on the human development index (e.g. 159th out of 189 countries in 2019). The government of Uganda relies strongly on donor funding from humanitarian agencies in the USA, the UK, Sweden, Canada, and Germany to support its land distribution program. External donor funding has nevertheless been very volatile. For example, at the end of 2017, the United Nations High Commission for Refugees (UNHCR) was only able to raise 39% of the required funds for the refugee response in Uganda. Also, the 2017 solidarity summit supporting Uganda's contribution to hosting refugees raised only USD 350 million out of the targeted USD 2 billion. The shortfall in external funding further constrains Uganda's efforts to support refugees using a meager budget.

Also, despite the excellent gesture of land distribution to refugees, the allocated plots of land (about 30 m by 30 m used for residential plots) are of poor quality and small in size for refugees to be self-reliant through farming (Bohnet/Schmitz 2019). Refugees cannot engage in production sufficient to meet their food needs, leaving them in dire situations (Coggio 2019). Before 2016, refugee households received residential plots of agricultural land of about 50 m by 50 m in area and a homestead plot of 20 m by 30 m in one of the districts (United Nations Development Programme 2018). In the absence of insufficient land provision by the government, land arrangements based on suitable contractual arrangements between hosts and refugees may offer alternative opportunities for land access.

4.1.2 Study Area

The study setting was Adjumani district, situated in Northern Uganda (Fig. 4.2). Adjumani has been plagued by civil tensions emanating internally from ethnic conflicts and externally from Southern Sudan. Also, many residents in the Adjumani district have previously been displaced due to internal conflicts. Currently, Adjumani

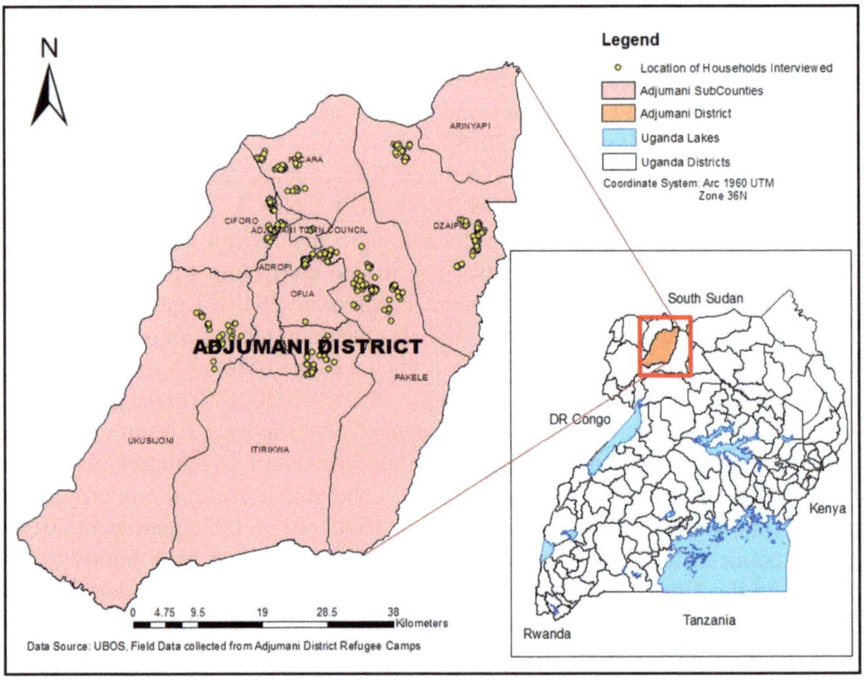

Fig. 4.2 A map of Adjumani district showing the distribution of the households in the study. *Source* Author's construction

has the highest refugee ratio to the host population (43:57) compared to other refugee-hosting districts with the country's newest and largest refugee settlements. The study was conducted in 11 refugee settlements and surrounding host communities, namely Elema, Boroli, Mugula, Oliji, Alere, Agojo, Maji, Merieyi, Ayilo, and Pagirinya settlements in Adjumani district. The distribution of the sampled households in the different refugee settlements is shown in Fig. 4.2.

4.2 Review of Literature

The level of trust in any society strongly predicts many economic and political outcomes (Bauer et al. 2018; Glaeser et al. 2000; Karlan 2005). Many social relations hinge on trust, trustworthiness, and altruism, which is crucial in the presence of market failures when contracts are difficult to enforce (Karlan 2005). When transactions seem complex, trust and social preferences will allow for transactions to be completed informally and at lower costs (Bellemare/Kröger 2007). Trust largely depends on individual attitudes, duration of acquaintanceships, and geographic similarity between groups (Glaeser et al. 2000; Karlan 2005).

Regarding social preferences, economic experiments show that people do not necessarily choose options that maximize their monetary pay-offs when their actions could affect the pay-offs of others (Charness/Rabin 2002). These actions are driven by the desire to reduce differences in pay-offs (difference aversion), reciprocity (raise or lower pay-offs depending on how others behave), and maximize social welfare (Charness/Rabin 2002; Fisman et al. 2007; Rabin 1993). Social preference models that depict prosocial behavior incorporate fairness concerns such as difference aversion and reciprocity when individuals care for their pay-offs and pay-offs received by others (Fehr/Schmidt 1999). Behavior such as trust will emanate from expectations of trustworthiness (expectations of returns) from the other party and satisfaction from being kind to others, referred to as unconditional kindness (Ashraf et al. 2006; Rabin 1993).

Prosocial behavior of individuals has been linked to outcomes such as creditworthiness (Karlan 2005), political allegiance (Fisman et al. 2007), and market integration (Jakiela 2011), and it is the fundamental driver of consumption savings and investments (Voors et al. 2012a, b). Karlan (2005) uses investment games to explore whether creditworthiness in microfinance institutions signals trustworthiness. The studies find that trustors give significantly more to (and believe they will receive more from) microfinance borrowers. Jakiela (2011) uses dictator games to examine the relationship between market integration and individual choices, and finds that giving in the dictator game is significantly associated with market integration (proximity to roads). A related paper by Henrich et al. (2010) finds that fairness varies with the extent of market integration (percentage of purchased calories). They also find that religiosity is associated with fairness, although not across all measures. Prosocial behavior may vary by gender (Bellemare/Kröger 2007; Chaudhuri et al. 2013b), exposure to violence (Bauer et al. 2018; Voors et al. 2012a, b), genetics (Kosfeld et al. 2005), environment (Cesarini et al. 2008), internalized norms and audience effects (Andreoni/Bernheim 2009; Kimbrough/Vostroknutov 2016). For example, Haselhuhn et al. (2015) show that women are more likely to trust and regain trust once lost, while those who have had previous experience of violence may be more altruistic towards those fleeing from violence than people with no such experience (Voors et al. 2012a, b).

4.3 Methodology

4.3.1 Conceptual Framework and Hypothesis

Many contractual arrangements in rural areas in developing countries may rely greatly on social relations and behavioral attributes of trust, reciprocity, and altruism. These attributes are crucial in verifying, enforcing, and monitoring undocumented contracts (Binswanger/Rosenzweig 1981; Ghatak/Karaivanov 2014; Odera 2013). For example, landlords in a sharecropping land arrangement are more likely to choose trustworthy tenants to minimize the possibility of under-reporting the output and shirking (Holden/Otsuka 2014). Evidence also shows that past exposure to violence increases prosociality (Hartman/Morse 2018; Voors et al. 2012a, b). Voors et al. (2012a, b) found that individuals exposed to violence in Burundi displayed more altruistic behavior towards their neighbors. Similarly, Hartman/Morse (2018) find that Liberian host communities exposed to violence are empathetic and generous. Host community members exposed to war may be charitable to refugees and likely to influence their willingness to engage in any land arrangements with refugees. In this regard, it was hypothesized that higher levels of trust and social preferences (expectations of trustworthiness and altruism) by the hosts are associated with an increased likelihood of engaging in informal land arrangements. In other words, trusting and altruistic hosts are more willing to engage or have previously been involved in land arrangements than non-trusting and selfish hosts. Similarly, refugees' reciprocity and altruism are associated with an increased probability of prior participation in informal land arrangements.

4.3.2 Variables and Measurements

For hosts, the main independent variables are trust and social preferences (altruism and expectations of trustworthiness), both of which are elicited from the games. Trust is measured by the proportion of the endowment that the trustor (hosts) sends to their partners. In contrast, the expectation of trustworthiness is measured by the average amount that the sender anticipates in return from the trust game (solicited using the strategy method). Altruism is the proportion of the endowment that the sender in the dictator game transfers to the receiver with no anticipation of receiving anything back. For refugees, the independent variables of interest are altruism and trustworthiness. Altruism is the proportion of the endowment that refugees send to their partners in the trust game. Trustworthiness is the average amount that refugees send back in the trust game. According to the literature, other independent variables that are likely to affect the willingness or previous engagement of hosts in land arrangements include age, the gender of the household head, the level of education, and the household's wealth (Allen/Lueck 1992; Ghatak/Karaivanov 2014; Holden/Otsuka 2014; Yami/van Asten 2018).

The dependent variables are: (1) present willingness by hosts to engage in any one of the existing land arrangements in the area (2) whether the hosts have previously engaged in land arrangements or not and (3) whether refugees have previously engaged in any land arrangement or not. The existing land arrangements between hosts and refugees in Adjumani district include sharecropping, land renting for a specified period, land, labor exchange, and giving refugees or hosts free land for a specified period.

4.3.3 Estimation

To estimate the effect of trust and social preferences on the willingness of host and refugee communities to engage in land arrangements, the following equation was used:

$$Y_h = \beta_0 + \beta_1 T_{ih} + \beta_2 R_{i_h} + \beta_3 A_{i_h} + \beta_4 X_h + \beta_5 D_i + \beta_6 E_h + \epsilon_h \tag{4.1}$$

Y_h is the willingness of hosts to engage in informal land arrangements with refugees. In another estimation, Y_h is whether the household has previously engaged in any land arrangement or not. T is a measure of trust of individual i from household h. It is a binary variable equal to one if the trustor (hosts) sends positives amounts and equal to zero if the trustor sends nothing to their partner. β_1 is the magnitude of association between trust and willingness to engage in or previous engagement in informal land transactions with refugees. R_{ih} is the measure of the host's expected reciprocity. Hosts were asked what they expected their partners to return to them after they made transfers in the trust game. β_2 is the association between expected reciprocity and willingness to engage in informal land transactions with refugees. A_{ih} measures altruism, which is a dummy variable depending on whether a household transferred positive amounts or not in the dictator game. Coefficient β_3 is the association between altruism and willingness to engage in informal land transactions with refugees. X_h is a vector of other household characteristics, such as household size, the land size held by the household, wealth status and the educational level of the household head. D_i are the characteristics of the player (education level and age). E_h measures the perceived ratio of the socioeconomic status of hosts to refugees. Lastly, ϵ_h is the error term. Equation (4.1) was estimated using a binary probit model.

It is likely that some households which have previously engaged in land arrangements with either hosts or refugees are currently unwilling to engage. At the same time, some are willing to continue to engage with refugees. To explore the role of trust and social preferences in the dynamism between previous engagement and present willingness to engage in land arrangements, four choices were constructed: (1) hosts who have ever and are currently willing to have a land arrangement with refugees, (2) hosts who have previously engaged in but are not currently willing to have any land arrangements with refugees, (3) hosts who have never had any land arrangements with refugees but are currently willing to engage in them, (4) hosts who have never had any land arrangements with refugees and are not currently willing to engage in them. The four choices are discrete, and the multinomial logit model was used to estimate the likelihood of a household being associated with one option over another. The multinomial logit model makes the assumption that the error terms should be independently and identically distributed across the four alternatives (Everts 2003).

4.3.3.1 Robustness Checks

Endogeneity in estimating the association between trust and social preferences and the willingness to engage in informal land arrangements is likely to be a problem. Hosts who have previously engaged in informal land arrangements with refugees already have prior reasons for trusting or not trusting, introducing bias in estimating the effect of trust and social preferences on their willingness to engage in informal land arrangements. As a sensitivity test, households that had previously engaged in any informal land arrangements with a refugee were excluded from the analysis and the results were compared.

4.3.4 The Experiment

4.3.4.1 Trust and Dictator Games

Berg et al. (1995) proposed the two-player sequential trust game with no contract to enforce agreement (Johnson/Mislin 2011). The trust game involves two anonymously paired players; a sender and receiver. The sender decides on what proportion of his endowment (as a measure of trust) (s)he should send to the receiver with the anticipation that the sender will reciprocate the trust or return the endowment from unconditional kindness. The amount transferred is tripled, and the receiver decides how much to send back to the trustor (as a measure of trustworthiness). The dictator game measures unconditional kindness (altruism) (Ashraf et al. 2006). The dictator and the receiver in the dictator game split a prize normalized to have a unit value. The dictator decides what proportion of his endowment to give to the receiver with no anticipation of receiving anything back. In our study, we used the within-subject design in which each participant played both the trust and dictator games in random order.

4.3.4.2 Experimental Procedures and Instructions

The trust and dictator games were conducted in accordance with the written procedures of Bauer et al. (2018). Bauer et al. (2018) adapted the written protocols of Henrich et al. (2006a, b). Both games were played separately by refugees and host communities. Refugees played as trustees/receivers in the trust game and as senders in the dictator game. Hosts played as trustors in the trust game and also played as senders in the dictator game. Trustors were endowed with slips equivalent to Uganda shillings (UGX) 2,000 and had the opportunity to send either UGX 0, 1,000, or the entire UGX 2,000 endowment. The amount transferred by the trustors was tripled and given to the trustees, who had the chance of sending back UGX 3,000 if the trustor sent UGX 1,000 and up to UGX 6,000 if the trustor sent them UGX 2,000. Hosting communities were also asked to place in the envelopes how much they expected from their partner if they transferred UGX 1,000 (tripled amount 3,000) and UGX 2,000 (tripled amount UGX 6,000). Both groups played separately in different demarcated areas. To control for learning effects from playing the game in the same order, individuals were randomly assigned to the game (either trust or dictator game) that they would play first.

Before the start of the game, all rules were explained to the group of refugees and host communities, for example: (i) that the game would remain anonymous, (ii) that the cards or slips represented UGX 1,000 notes which would be replaced with real money after the game (iii) that payments would be from one of the randomly chosen two games, (iv) that expectations would be paid at the rate of UGX 500 for every correct prediction, (v) that envelopes of different colors would be used for the amount of money that the players decided to transfer or retain and for expectations. Instructions for playing the game were provided first at the group level and subsequently at the individual level. The players' comprehension and understanding of the game was tested and those who did not seem to understand the experiment were dropped and replaced.

4.3.4.3 Sampling Technique and Sample Size

A multistage sampling technique was used, whereby in the first stage refugee settlements were randomly selected based on whether they had been in existence for two years, five years, or more than five years. Also randomly selected were two of the five hosting local council areas (lowest administrative units in Uganda) within a vicinity of 15 km from refugee settlements. In the second stage, refugee and host households were randomly selected from the settlements and local council areas using probability proportional to size sampling. In total, the study covered 628 refugee and host community households, although the final sample with complete analysis only contained 619 households (288 refugee households and 331 host households). 589 families participated in the field experiments (272 refugees and 317 hosts).

4.3.5 Survey Data and Sample Characteristics

The information required for the study was also collected from a household survey and focus group discussions in each of the refugee settlements and local council areas of the host communities. The household survey and focus group discussions were conducted between April and May 2018, while the field games were held in June 2018. The focus group discussions solicited information on the available land arrangements in the area, access to infrastructure and refugees, and hosts' perceptions of refugee influx in the area. A survey solicited information on household demographic characteristics, consumption patterns, and welfare. Table 4.1 provides

Table 4.1 Summary statistics of variables used

Variables	(1)	(2)	(3)	(4)	(5)
	N	Mean	Standard deviation	Minimum	Maximum
1. The ratio of perceived economic, social status of oneself to a neighboring refugee	619	1.072	0.893	0.100	9
2. The ratio of perceived economic, social status of oneself to a neighboring host community	619	0.925	0.844	0.100	10
3. Household head is female (d, 1 = Yes)	589	0.628	0.484	0	1
4. Age of player	624	38.48	14.86	22	90
5. Average amount transferred in trust game by hosts	317	981.1	578.9	0	2,000
6. Amount transferred in dictator game (refugees and hosts)	589	787.8	626.1	0	2,000
7. Hosts' beliefs of the expected average amount to be reciprocated	318	50.76	19.53	0	100
8. Average percentage reciprocated in trust game by refugees	272	37.29	18.45	0	100
9. Refugees' expectations of amount to be transferred in trust game	272	1,092	525.0	0	2,000
10. Years of schooling of the household head	585	4.844	4.104	0	17
11. Distance to district headquarters	619	8.572	4.795	1	16
12. Number of shops in the locality	619	6.596	3.412	1	12
13. Logarithm of total productive assets	624	2.967	4.418	0	13.62
14. Ever participated in land arrangement with refugees (d, 1 = yes)	628	0.253	0.435	0	1
15. Ever participated in land arrangement with host community (d, 1 = yes)	628	0.347	0.476	0	1
16. Willingness to offer refugees land freely (d, 1 = yes)	628	0.347	0.476	0	1
17. Willingness to rent land to refugees (d, 1 = yes)	628	0.121	0.326	0	1

(continued)

Table 4.1 (continued)

Variables	(1)	(2)	(3)	(4)	(5)
	N	Mean	Standard deviation	Minimum	Maximum
18. Willingness to engage in land labor arrangements (d, 1 = yes)	628	0.0701	0.255	0	1
19. Willingness to engage in other land arrangements (d, 1 = yes)	628	0.0303	0.171	0	1
20. Ever engaged in any land arrangement (d, 1 = yes)	628	0.473	0.500	0	1
21. Willingness to engage in any non-market land transactions (d, 1 = yes)	628	0.433	0.496	0	1

Numbers in parentheses are standard deviations. N refers to the number of respondents

the summary statistics for the variables used in the study. The average amount transferred by the hosts in the trust game was UGX 981.1,[1] while the average amount transferred in the dictator game by all players (both refugees and hosts) was UGX 787.7. Hosts' expectations of reciprocity were 50.76% of the tripled amount that they transferred. This amount was somewhat higher than the actual average reciprocated amount by refugees (37.29%). Refugees' expectations of the amount their partners would transfer in the trust game as a measure of expected trust was an average of UGX 1,092, representing about 54.6% of the endowment.

4.4 Results

4.4.1 Descriptive Statistics

Hosts and refugees were asked if they had ever engaged in any land arrangements with refugees, hosts, or both. They were also asked if they were currently willing to engage in each of the following land arrangements: (1) free land arrangements (cultivate the land for free for a specified period), (2) offer land in exchange for labor, (3) rent land for a specified period, and (4) other unspecified informal land arrangements. Overall, 47.3% of both refugees and hosts had ever engaged in any land arrangements, and 43.3% were currently willing to engage in some form of land arrangements. Specifically, 34.7% of hosts were willing to engage in free land arrangements with refugees. 12.1% were ready to rent out their land, 7% were willing to engage in

[1] When the study was conducted, 1 USD = UGX 3,600; therefore UGX 981.1 was approx. 0.27 USD. For simplicity, the use of UGX is maintained throughout this book.

land labor arrangements, and 3% were willing to engage in other unspecified land arrangements.

4.4.1.1 Previous Engagement Land Arrangements by the Host Community

The results presented in Table 4.2 show characteristics of hosts based on whether they had ever had any land arrangements with refugees in the past or not. The results show no statistical difference in the amounts transferred in the dictator game by the hosts' previous engagement in informal land arrangements. There were also no significant differences in trust, expectations of reciprocity, or altruism arising from previous participation in land arrangements with refugees. Regarding other characteristics, females were significantly less likely to have engaged in any land arrangements with refugees than males: 34.9% of females had had a land arrangement with refugees compared with 58.8% of male-headed households of hosting communities. There were also significant differences in years of schooling of the household head with regard to engagement in land arrangements with refugees. The relative perceived socioeconomic status of self (host community) to refugees and fellow hosts and the value of productive assets was not statistically different between hosts willing to engage in land arrangements and those unwilling to engage in land arrangements.

4.4.1.2 Host Community Willingness to Participate in Land Arrangements

Table 4.3 shows the characteristics of hosts by their willingness to engage in land arrangements. 71.5% of hosts were willing to engage in land arrangements with refugees. Specifically, 61.4% were willing to engage in free land arrangements, 12.3% in land labor exchange, and another 5% in other unspecified land arrangements. There were significant differences in trust by hosts willing to engage in informal land arrangements. Hosts willing to engage in land arrangements with refugees transferred UGX 1,090 (about 54.5% of their UGX 2,000 endowment) to their partner, while hosts unwilling to engage in any land arrangements with refugees transferred a lesser amount of UGX 913.26. Other behavior measures, such as expectations of trustworthiness and beliefs of expected trust, were not significantly different between hosts willing or unwilling to engage in informal land arrangements. Other variables, such as gender of the household head and the ratio of perceived socioeconomic status compared to refugees, showed a significant difference between willingness to engage in informal land transactions. For example, those willing to engage in informal land transactions perceived themselves to be of a higher social and economic status than their neighbors.

Table 4.2 Characteristics of hosts based on whether they had ever had any land arrangements with refugees or not

	Had any informal land arrangements with refugees (%)			
	Yes (46.2%)	No	All	t value
Trust: amount transferred in the trust game (UGX)	1037.5(645.21)	962.02(554.86)	981.07(578.86)	−1.01
Expectations of partner's reciprocity (average percent)	54.219(20.88)	49.61(18.96)	50.76(19.53)	−1.82
Altruism: amount transferred in the dictator game	739.726(643.85)	788.24(617.19)	765.82(629.11)	0.68
Household head is female	0.349(0.49)	0.588(0.49)	0.477(0.50)	4.35
Age of the household head	38.06(14.2)	37.33(14.46)	37.67(14.33)	0.45
Years of schooling	6.234(3.82)	4.953(3.50)	5.543(3.70)	3.11
Ratio of perceived economic status of oneself to refugees	1.14(1.10)	1.01(0.79)	1.074(0.95)	−1.16
Ratio of perceived economic status of oneself to host community	1.088(0.69)	1.032(0.80)	1.058(0.75)	−0.66
Value of productive assets (UGX)	8294.521(28626.95)	10305.88(43181.2)	20011.36(37129.79)	0.479

Source Author's own construction
The numbers in parentheses are standard deviations

4.4.1.3 Previous Engagement and Future Willingness to Engage in Land Arrangements

Descriptive statistics show that 187 families (29.8%) had engaged in and were currently willing to engage in informal land arrangements. 110 households (17.5%) had previously engaged in such arrangements but were not currently willing to engage

Table 4.3 Characteristics of hosts by their willingness to engage in land arrangements with refugees

Willingness to engage in any land arrangement with refugees				
	Yes (N = 226)	No (N = 90)	All (N =316)	t value of the difference
Trust: amount transferred in the trust game (UGX)	1090.9(562.73)	913.26(579.67)	981.07(578.86)	−2.68
Altruism: amount transferred in the dictator game	769.91(632.57)	755.56(623.71)	765.82(629.11)	−0.183
Expected partner's reciprocity (average percent)	52.92(19.28)	49.45(19.60)	50.76(19.53)	1.53
Beliefs in partner's expectation of trust	1108.33(498.67)	1070.7(498.78)	1084.9(498.28)	0.652
Household head is female	0.39(0.49)	0.68(0.47)	0.47(0.50)	4.625
Age of the household head	36.69(13.69)	40.11(15.63)	37.66(14.33)	1.92
Years of schooling	5.897(3.64)	4.66(3.69)	5.54(3.69)	−2.72
Ratio of perceived socio-economic status of oneself to host	1.08(1.01)	1.057(0.752)	1.074(0.945)	0.195
Ratio of perceived socio economic status of oneself to refugee	1.12(0.837)	0.893(0.436)	1.05(0.753)	−2.445
Total value of productive assets	10995.58(10995.58)	5311.11(12255.38)	9376.58(37129.79)	−1.229

Source Author's own construction
The numbers in parentheses are standard deviations

in them, while 85 families (13.5%) had never engaged in such arrangements but were willing to engage in them. Lastly, 246 (39.17%) families had never participated in and were not willing to engage in any land arrangements. Refugees dominated the last category because they lacked land. For host communities, 162 households (51.3%) had engaged and were willing to engage again in informal land arrangements. 40 families (17.5%) had participated in the past and were no longer willing to engage in non-market land transactions. 64 families (20.6%) had never engaged but were willing to engage in land arrangements. Lastly, 50 families (15.82%) had never participated in and were unwilling to participate in any non-market land transactions.

The highest proportion of hosts who sent all their initial endowment of UGX 2,000 in the trust game was those who had engaged in informal land transactions and were willing to engage in them in the future, suggesting that they trusted a lot more (Appendix, Fig. 4.3). Those who had never been involved in any land arrangement and were willing to engage sent the highest proportion of a 50/50 split of their endowment (UGX 1,000). It is probable that these were individuals with an aversion to inequity. Players who had previously engaged in informal land transactions but were unwilling to engage in them anymore represented the highest proportion of players who sent nothing from their endowment, suggesting that they trusted people less (27.12%). Those who had never engaged and were not willing to engage in information land transactions had the next highest proportion of players who sent zero shilling of their endowment. Overall, those unwilling to engage in any land arrangements with refugees showed the highest degree of caution (transferred zero in the trust game).

Hosts who had never participated and were unwilling to engage in any informal land arrangements sent the highest proportion of their endowment to their partners, followed by households who had never engaged but were willing to engage (Appendix, Fig. 4.4). The figures seem to illustrate the possibility that host communities who have never engaged with refugees in any land arrangement may be more altruistic than those who have engaged with them in the past, perhaps because they are clueless about the latter's behavior and socioeconomic status. Indeed the median and mean of the perceived ratio of one's own socioeconomic status to that of neighbors who are refugees were slightly higher for hosts who had never engaged with refugees. For hosts who had previously engaged with refugees, their perceived socioeconomic ratio to refugees was somewhat lower than that of hosts who had never engaged with refugees. Their expectations of reciprocity were also low. The results seem to show that intrinsic behavior revealed through experiments is somehow linked to some outcomes that people respond to in experiments.

Reciprocating trust is crucial for informal transactions. To trust substantially, an individual's expectations of their partner's reciprocation of their trust is an important determinant. Hosts who have previously engaged in informal land transactions with refugees but are unwilling to engage anymore have the highest proportion of players whose beliefs about expected reciprocity or trustworthiness of their partners is zero. In other words, their expectations of reciprocity by refugees are low in the trust game, perhaps given their previous engagement. Hosts who have previously engaged with refugees and are currently willing to or who have never participated but are willing to engage with refugees have firmer beliefs in reciprocation of trust by refugees.[2] The survey results on trust also show that 20.5% of hosts have previously been involved with refugees and are unwilling to trust refugees anymore. 12% of hosts who have never encountered and are not willing to engage trust refugees. 9.3% of hosts who have been involved with refugees and are willing to engage trust refugees. Lastly, 8.3% of the hosts have not been involved in the past but are willing to trust refugees.

4.4.2 Econometric Estimation

The purpose of the games was to examine whether trust, trustworthiness, and altruism are associated with the increased likelihood of hosts to engage in land arrangements with refugees. The hypothesis was that the more 'trusting' hosting communities and the more trustworthy refugees were likely and currently willing to engage in land arrangements with refugees.

Table 4.4 shows the results of the analysis of factors associated with the host's present willingness to engage in land arrangements with refugees using a full and a reduced sample that excludes families that have engaged in informal land arrangements in the past. These results show that having trust is associated with a 20% increase in willingness to engage in land transactions compared to less trusting families (who make no transfer in the trust game). The results are consistent, albeit of a lower magnitude when families that have previously had land engagements are excluded from the sample. This shows that trust is crucial for the host's willingness to engage in informal land transactions.[3]

The gender of the household head and the total value of the household assets were also associated with greater willingness to engage in land transactions with refugees. Females were associated with 16% less willingness to engage in land transactions with refugees than their male counterparts. Also, a 10% increase in the value of total assets that the household owned was associated with a 0.01% increase in willingness to engage in land transactions with refugees. The perceived ratio of socioeconomic status of hosts to refugees was also associated with a higher likelihood of engaging in land transactions with refugees. If hosts perceived that refugees were better off than they were, this was associated with less willingness by hosts to engage in land transactions with refugees.

[2] The previous treatment in playing the dictator and trust game was the random assignment to information that one was playing with either a refugee or a member of the host community. This did not predict whether hosts or refugees have ever engaged in any informal land transaction in the past or their willingness to engage in the future, and therefore does not affect the analysis.

[3] Due to the limited sample, it is not possible to distinguish between trust towards refugees or trust towards hosts.

Table 4.4 A probit analysis of factors associated with the current willingness of hosts to engage in informal land arrangements with refugees (margins)

Variables	Willingness to engage in land arrangements (full sample)			Willingness to engage in a land arrangement (sample excludes those who have ever engaged)		
	(1)	(2)	(3)	(4)	(5)	(6)
Transferred in the dictator game (dummy; 1 = Yes)	−0.092* (0.047)	−0.075 (0.047)	−0.078* (0.046)	−0.095 (0.070)	−0.084 (0.070)	−0.098 (0.067)
Transferred a positive amount in the trust game (dummy; 1 = Yes)	0.183*** (0.070)	0.205** (0.085)	0.201** (0.083)	0.163** (0.065)	0.174* (0.096)	0.132* (0.073)
Average expected trustworthiness (percentage)		0.001 (0.002)	0.001 (0.002)		0.002 (0.002)	0.002 (0.002)
Household size		−0.019** (0.010)	−0.014 (0.009)		−0.024* (0.012)	−0.015 (0.010)
Household head is female (d, 1 = yes)		−0.204*** (0.077)	−0.160** (0.070)		−0.115 (0.107)	−0.052 (0.091)
Age of the household head		−0.002 (0.003)	−0.002 (0.002)		−0.003 (0.002)	−0.001 (0.002)
Years of schooling		0.005 (0.008)	0.001 (0.008)		0.003 (0.009)	0.002 (0.007)
Log of total assets		0.016*** (0.006)	0.013** (0.006)		0.009 (0.008)	0.005 (0.006)
Ratio of socioeconomic status of self to refugees			0.183*** (0.024)			0.191*** (0.033)
The ratio of socioeconomic status of self to hosts			−0.114*** (0.034)			−0.087*** (0.031)
Pseudo R squared	0.017	0.101	0.171	0.018	0.081	0.164
Observations	314	302	302	234	224	224

Source Author's own construction
Notes The numbers in parentheses are standard errors, and the analysis is clustered at the village level with settlement fixed effects. *** $p < 0.01$, ** $p < 0.05$, * $p < 0.1$. represent statistical significance at 1%, 5% and 10% respectively

4.4.2.1 The Combined Decisions of Previous Engagement and Current Willingness to Engage in Informal Land Transactions

Table 4.5 reports the results of the multinomial logit model, comparing factors associated with previous engagement and current willingness to engage in land transactions with refugees. The base outcome is households who have never had and are unwilling to engage in any land transactions with refugees. The results show that people who transfer positive amounts in the dictator game are associated with the option of not

Table 4.5 A multinomial logit model comparing factors associated with previous engagement and current willingness for host communities to engage in informal land arrangements with refugees (margins)

Variables	Ever had a land arrangement and presently willing (N = 162)		Ever had a land engagement and not willing to engage with refugees (N = 40)		Never had a land engagement and willing to engage with refugees (N =64)	
	(1)	(2)	(3)	(4)	(5)	(6)
Made a transfer in the dictator game (dummy; 1 = yes)	0.012 (0.041)	0.026 (0.045)	0.036 (0.063)	0.046 (0.058)	−0.093** (0.041)	−0.099** (0.041)
Made a transfer in the trust game (dummy; 1 = yes)	0.067 (0.066)	0.093 (0.073)	−0.128* (0.075)	−0.136* (0.074)	0.143** (0.065)	0.152** (0.069)
Household head is female	−0.247*** (0.056)	−0.211*** (0.045)	−0.004 (0.063)	0.026 (0.061)	−0.002 (0.062)	0.009 (0.073)
Age of the household head		−0.001 (0.003)		0.002 (0.002)		−0.002 (0.001)
Years of schooling		0.006 (0.009)		0.010* (0.006)		0.002 (0.006)
Log of total assets		0.018*** (0.006)		0.001 (0.004)		−0.001 (0.004)
Pseudo R squared	0.055	0.079	0.055	0.079	0.055	0.079
Observations	314	310	314	310	314	310

Source Author's own construction

The base outcome is hosts who have "Never had a land arrangement with refugees and are not presently willing to engage in any land arrangement" (N = 50). Standard errors are in parentheses. *** $p<0.01$, ** $p<0.05$, * $p<0.1$. represent statistical significance at 1%, 5% and 10% respectively

having engaged and not being currently willing to engage in land arrangements. This is compared to their counterparts who have never engaged in but are currently willing to engage in land arrangements with refugees. Specifically, there is a 10% likely association between the transfer of positive amounts in the dictator game (altruism) and the option of not previously engaging and not currently being willing to engage in any informal land transactions with refugees. This suggests that altruistic hosts are not necessarily involved in or willing to engage in land transactions with refugees, contradicting previous assumptions. The results also show that individuals who transfer positive amounts in the trust game are more likely to be associated with never engaged but presently willing to engage in land transactions with refugees. Specifically, there is a 15% more likely association between individuals who transfer positive amounts in the trust game and the willingness to engage in land transactions with refugees when they have not been involved in the past. Although marginally significant, trust is less associated with individuals from households who have previously engaged and are currently unwilling to engage with refugees, suggesting that hosts need to trust refugees before engaging in any informal land arrangements.

Apart from trust and altruism, the results show that female-headed households are associated with less willingness to engage in informal land arrangements with refugees at the time of the survey. They are more likely to be in the category of never been involved and unwilling to engage. Evidence shows that female-headed households are less likely to be involved in risky contractual arrangements because of their low bargaining power and tendency to be risk-averse (Gebregziabher/Holden 2011; Holden/Otsuka 2014). On the other hand, a 10% increase in the total assets is associated with a 0.2 percentage point higher likelihood of having ever had a land engagement with refugees and being willing to engage in informal land transactions with refugees. Therefore wealthy households are more likely to engage in casual land arrangements with refugees.

4.4.2.2 Refugees' Previous Engagement in Land Arrangements

About 35% of refugees have ever engaged in a land transaction with either a host or fellow refugees. The descriptive statistics show that reciprocity is higher for those refugees who have never participated in any land transaction with either refugees or hosts. Expectations of trust and transfers in the dictator game that signals altruism are higher for refugees who have never participated in any land engagements (Figs. 4.5 and 4.6, in Appendix). For example, 12.3% of refugees who have ever engaged in any land arrangement expect their partners to transfer a zero amount of their endowment compared to 3.6% who have never been involved in any land arrangement. The differences are, nevertheless, not significant. One factor that is quite different between refugees engaged in land transactions and those who have not is the years of schooling (Appendix, Table 4.6). The former has, on average, 4.9 years of education compared to 3.5 years of education for the latter.

Table 4.7 in the Appendix shows that social preferences are less associated with refugees' participation in land transactions. Altruism and trustworthiness are not associated with refugees' likely engagement in the informal land market. The hypothesis that participation in informal land transactions signals that refugee are trustworthy is therefore rejected. The gender, age, and years of schooling of the household head are the significant factors associated with refugees' participation in non-market land transactions. Female-headed households are 18.7% less associated with involvement in non-market land transactions than male-headed households. An additional year to the household head's age is associated with refugees' likely participation in informal land transactions by 0.5 percentage points. Also, one other year of schooling for a refugee household's head is related to an increase in the likely participation in non-market land transactions by 2.5%.

4.4.3 Discussion

The results show that trust and high expectations of trustworthiness are associated with an increased likelihood of hosts engaging in land transactions with refugees. Trust is crucial for many operations that remain informal and noncontractual. Given that most land transactions in the study setting remain informal, trust ensures that contracting parties do not renege on the agreements. In the focus group discussions, some hosts associated refugees with theft, showing their lack of trust in the latter. It's also likely that hosts who have previously been engaged in informal land arrangements with refugees will no longer have the will if refugees abused their trust. Trust is mainly due to individual attitudes and the existing relationship between players, including cultural similarity, duration of acquaintanceships, and geographic similarity (Glaeser et al. 2000; Karlan 2005). Hosts may place more trust in refugees who have stayed longer with them than in newcomers because longer-term refugees have learned and adopted the hosts' existing norms from repeated social interactions. With time, hosts' negative perceptions of refugees might also change due to repeated social and economic interactions and information received from peers and the media. Any efforts towards building trust may involve increasing opportunities for social and economic interactions.

Literature suggests that previous exposure to violence increases prosociality towards people also affected by violence (Hartman/Morse 2018; Voors et al. 2012a, b), resulting from empathy or from the desire to reciprocate good deeds. This study hypothesized that hosts who were once forcibly displaced are more likely to be empathetic to refugees in their communities. It was thought that sympathetic concerns are likely to drive land arrangements, such as giving refugees free land for cultivation. However, the results do not support charitable concerns as a driver of land transactions between hosts and refugees. Perhaps, as Hartman/Morse (2018) suggest, norms of reciprocity are likely to be higher amongst closely-knit groups. If this is the case, hosts may be more aligned to reciprocating trust with fellow hosts than with refugees. Indeed, in a separate analysis, altruism is found to be associated with land arrangements between hosts and fellow hosts and not with refugees.

The results further show that if hosts perceive that refugees are better off, they are less willing to engage in informal land transactions with refugees. It is plausible to think that hosts view refugees as competitors for the scarce resources and think that they are likely to be better off. Kreibaum (2016) finds that hosting communities surrounding refugee settlements in Uganda harbor negative views on their present economic situation and feel neglected by the central government. Such feelings may cause resentment of refugees by hosts. Indeed, the results reported in this chapter show a negative association between hosts who perceive that refugees are socially and economically better off and willingness to engage in informal land transactions.

Other factors explaining the host's willingness to engage or actual engagement in informal land arrangements include the value of assets owned, the gender of the household head, and the perceived relative socioeconomic status of hosts to neighboring refugees. Wealthier hosts are also more likely to have participated or be willing to engage in casual land arrangements with refugees. This is not surprising, as wealthier households have the land resources to engage in land arrangements with refugees. For example, in land renting agreements, households poor in non-land resources such as farm equipment and labor may find it difficult to participate (Holden/Otsuka 2014). Evidence also shows that wealthier households are more likely to benefit from refugee influxes because they are better positioned to tap into the available opportunities (Maystadt/Verwimp 2014). Female household heads are less likely to have been involved or be eager to engage in informal land arrangements. Female-headed households are associated with 16% less willingness to engage in informal land transactions with refugees than their male counterparts. This might be due to the fact that female-headed households lack access to land or do not have land rights and might consider engaging in land arrangements with refugees a risky venture. In some areas of Northern Uganda, females access land use rights through their husbands or, in the absence of a spouse, through their patrilineal family. This arrangement places females in a disadvantaged position regarding land access (Adelman/Peterman 2014; Whyte/Acio 2017). Most research also shows that women tend to take on less risky ventures (Harris et al. 2006). In this case, given that refugees may only temporarily be settled (Zhu et al. 2016a, b), they might consider it risky to engage in land transactions with them.

For refugees, their high trustworthiness is not associated with their previous engagement in land transactions. For reporting and monitoring purposes, it was anticipated in this study that informal land arrangements would discriminate against untrustworthy refugees, based on evidence that trustworthy individuals might be preferred to dishonest individuals in many casual land arrangements (Holden/Otsuka 2014). The results show informal institutions' failure to ration land to only trustworthy refugees.

As a limitation of the study, trust and social preferences are intrinsic characteristics influenced by observable and unobservable factors, some of which may explain the willingness of the individual to engage in informal land arrangements. To the extent possible, the study controls most of the observable factors but, given its cross-sectional nature, was unable to control for unobserved factors. In this regard, the explanations are limited to associations rather than attributing changes in the willingness to engage in informal land arrangements to trust and social preferences.

4.5 Conclusion and Policy Recommendations

Given the intensified resurgence of conflicts all around the globe (in particular in Africa) and consequent migration flows, governments in many low/middle-income countries (LMICs) design policies to support and integrate refugees. Humanitarian approaches to supporting refugees are leaning towards novel program designs that allow refugees to "assist themselves" amid protracted displacement, waning humanitarian assistance, and the inclusivity Agenda 2030 (United Nations Development Programme 2018; Zhu et al. 2016a, b). Providing land to refugees for residential and agricultural purposes is one avenue for achieving self-reliance and local integration (United Nations Development Programme 2018). However, host countries are often land-constrained and/or do not have a fully fleshed land law and registrar system. Therefore, government land provision (as is the case in Uganda) may be insufficient and constraining to Government resources; private land arrangements between hosts and refugees offer alternative ways by which refugees can access land.

This study examined how trust and social preferences may encourage private land arrangements in Uganda. Uganda has been conflict-prone for decades in the past in its northern part and has recently experienced a high influx of refugees from South Sudan and the Democratic Republic of the Congo. Experimental methods were used to measure trust and social preferences among and between refugees and hosts in the Northern Region of Uganda. Informal land arrangements that are common in the developing world in rural areas are usually undocumented and may rely to a great extent on social relations of trust and reciprocity. Hosting communities that have previously been forcibly displaced due to internal conflicts may exhibit norms of reciprocity and altruism towards those currently displaced by war due to empathetic concerns. Therefore, it was hypothesized that (1) trusting and altruistic hosts are willing or more likely to have engaged in land arrangements with refugees, unlike non-trusting and altruistic hosts; (2) trustworthy refugees are also more likely to have engaged in land arrangements with refugees.

The results of the research support these hypotheses. In detail, the quantitative analysis showed that trust and social preferences largely explain previous engagement of hosts in land arrangements and their willingness to do so in the future. Based on evidence that trust and trustworthiness are likely to be high when individuals are closer socially (Glaeser et al. 2000), opportunities that increase socioeconomic interactions between refugees and hosts, such as social events and social groups, may be a worthwhile approach. Other interventions that build mutual trust between refugees and hosts include spreading positive information that helps to combat negative stereotypes. These programs could complement government land provision and offer a cost-efficient way to create mutual benefits. In addition, private arrangements between hosts and refugees are less likely to cause resentment against refugees among host communities and will therefore contribute to social peace in these areas.

Although this research provides only a case study on refugee-host interactions and refugee support policies, the findings may also have wider implications for other areas and contexts. Specifically, they may be essential to host countries that have suffered from conflict and forced migration in the past and that are therefore more sympathetic toward refugees. Nevertheless, the context of the study remains specific since the culture and language of hosts and refugees are relatively close in the study.

Appendix

See Figs. 4.3, 4.4, 4.5 and 4.6; Tables 4.6 and 4.7.

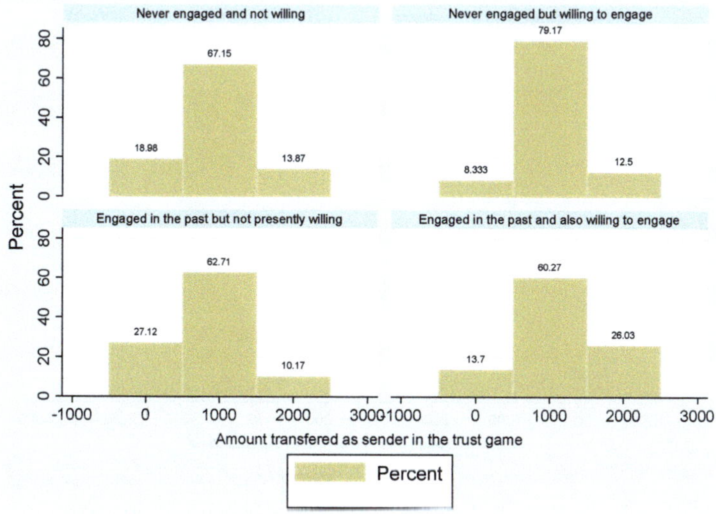

Fig. 4.3 Showing hosts' transfers in the trust game by previous engagement and future willingness to engage in informal land arrangements. *Source* Author's construction

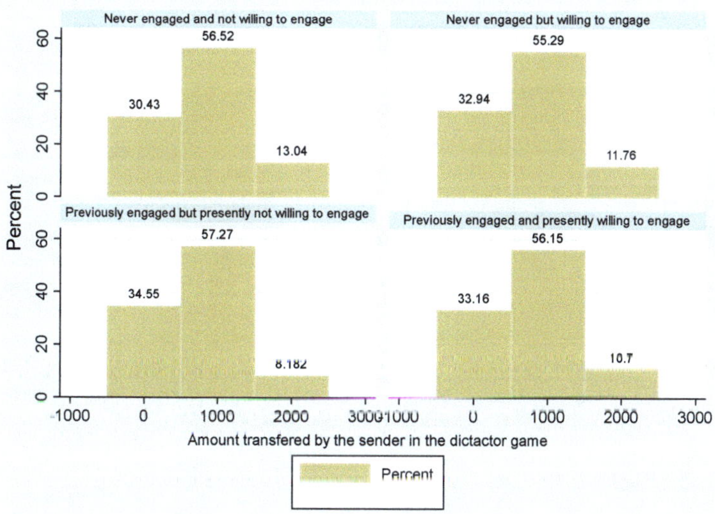

Fig. 4.4 Showing hosts' transfers in the dictator game by previous engagement and willingness to engage in informal land arrangements. *Source* Author's construction

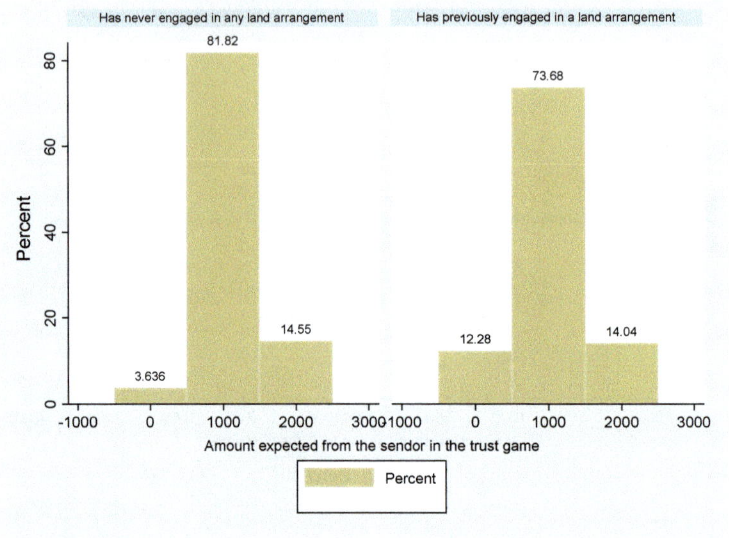

Fig. 4.5 Refugees' expectation of trust by previous land engagement. *Source* Author's construction

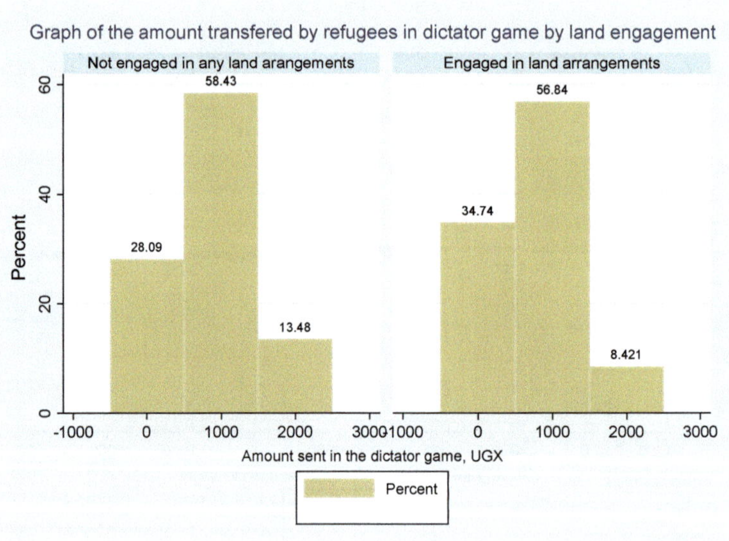

Fig. 4.6 Amount transferred by refugees in the dictator game by previous land engagement. *Source* Author's construction

Table 4.6 Characteristics of refugees by engagement in informal land transactions

	Ever participated in land transaction			
	Yes (N = 95)	No (N = 178)	All (N = 273)	t value of the difference
Average trustworthiness	36.46(17.92)	38.55(19.24)	37.29(18.45)	0.911
Expectations of trust	1072.28(567.46)	1122.64(451.51)	1091.91(525.03)	0.771
Altruism (amount sent in the dictator game)	736.84(605.12)	853.93(629.78)	813.19(622.71)	1.483
Gender of the household head	0.768(0.424)	0.820(0.385)	0.802(0.399)	1.022
Age of the household head	40.358(12.884)	37.758(15.414)	38.663(14.612)	1.403
Years of schooling	4.915(4.511)	3.548(4.279)	4.029(4.403)	2.459
Total value of productive assets	12384.21(84419.69)	2665.73(8858.54)	6047.61(50353.47)	1.523
Ratio of perceived socioeconomic status of self to refugee	1.145(0.787)	1.021(0.909)	1.065(0.869)	−1.119
Ratio of perceived socio economic status of self to host	0.831(0.897)	0.731(0.965)	0.765(0.942)	0.83

4.6 Limitations and Suggestions for Further Research

This book is not without limitations, and this section highlights some of them and suggests future research to build on the study's objectives. The first chapter acknowledges that only document reviews were used in the attempt to explain the drivers of armed conflicts in the region. Further research could tackle the depth of the motivations and disincentives through primary research from key informant interviews and focus group discussions. In Chap. 2, the prosocial attributes between refugees and hosts were examined to understand discrimination based on the social identity of being a refugee or a host using trust and dictator games. It is essential to ascertain the extent to which hosts trust refugees and how refugees reciprocate the trust for any meaningful transaction to happen, which this study does. For comparability between refugees and hosts, further research could allow hosts and refugees to play both the roles of senders and receivers in the trust game. Additionally, an opportunity exists to examine how cooperative behavior between refugees and hosts could impact the management and use of natural resources, which is currently a key concern given the

Table 4.7 A probit model of factors associated with refugees' engagement in land transactions (margins)

Variables	If a refugee household has ever participated in an informal land transaction			
	(1)	(2)	(3)	(4)
Transferred in the dictator game (dummy; 1 = yes)	−0.069 (0.057)	−0.019 (0.071)	−0.017 (0.067)	−0.018 (0.070)
Average percentage trustworthiness		−0.001 (0.002)	−8.82e−05 (0.002)	0.000 (0.002)
Household head is female (d, 1 = yes)			−0.192*** (0.071)	−0.187*** (0.07)
Age of the household head			0.006*** (0.002)	0.006*** (0.002)
Years of schooling			0.027*** (0.010)	0.025** (0.010)
The logarithm of total assets			0.004 (0.006)	0.004 (0.006)
Log perceived ratio of socioeconomic status of self to members of the host community				−0.017 (0.045)
Log perceived ratio of socio-economic status of self to refugees				0.062* (0.037)
Pseudo R squared	0.003	0.002	0.105	0.110
Observations	272	270	270	270

increased influx of refugees in Uganda and other countries. This chapter focuses on the contractual land transactions between refugees and hosts. The size of land transacted through such arrangements was not examined in this study. Further research could extend this concept of land transactions between refugees and hosts to focus on the size and how it impacts food security. For example, a randomized control trial could be used to assess the impact of refugees acquiring additional land on welfare outcomes.

Despite the limitations, the research from the different chapters of the book remains novel. It contributes to academic, policy, and development understandings of motives of conflict in Sub-Saharan Africa, recovery of households from protracted armed conflicts, social preferences between refugees and hosts, and what they mean for informal contractual arrangements.

References

Acemoglu, D., Vindigni, A., & Ticchi, D. (2010). Persistence of Civil Wars. *European Economic Association*, *8*(May), 664–676.

Adelman, S., & Peterman, A. (2014). Resettlement and gender dimensions of land rights in post-conflict Northern Uganda. *World Development*, *64*, 583–596. https://doi.org/10.1016/j.worlddev.2014.06.031

Ager, A., & Strang, A. (2008). Understanding Integration: A Conceptual Framework. *Journal of Refugee Studies*, *21*(2), 166–191. https://doi.org/10.1093/jrs/fen016

Ahabwe, G., & Depio, S. (2019). *How Effective is the Self-Reliance Agenda in Uganda's* (Issue 107).

Akerlof, G. A., & Kranton, R. E. (2000). Economics and Identity. *Economics and Identity*, *CXV*(3), 715–753.

Akresh, R., Lucchetti, L., & Thirumurthy, H. (2012). Wars and child health: Evidence from the Eritrean – Ethiopian conflict. *Journal of Development Economics*, *99*(2), 330–340. https://doi.org/10.1016/j.jdeveco.2012.04.001

Allen, D., & Lueck, D. (1992). Contract Choice in Modern Agriculture: Cash Rent versus Cropshare. *The Journal of Law and Economics*, *35*(2), 397–426. http://www.jstor.com/stable/725546

Allen, T. (1991). Understanding Alice: Uganda's Holy spirit Movement in Context. *Journal of the International African Institute*, *61*(3), 370–399. https://www.jstor.org/stable/1160031?seq=1#metadata_info_tab_contents

Allen, T., & Koen, V. (2010). *The Lord's Resistance Army: Myth and Reality* (T. Allen & K. Vlassenroot (eds.); Issue November). Zed Books Ltd. http://www.zedbooks.co.uk/

Andreoni, J., & Bernheim, D. (2009). Social image and the 50–50 norm: a theoretical and experimental analysis of audience effects. *Econometrica*, *77*(5), 1607–1636. https://doi.org/10.3982/ECTA7384

Andreoni, J., & Miller, J. (2002). Giving According to GARP: An Experimental Test of the Consistency of Preferences for Altruism. *Econometrica*, *70*(2), 737–753.

Annan, J., Blattman, C., Mazurana, D., & Carlson, K. (2011). Civil war, reintegration, and gender in northern Uganda. *Journal of Conflict Resolution*, *55*(6), 877–908. https://doi.org/10.1177/0022002711408013

Ashraf, N., Bohnet, I., & Piankov, N. (2006). Decomposing trust and trustworthiness. *Experimental Economics*, *9*(3), 193–208. https://doi.org/10.1007/s10683-006-9122-4

Ashraf, N., Gine, X., & Karlan, D. (2009). Finding missing markets (and a disturbing epilogue): Evidence from an export crop adoption and marketing intervention in Kenya. *American Journal of Agricultural Economics*, *91*(November), 973–990. https://doi.org/10.1111/j.1467-8276.2009.01319.x

Bakwesegha, C., Brubaker, R., Connor, W., Ellis, A., Esman, M., Hannan, H., Hechter, M., Kalin, W., Lemarchand, R., Lund, Michaels, S., van der Stoel, M., Miall, H., Zartmann, William, I., Ropers, N., Rothchild, D., Tishkov, Valery, A., Vinas, A., & Waldman, P. (2004). Facing Ethnic Conflicts: Toward a New Realism. In G. Wimmer (Ed.). *Toward a new realism*. Rowman & Littlefield Publishers, 2004. https://books.google.de/books?id=DdtOAQAAQBAJ&dq=conrad+schetter+conflict&lr=&source=gbs_navlinks_s

Barr, A. (2003). Trust and expected trustworthiness: Experimental evidence from Zimbabwean villages. *Economic Journal*, *113*(489), 614–630. https://doi.org/10.1111/1468-0297.t01-1-00150

Bauer, M., Blattman, C., Chytilová, J., Henrich, J., Miguel, E., & Mitts, T. (2016). Can War Foster Cooperation? *Journal of Economic Perspectives*, *30*(3), 249–274. https://doi.org/10.1257/jep.30.3.249

Bauer, M., Fiala, N., & Levely, I. (2018). Trusting Former Rebels: An Experimental Approach to Understanding Reintegration after Civil War. *Economic Journal*, *128*(613), 1786–1819. https://doi.org/10.1111/ecoj.12503

Baumgartner, T., Götte, L., Gügler, R., & Fehr, E. (2012). The mentalizing network orchestrates the impact of parochial altruism on social norm enforcement. *Human Brain Mapping*, *33*(6), 1452–1469. https://doi.org/10.1002/hbm.21298

Bellemare, C., & Kröger, S. (2007). On representative social capital. *European Economic Review*, *51*(1), 183–202. https://doi.org/10.1016/j.euroecorev.2006.03.006

Bellows, J., & Miguel, E. (2006). War and institutions: New evidence from Sierra Leone. *American Economic Review*, *96*(2), 394–399. https://doi.org/10.1257/000282806777212323

Bellows, J., & Miguel, E. (2009). War and local collective action in Sierra Leone. *Journal of Public Economics*, *93*(11–12), 1144–1157. https://doi.org/10.1016/j.jpubeco.2009.07.012

Bennett, D. S., & Stam, A. C. (2016). The Duration of Interstate Wars, 1816–1985 Author(s): D. Scott Bennett and Allan C. Stam III Source: The American Political Science Review, Vol. 90, No. 2 (Jun., 1996), pp. 239–257 Published by: American Political Science Association Stabl. *The American Political Science Review*, *90*(2), 239–257.

Berg, J., Dickhaut, J., & McCabe, K. (1995). Trust, reciprocity, and social history. *Games and Economic Behavior*, *10*(1), 122–142. https://doi.org/10.1006/game.1995.1027

Bernhard, H., Fischbacher, U., & Fehr, E. (2006). Parochial altruism in humans. *Nature*, *442*(7105), 912–915. https://doi.org/10.1038/nature04981

Besley, T., & Persson, T. (2008a). The Incidence of Civil War: Theory and Evidence. In Intergovernmental Panel on Climate Change (Ed.), *NBER Working paper series* (Vol. 14585). Cambridge University Press. https://doi.org/10.3386/w14585

Besley, T., & Persson, T. (2008b). The Incidence of Civil War: Theory and Evidence. In Intergovernmental Panel on Climate Change (Ed.), *NBER Working paper series* (Vol. 14585). Cambridge University Press. https://doi.org/10.3386/w14585

Binswanger, H. P., & Rosenzweig, M. R. (1981). Contractual arrangements, Employment and wages in rural labor markets: A critical review. In *Studies in employment & rural development series* (Issue SER 67). http://documents.worldbank.org/curated/en/412971467997610342/Contractual-arrangements-employment-and-wages-in-rural-labor-markets-a-critical-review

Blattman, C., & Annan, J. (2010). The Consequences of Child Soldiering. *Review of Economics and Statistics*, *92*(4), 882. https://doi.org/10.1162/REST_a_00036

Blattman, C., & Miguel, E. (2010). Civil War. *Journal of Economic Literature*, *48*(1), 3–57. https://doi.org/10.1257/jel.48.1.3

Bloem, J. (2019). Good Intentions Gone Bad? The Dodd-Frank Act and Conflict in Africa's Great Lakes Region. In *HiCN*.

Bohnet, H., & Schmitz, C. P. (2019). *Uganda: A role model for refugee integration?* (No. 2; 2019).

Brosché, J., & Höglund, K. (2016). Crisis of governance in South Sudan: Electoral politics and violence in the world's newest nation. *Journal of Modern African Studies*, *54*(1), 67–90. https://doi.org/10.1017/S0022278X15000828

Brück, T., D'Errico, M., & Pietrelli, R. (2018). The effects of violent conflict on household resilience and food security: Evidence from the 2014 Gaza conflict. *World Development*, *2018*. https://doi.org/10.1016/j.worlddev.2018.05.008

Bundervoet, T., Verwimp, P., & Akresh, R. (2009). Health and civil war in rural Burundi. *Journal of Human Resources*, *44*(2), 536–563. https://doi.org/10.3368/jhr.44.2.536

Burke, M., & Young, P. (2009). Social Norms. In A. Bisin, J. Benhabib, & M. Jackson (Eds.), *The Handbook of Social Economics* (pp. 1–51).

Burks, S. V., Carpenter, J. P., & Verhoogen, E. (2003). Playing both roles in the trust game.pdf. *Journal of Economic Behaviour and Organisation*, *51*, 195–216. https://doi.org/10.1016/S0167-2681(02)00093-8

Cameron, A. C., Gelbach, J. B., & Miller, D. L. (2007). *Nber Technical Working Paper Series*. *90*(August), 414–427. https://pdfs.semanticscholar.org/df0a/ff0cb4db55166abbf5e33696d67698f81d3d.pdf%5Cnhttp://www.mitpressjournals.org/doi/pdf/10.1162/rest.90.3.414

Cesarini, D., Dawes, C. T., Fowler, J. H., Johannesson, M., & Lichtenstein, P. (2008). Heritability of cooperative behaviour in the trust game. *PNAS*, *105*(10), 3721–3726. https://doi.org/10.1073/pnas.0710069105

Charness, G., & Rabin, M. (2002). Understanding Social Preferences with Simple Tests. *The Quarterly Journal of Economics*, *117*(3), 817–869. http://www.jstor.org/

Chaudhuri, A., Paichayontvijit, T., & Shen, L. (2013a). Gender differences in trust and trustworthiness: Individuals, single sex and mixed sex groups. *Journal of Economic Psychology*, *34*, 181–194. https://doi.org/10.1016/j.joep.2012.09.013

Chaudhuri, A., Paichayontvijit, T., & Shen, L. (2013b). Gender differences in trust and trustworthiness: Individuals, single sex and mixed sex groups. *Journal of Economic Psychology*, *34*, 181–194. https://doi.org/10.1016/j.joep.2012.09.013

Chen, Y., & Li, S. X. (2009). Group identity and social preferences. *American Economic Review*, *99*(1), 431–457. https://doi.org/10.1257/aer.99.1.431

Coggio, T. (2019). Can Uganda's Breakthrough Refugee-Hosting Model Be Sustained? *Migration Policy Institute*, 1–11. https://www.migrationpolicy.org

Collier, P. (1999). On the Economic Consequences of Civil War. *Oxford Economic Papers*, *51*(January 1999), 168–183.

Collier, P., & Hoeffler, A. (2004). Greed and grievance in civil war. *Oxford Economic Papers*, *56*(2004), 563–595. https://doi.org/10.1093/oep/gpf064

Collier, P., Hoeffler, A., & Söderbom, M. (2004). Collier 2004 – Duration of civil wars. *Journal of Peace Research*, *41*(3), 253–273.

Cox, J. C. (2004a). How to identify trust and reciprocity. *Games and Economic Behavior*, *46*(2), 260–281. https://doi.org/10.1016/S0899-8256(03)00119-2

Cox, J. C. (2004b). How to identify trust and reciprocity. *Games and Economic Behavior*, *8256*(03), 260–281. https://doi.org/10.1016/S0899-8256(03)00119-2

Cramer, C. (2002). Homo Economicus Goes to War: Methodological Individualism, Rational Choice and the Political Economy of War. *World Development*, *30*(11), 1845–1864. https://doi.org/10.1016/S0305-750X(02)00120-1

Cunningham, D. E., Gleditsch, K. S., & Salehyan, I. (2009). It Takes Two: A Dyadic Analysis of Civil War Duration and Outcome. *Journal of Conflict Resolution*, *53*(4), 570–597. https://www.jstor.org/stable/20684603?seq=1#metadata_info_tab_contents

Cuvelier, J., Van Bockstaal, S., Vlassenroot, K., & Iguma, C. (2014). Analyzing the Impact of the Dodd-Frank Act on Congolese Livelihoods. In *Conflict Prevention and Peace Forum* (Vol. 1, Issue November). https://doi.org/10.1017/CBO9781107415324.004

d'Errico, M., Winters, P., & Romano, D. (2024). Assessing Uganda's Progressive Refugee Policy in the Era of COVID-19: Introduction to the Special Issue. *Journal of Development Studies*, *60*(3), 351–359. https://doi.org/10.1080/00220388.2023.2282364

Deininger, K., & Feder, G. (2001). Chapter 6 Land institutions and land markets. In B. Gardner & G. Rausser (Eds.), *Handbook of Agricultural Economics* (2001st ed., Vol. 1, Issue PART A, pp. 287–331). Elsevier Science B.V. https://doi.org/10.1016/S1574-0072(01)10009-5

Denison, R. F., & Muller, K. (2016). The evolution of cooperation. *Scientist*, *30*(1). https://doi.org/10.5840/tpm201467114

Dessalegn, A. G. (2017). The Cause and Consequence of Conflict in South Sudan. *International Journal of Political Science and Development*, *5*(1), 15–21. https://doi.org/10.14662/IJPSD2016.063

Development Pathways. (2018). *Analysis of Refugee Vulnerability in Uganda and Recommendations for Improved Targeting of Food Assistance* (Issue April 2018).

di Montenegro, T. X. (2017). *China's Interest in Africa: Conflict or Stability?* [Florida International University]. https://doi.org/10.25148/etd.FIDC001790

Elwert, G. (2018). Intervention in markets of violence. In *Potentials of disorder* (Issue September 2001, pp. 219–242). Manchester University Press. https://doi.org/10.7765/9781526137586.00017

Eswaran, M., & Kotwal, A. (1985). A Theory of Contractual Structure in Agriculture. *The American Economic Review*, *75*(3), 352–367.

Everett, J. A. C., Faber, N. S., & Crockett, M. (2015). Preferences and beliefs in ingroup favoritism. *Frontiers in Behavioral Neuroscience*, *9*(FEB), 1–21. https://doi.org/10.3389/fnbeh.2015.00015

Everts, E. (2003). Identifying a particular family humor style: A sociolinguistic discourse analysis. *Humor – International Journal of Humor Research, 16*(4), 752. https://doi.org/10.1515/humr.2003.021

FAO. (2018). *Food Security, Resilience and Well-Being Analysis of Refugees and Host Communities in Northern Uganda*. https://doi.org/10.11975/j.issn.1002-6819.2015.24.025

FAO, & World Food Program. (2018). *Monitoring food security in countries with conflict situations: A joint FAO/WFP update for the United Nations Security Council* (Issue 3).

Fearon, J. D. (1995). Rationalist Explanations for War Author. *International Organization, 49*(3), 379–414.

Fehr, E. (2009). On the Economics and Biology of Trust. *European Economic Association, 7*(2–3), 235–266.

Fehr, E., Fischbacher, U., & Gächter, S. (2002). Strong reciprocity, human cooperation, and the enforcement of social norms. *Human Nature, 13*(1), 1–25. https://doi.org/10.1007/s12110-002-1012-7

Fehr, E., & Schmidt, K. M. (1999). A Theory of Fairness, Competition, and Cooperation. *The Quarterly Journal of Economics, 114*(3), 817–868. https://doi.org/10.1162/003355399556151

Fershtman, C., & Gneezy, U. (2001a). Discrimination in a Segmented Society: An Experimental Approach. *The Quarterly Journal of Economics*. https://rady.ucsd.edu/faculty/directory/gneezy/pub/docs/discrimination-society.pdf

Fershtman, C., & Gneezy, U. (2001b). Discrimination in a Segmented Society: An Experimental Approach. *The Quarterly Journal of Economics*.

Fisman, B. R., Kariv, S., & Markovits, D. (2007). Individual Preferences for Giving. *The American Economic Review, 97*(5).

Fisman, R., Jakiela, P., & Kariv, S. (2017). Distributional preferences and political behavior. *Journal of Public Economics, 155*, 1–10. https://doi.org/10.1016/j.jpubeco.2017.08.010

García, A. D. (2020). Armed groups, IHL and the invisible world: How spiritual beliefs shape warfare. *International Review of the Red Cross, 102*(915), 1179–1199. https://doi.org/10.1017/S1816383121000229

Gates, S. (2015). Recruitment, Retention, and Religion in Rebel Groups. In *"Peace, Conflict, and Development", ESOP*, (Issue March 2015).

Geanakoplosand, J., Pearce, D., & Ennio, S. (1989). Psychological Games and Sequential Rationality. *Games and Economic Behaviour, 1*(1989), 60–79.

Gebregziabher, G., & Holden, S. T. (2011). Distress rentals and the land rental market as a safety net: Contract choice evidence from Tigray, Ethiopia. *Agricultural Economics, 42*(SUPPL. 1), 45–60. https://doi.org/10.1111/j.1574-0862.2011.00551.x

Ghatak, M., & Karaivanov, A. (2014). Contractual structure in agriculture with endogenous matching. *Journal of Development Economics, 110*, 239–249. https://doi.org/10.1016/j.jdeveco.2013.05.005

Ghobarah, H. A., Huth, P., & Russett, B. (2003). and Maim the Shooting Wars Kill Civil People-Long After Stops. *The American Political Science Review, 97*(2), 189–202. http://www.jstor.org/stable/3118203

Glaeser, E. L., Laibson, D. I., Scheinkman, J. A., & Soutter, C. L. (2000). Glaeser et al 2000_article.pdf. *Quarterly Journal of Economics, 115*(3), 811–846.

Grossman, H. (1991). A General Equilibrium Model of Insurrections. In *American Economic Review* (Vol. 81, Issue 4, pp. 912–921). https://doi.org/10.2307/2006650

Guerrero, S. (2009). The Effects of the War in Iraq on Nutrition and Health: An Analysis Using Anthropometric Outcomes of Children. *SSRN Electronic Journal, 14056*. https://doi.org/10.2139/ssrn.1359161

Guerrero Serdan, G. (2009). The Effects of the War in Iraq on Nutrition and Health: An Analysis Using Anthropometric Outcomes of Children. *SSRN Electronic Journal, 14056*. https://doi.org/10.2139/ssrn.1359161

Harris, C., Jenkins, M., & Glaser, D. (2006). Gender Differences in Risk Assessment: Why do women take fewer risks than men? *Judgement and Decision Making, 1*(1), 48–63. http://journal.sjdm.org/jdm06016.pdf

Hartman, A. C., & Morse, B. S. (2018). Violence, Empathy and Altruism: Evidence from the Ivorian Refugee Crisis in Liberia. *British Journal of Political Science*, 1–25. https://doi.org/10.1017/S0007123417000655

Haselhuhn, M. P., Kennedy, J. A., Kray, L. J., Van Zant, A. B., & Schweitzer, M. E. (2015). Gender differences in trust dynamics: Women trust more than men following a trust violation. *Journal of Experimental Social Psychology, 56*, 104–109. https://doi.org/10.1016/j.jesp.2014.09.007

Henrich, J., Boyd, R., & Bowles, S. (2005). "Economic Man" in Cross-Cultural Perspective: Ethnography and Experiments from 15 Small-Scale Societies. *Behavioral and Brain Sciences, 28*(2005), 795–855.

Henrich, J., Ensminger, J., Mcelreath, R., Barr, A., Barrett, C., Bolyanatz, A., Cardenas, J. C., Gurven, M., Gwako, E., Henrich, N., Lesorogol, C., Marlowe, F., Tracer, D., & Ziker, J. (2010). Markets, Religion, Community size, and the Evolution of Fairness and Punishment. *Science, 327*(March 2010), 1480–1484. https://doi.org/10.1126/science.1182238

Henrich, J., McElreath, R., Barr, A., Ensminger, J., Barrett, C., Bolyanatz, A., Cardaroas, J. C., Gurven, M., Gwako, E., Henrich, N., Lesoronol, C., Marlowe, F., Tracer, D., & Ziker, J. (2006a). Costly punishment across human societies. *Science, 312*(5781), 1767–1770. https://doi.org/10.1126/science.1127333

Henrich, J., McElreath, R., Barr, A., Ensminger, J., Barrett, C., Bolyanatz, A., Cardenas, J. C., Gurven, M., Gwako, E., Henrich, N., Lesorogol, C., Marlowe, F., Tracer, D., & Ziker, J. (2006b). Costly punishment across human societies. MATERIAL RESPALDO. *Science (New York, N.Y.), 312*(5781), 1767–1770. https://doi.org/10.1126/science.1127333

Hirshleifer, J. (1995). Theorizing about conflict. In K. Hartley & T. Sandler (Eds.), *Handbook of Defense Economics* (Vol. 1, pp. 165–189). Elsevier. https://doi.org/10.1016/S1574-0013(05)80009-2

Hoeffler, A. (2012). On the Causes of Civil War. In *Oxford Economic Papers* (Vol. 50). Oxford University Press. https://doi.org/10.1093/oxfordhb/9780195392777.013.0009

Holden, S. T., & Otsuka, K. (2014). The roles of land tenure reforms and land markets in the context of population growth and land use intensification in Africa. *Food Policy, 48*, 88–97. https://doi.org/10.1016/j.foodpol.2014.03.005

Hovil, L. (2001). *Refuges and the Security Situation in Adjumani District* (Refugee Law Project, Issue 2).

Jakiela, P. (2011). Using economic experiments to measure informal institutions. In W. University (Ed.), *The Legacy and Work of Douglass C. North: Understanding Institutions and Development Economics* (pp. 248–265). Department of Economics, Washington University. https://doi.org/10.1017/CBO9781107300361.013

Johnson, N. D., & Mislin, A. A. (2011). Trust games: A meta-analysis. *Journal of Economic Psychology, 32*(5), 865–889. https://doi.org/10.1016/j.joep.2011.05.007

Joras, U., & Schetter, C. (2004). Hidden ties: Similarities between Research and Policy Approaches to Ethnic Conflicts. In G. Wimmer & U. D. Howowitz (Eds.), *Facing Ethnic Conflicts. Towards a New Realism* (pp. 315–332). Lanham, Rowman & Littlefield.

Jourdan, L. (2011). Mayi-Mayi: Young rebels in Kivu, DRC. *Africa Development, 36*(3–4), 89–111.

Karlan, D. S. (2005). Using Experimental Economics to Measure Social Capital and Predict Financial Decisions. *American Economic Review, 95*(5 (Dec., 2005)), 1688–1699. https://www.jstor.org/stable/4132772

Keswell, M., & Carter, M. R. (2014). Poverty and land redistribution. *Journal of Development Economics, 110*, 250–261. https://doi.org/10.1016/j.jdeveco.2013.10.003

Kimbrough, E. O., & Vostroknutov, A. (2016). Norms Make Preferences Social. *Journal of the European Economic Association, 14*(3), 608–638. https://doi.org/10.1111/jeea.12152

Kisangani, E. (2003). Conflict in the Democratic Republic of Congo: A mosaic of insurgent groups. *International Journal of World Peace, 20*(3), 51–80. www.jstor.org/stable/20753410

Kosfeld, M., Heinrichs, M., Zak, P. J., Fischbacher, U., & Fehr, E. (2005). Oxytocin increases trust in humans. *Nature, 435*(7042), 673–676. https://doi.org/10.1038/nature03701

Kosfeld, M., & Rustagi, D. (2015). Leader punishment and cooperation in groups: Experimental field evidence from commons management in Ethiopia. *American Economic Review, 105*(2), 747–783. https://doi.org/10.1257/aer.20120700

Kreibaum, M. (2016). Their Suffering, Our Burden? How Congolese Refugees Affect the Ugandan Population. *World Development, 78*, 262–287. https://doi.org/10.1016/j.worlddev.2015.10.019

Lemarchand, R. (2008). The Burundi Killings of 1972. In *Online Encyclopedia of Mass Violence* (Issue June). https://www.sciencespo.fr/mass-violence-war-massacre-resistance/en/document/burundi-killings-1972.html

Loewenstein, G., & Thompson, L. (1989). Social utility and Decision making in interpersonal contexts. *Journal of Personality and Social Psychology, 57*(3), 426–441.

Ma, T. (2009). China and Congo's coltan connection. In *Project 2049 Institute.*

Martiniello, G. (2010). African land questions, agrarian transitions and the state: the contradictions of neo-liberal land reforms. *Review of African Political Economy, 37*(125), 387–389. https://doi.org/10.1080/03056244.2010.511784

Maystadt, J.-F., & Verwimp, P. (2014). Winners and Losers among a Refugee-Hosting Population. *Economic Development and Cultural Change, 62*(4), 769–809. https://doi.org/10.1086/676458

Melander, E., Pettersson, T., & Themnér, L. (2016). Organized violence, 1989–2015. *Journal of Peace Research, 53*(5), 727–742. https://doi.org/10.1177/0022343316663032

Merkx, J. (2000). Document. Refugee identities and relief in an African borderland: a study of northern Uganda and southern Sudan. In *New issues in Refugee Research* (Vol. 21, Issue 19). https://doi.org/10.1093/rsq/21.1_and_2.113

Mkandawire, T. (2002). The terrible toll of post-colonial "rebel movements" in Africa: Towards an explanation of the violence against the peasantry. *Journal of Modern African Studies, 40*(2), 181–215. https://doi.org/10.1017/S0022278X02003889

Mkandawire, T. (2015). Neopatrimonialism and the Political Economy of Economic Performance in Africa: Critical Reflections. *World Politics, 67*(3), 563–612. https://doi.org/10.1017/S004388711500009X

Ngaruko, F., & Nkirunziza, J. (2000). An economic interpretation of conflict in Burundi. *Journal of African Economies, 9*(3), 370–409. https://doi.org/10.1093/jae/9.3.370

Nindorera, W. (2012). *The CNDD-FDD in Burundi: The path from armed to political struggle* (Issue 10).

Nkurunziza, J. D. (2015). Timing and Sequencing of Post-Conflict Reconstruction and Peace-building in Burundi. In *CRPD Working Paper* (Issue 34). https://doi.org/10.1093/acprof:oso/9780198757276.003.0013

Nkurunziza, J. D. (2022). The origin and persistence of state fragility in Burundi. In *State Fragility, Growth and Development* (Issue April). https://doi.org/10.4324/9781003297697-4

Nshimirimana, F. (2024). *Exclusionary Governance in Burundi:Implications for Democracy and Consolidating Peace.*

Nyadera, I. N. (2018). South Sudan conflict from 2013 to 2018: Rethinking the causes, situation and solutions. *African Journal on Conflict Resolution, 18*(2), 59–86.

O'Brien, A. (2009). Shots in the Dark: The 2008 South Sudan Civilian Disarmament Campaign. In *HSBA Working Paper.*

Odera, L. C. (2013). The Role of Trust as an Informal Institution in the Informal Sector in Africa. *Africa Development, 38*(3–4), 121 – 146.

Peterson, R. (2001). Resistance and Rebellion; Lessons from Eastern Europe. In *Cambrige University Press.* https://doi.org/10.1007/BF02430448

Pham, P. N., Vinck, P., & Stover, E. (2008). The Lord's Resistance Army and Forced Conscription in Northern Uganda. *Human Rights Quarterly, 30*(2008), 404–411.

Poole, L. (2019). *The refugee response in northern Uganda: Resources beyond international humanitarian assistance* (No. 2019; HPG Working Paper, Issue February). www.odi.org/hpg.

Powell, R. (2006). War as a commitment problem. *International Organization, 60*(1), 169–203. https://doi.org/10.1017/S0020818306060061

Rabbie, J. M., Schot, J. C., & Visser, L. (1989). Social identity theory: A conceptual and empirical critique from the perspective of a behavioural interaction model. *European Journal of Social Psychology, 19*(3), 171–202. https://doi.org/10.1002/ejsp.2420190302

Rabellino, D., Morese, R., Ciaramidaro, A., Bara, B. G., & Bosco, F. M. (2016). Third-party punishment: altruistic and anti-social behaviours in in-group and out-group settings. *Journal of Cognitive Psychology, 28*(4), 486–495. https://doi.org/10.1080/20445911.2016.1138961

Rabin, M. (1993). Incorporating fairness into game theory and economics. *The American Economic Review, 83*(5), 1281–1302. http://www.jstor.org/stable/2117561

Raleigh, C., Linke, A., Hegre, H., & Karlsen, J. (2010). Introducing ACLED-Armed Conflict Location and Event Data. *Journal of Peace Research, 47*(5), 651–660.

Refugee law project. (2022). Negotiating peace: Resolution of Conflicts in Uganda's West Nile Region. In *Refugee Law Project Working Paper* (Issue 12). https://doi.org/10.4324/9781003317487-18

Relief web. (2002). *Rwanda-Uganda: Interahamwe reported present in Uganda.* https://reliefweb.int/report/democratic-republic-congo/rwanda-uganda-interahamwe-reported-present-uganda

Rockmore, M. (2017). The cost of fear: The welfare effect of the risk of violence in Northern Uganda. *World Bank Economic Review, 31*(3), 650–669. https://doi.org/10.1093/wber/lhw025

Rockmore, M. (2020). Conflict-Risk and Agricultural Portfolios: Evidence from Northern Uganda. *The Journal of Development Studies, 2016*, 1–21. https://doi.org/10.1080/00220388.2019.1703953

Rufanges, C. J., & Aspa, J. M. R. (2016). *Democratic Republic of Congo: A Review of 20 years of war* (Issue April). https://escolapau.uab.cat/img/programas/alerta/alerta/RDCongo_20AnosGuerra_I.pdf

Saferworld. (2010). Karamoja conflict and security assessment. In *Report* (Issue September).

Shemyakina, O. (2011). The effect of armed conflict on accumulation of schooling: Results from Tajikistan. *Journal of Development Economics, 95*(2), 186–200. https://doi.org/10.1016/j.jdeveco.2010.05.002

Sigman, R., & Lindberg, S. I. (2017). Neopatrimonialism and Democracy: An Empirical Investigation of Africa's Political Regimes. *SSRN Electronic Journal, January*. https://doi.org/10.2139/ssrn.3066654

Skaperdas, S. (2008). An economic approach to analyzing civil wars. *Economics of Governance, 9*(1), 25–44. https://doi.org/10.1007/s10101-007-0043-2

State Parties to the 1951 Convention relating to the Status of Refugees and the 1967 Protocol, (2011). https://doi.org/10.1093/rsq/hdn023

Tajfel, H., Billig, M. G., & Bundy, R. (1971). Social categorization and intergroup behaviour. *European Journal of Social Pszchology, 1*(2), 149–178. https://doi.org/10.1002/ejsp.2420010202

The Fund For Peace. (2019). *Fragile States Index Annual Report 2019.* www.fundforpeace.org

Titeca, K. (2024). Uganda and the DRC conflict: the interests driving Kampala's involvement. *The Conversation*, 23–26.

Uganda Bureau of Statistics. (2024a). National Population and Housing Census 2024: Preliminary Results. In *National Population and Household Census* (Vol. 256, Issue June).

Uganda Bureau of Statistics. (2024b). National Population and Housing Census 2024. In *Census 2024.* http://libdcms.nida.ac.th/thesis6/2010/b166706.pdf

UN, & African Union. (2011). *Fifth Anniversary of the signing of the Peace, Security and Cooperation Framework (PSCF)* (Vol. 46, Issue 0).

UNDP. (2017). *Summary of Study Uganda ' S Contribution To.* https://data2.unhcr.org/en/documents/download/64687

UNECA. (2015). *Conflicts in the Democratic Republic of Congo: Causes, impact and implications for the Great Lakes region.* Routledge. https://www.uneca.org/sites/default/files/PublicationFiles/conflits_in_drc_eng_25sept_rev1.pdf

UNECA. (2016). Conflict in the democratic Republic of Congo: Causes, impact and implications for the Great Lakes region. In *Routledge Handbook of Security Studies: Second Edition*. https://doi.org/10.4324/9781315753393

UNHCR. (2018). *South Sudan Regional Refugee Response Plan* (Issue December). http://reporting.unhcr.org/sites/default/files/2018SouthSudanRegionalRefugeeResponsePlan-Jan-Dec 2018%28January2018%29_0.pdf

UNHCR. (2019a). *Global Trends Forced Displacemnet in 2018*. www.unhcr.org/5c6fb2d04

UNHCR. (2019b). Uganda Country Refugee Response Plan. *The UN Refugee Agency, Jan 2019-Dec 2020*, 72. http://reporting.unhcr.org/sites/default/files/UgandaCountryRRP2019-20%28January 2019%29.pdf

United Nations Development Programme. (2018). *Understanding land dynamics and livelihood in refugee hosting districts of northern Uganda*.

United Nations High Commision for Refugees (UNHCR), & Government of Uganda (GoU). (2019). *Refugee and Host Population by District*. Uganda Comprehensive Refugee Response Portal. https://data2.unhcr.org/en/country/uga

Venugopalan, H. (2016). Understanding the Conflict in Congo. In *ORF ISSUE BRIEF* (Issue May). https://www.orfonline.org/wp-content/uploads/2016/05/ORF_IssueBrief_139_Venugopalan_Final.pdf

Vlassenroot, K., & Van Acker, F. (2001). War as Exit from Exclusion? The Formation of Mayi-Mayi Militias in Eastern Congo. *Afrika Focus, 17*(1–2), 51–77. https://doi.org/10.21825/af.v17i1-2.5426

von Braun, J., Teklu, T., & Webb, P. (1998). *Famine in Africa. Causes, Response and Prevention*. The John Hopkins Univerisity Press.

Voors, M. J., Nillesen, E. E. M., Verwimp, P., Bulte, E. H., Lensink, R., & Soest, D. P. Van. (2012a). Violent Conflict and Behavior: A field experiment in Burundi. *American Economic Review, 102*(2), 941–964.

Voors, M. J., Nillesen, E. E. M., Verwimp, P., Bulte, E. H., Lensink, R., & Van Soest, D. P. (2012b). Violent Conflict and Behaviour: a field experiment in Burundi. *Source: The American Economic Review, 102*(2), 941–964. https://doi.org/10.1257/aer.102.2.941

Wallensteen, P., & Axell, K. (1993). Armed Conflict at the End of the Cold War , 1989-92. *Journal of Peace Research, 30*(3), 331–346.

Werner, K., & Lambsdorff, J. G. (2019). Emotional Numbing and Lessons Learned after a Violent Conflict – Experimental Evidence from Ambon, Indonesia. *The Journal of Development Studies*, 1–15. https://doi.org/10.1080/00220388.2019.1590550

Whyte, S. R., & Acio, E. (2017). Generations and Access to Land in Postconflict Northern Uganda: Youth Have No Voice in Land Matters. *African Studies Review, 60*(3), 17–36. https://doi.org/10.1017/asr.2017.120

World Bank. (2015). *Forced Displacement in the Great Lakes Region*. http://hdl.handle.net/10986/21708

World Bank. (2016). *The Uganda Poverty Assessment Report 2016. Farms, cities and good fortune: assessing poverty reduction in Uganda from 2006 to 2013*. http://pubdocs.worldbank.org/en/890971474327477241/Uganda-Poverty-Assessment-Report-2016-Overview.pdf

WorldBank. (2016). *The Uganda Poverty Assessment Report, 2016: Farms, Cities and good fortune: assessing poverty reduction in Uganda from 2006 to 2013*.

Yami, M., & van Asten, P. (2018). Relevance of informal institutions for achieving sustainable crop intensification in Uganda. *Food Security, 10*(1), 141–150. https://doi.org/10.1007/s12571-017-0754-3

Young, J. (2016). Popular struggles and elite co-optation: the Nuer White Army in South Sudan's Civil War. In E. LeBrun (Ed.), *Small Arms Survey*. Graduate Institute of International and Development studies.

Zhu, H., Filipski, M., Valli, J., Gonzalez, E., Gupta, A., & Taylor, J. E. (2016). *Economic Impact of Refugee Settlements in Uganda* (Issue November).

Zhu, H., Taylor, J. E., Gupta, A., Filipski, M., Valli, J., & Gonzalez, E. E. (2016). Economic Impacts of Giving Land to Refugees. In *Agricultural and Applied Economics Association 2018 Annual Meeting*. Agricultural and Applied Economics Association. https://doi.org/10.22004/ag.econ.274212

Bibliography

Acemoglu, D., Vindigni, A., & Ticchi, D. (2010). Persistence of Civil Wars. *European Economic Association*, *8*(May), 664–676.

Adelman, S., & Peterman, A. (2014). Resettlement and gender dimensions of land rights in post-conflict Northern Uganda. *World Development*, *64*, 583–596. https://doi.org/10.1016/j.worlddev.2014.06.031

Ager, A., & Strang, A. (2008). Understanding Integration: A Conceptual Framework. *Journal of Refugee Studies*, *21*(2), 166–191. https://doi.org/10.1093/jrs/fen016

Ahabwe, G., & Depio, S. (2019). *How Effective is the Self-Reliance Agenda in Uganda's* (Issue 107).

Akerlof, G. A., & Kranton, R. E. (2000). Economics and Identity. *Economics and Identity*, *CXV*(3), 715–753.

Akresh, R., Lucchetti, L., & Thirumurthy, H. (2012). Wars and child health: Evidence from the Eritrean – Ethiopian conflict. *Journal of Development Economics*, *99*(2), 330–340. https://doi.org/10.1016/j.jdeveco.2012.04.001

Allen, D., & Lueck, D. (1992). Contract Choice in Modern Agriculture: Cash Rent versus Cropshare. *The Journal of Law and Economics*, *35*(2), 397–426. http://www.jstor.com/stable/725546

Allen, T. (1991). Understanding Alice: Uganda's Holy spirit Movement in Context. *Journal of the International African Institute*, *61*(3), 370–399. https://www.jstor.org/stable/1160031?seq=1#metadata_info_tab_contents

Allen, T., & Koen, V. (2010). *The Lord's Resistance Army: Myth and Reality* (T. Allen & K. Vlassenroot (eds.); Issue November). Zed Books Ltd. http://www.zedbooks.co.uk/

Andreoni, J., & Bernheim, D. (2009). Social image and the 50–50 norm: a theoretical and experimental analysis of audience effects. *Econometrica*, *77*(5), 1607–1636. https://doi.org/10.3982/ECTA7384

Andreoni, J., & Miller, J. (2002). Giving According to GARP: An Experimental Test of the Consistency of Preferences for Altruism. *Econometrica*, *70*(2), 737–753.

Annan, J., Blattman, C., Mazurana, D., & Carlson, K. (2011). Civil war, reintegration, and gender in northern Uganda. *Journal of Conflict Resolution*, *55*(6), 877–908. https://doi.org/10.1177/0022002711408013

Ashraf, N., Bohnet, I., & Piankov, N. (2006). Decomposing trust and trustworthiness. *Experimental Economics*, *9*(3), 193–208. https://doi.org/10.1007/s10683-006-9122-4

Ashraf, N., Gine, X., & Karlan, D. (2009). Finding missing markets (and a disturbing epilogue): Evidence from an export crop adoption and marketing intervention in Kenya. *American Journal of Agricultural Economics*, *91*(November), 973–990. https://doi.org/10.1111/j.1467-8276.2009.01319.x

A. Adong, *Armed Conflicts and Forced Displacements in the Anthropocene*, The Anthropocene: Politik—Economics—Society—Science 41, https://doi.org/10.1007/978-3-032-04820-2

Bakwesegha, C., Brubaker, R., Connor, W., Ellis, A., Esman, M., Hannan, H., Hechter, M., Kalin, W., Lemarchand, R., Lund, Michaels, S., van der Stoel, M., Miall, H., Zartmann, William, I., Ropers, N., Rothchild, D., Tishkov, Valery, A., Vinas, A., & Waldman, P. (2004). Facing Ethnic Conflicts: Toward a New Realism. In G. Wimmer (Ed.), *Toward a new realism*. Rowman & Littlefield Publishers, 2004. https://books.google.de/books?id=DdtOAQAAQBAJ&dq=conrad+schetter+conflict&lr=&source=gbs_navlinks_s

Barr, A. (2003). Trust and expected trustworthiness: Experimental evidence from Zimbabwean villages. *Economic Journal, 113*(489), 614–630. https://doi.org/10.1111/1468-0297.t01-1-00150

Bauer, M., Blattman, C., Chytilová, J., Henrich, J., Miguel, E., & Mitts, T. (2016). Can War Foster Cooperation? *Journal of Economic Perspectives, 30*(3), 249–274. https://doi.org/10.1257/jep.30.3.249

Bauer, M., Fiala, N., & Levely, I. (2018). Trusting Former Rebels: An Experimental Approach to Understanding Reintegration after Civil War. *Economic Journal, 128*(613), 1786–1819. https://doi.org/10.1111/ecoj.12503

Baumgartner, T., Götte, L., Gügler, R., & Fehr, E. (2012). The mentalizing network orchestrates the impact of parochial altruism on social norm enforcement. *Human Brain Mapping, 33*(6), 1452–1469. https://doi.org/10.1002/hbm.21298

Bellemare, C., & Kröger, S. (2007). On representative social capital. *European Economic Review, 51*(1), 183–202. https://doi.org/10.1016/j.euroecorev.2006.03.006

Bellows, J., & Miguel, E. (2006). War and institutions: New evidence from Sierra Leone. *American Economic Review, 96*(2), 394–399. https://doi.org/10.1257/000282806777212323

Bellows, J., & Miguel, E. (2009). War and local collective action in Sierra Leone. *Journal of Public Economics, 93*(11–12), 1144–1157. https://doi.org/10.1016/j.jpubeco.2009.07.012

Bennett, D. S., & Stam, A. C. (2016). The Duration of Interstate Wars, 1816–1985 Author(s): D. Scott Bennett and Allan C. Stam III Source: The American Political Science Review, Vol. 90, No. 2 (Jun., 1996), pp. 239–257 Published by: American Political Science Association Stabl. *The American Political Science Review, 90*(2), 239–257.

Berg, J., Dickhaut, J., & McCabe, K. (1995). Trust, reciprocity, and social history. *Games and Economic Behavior, 10*(1), 122–142. https://doi.org/10.1006/game.1995.1027

Bernhard, H., Fischbacher, U., & Fehr, E. (2006). Parochial altruism in humans. *Nature, 442*(7105), 912–915. https://doi.org/10.1038/nature04981

Besley, T., & Persson, T. (2008a). The Incidence of Civil War: Theory and Evidence. In Intergovernmental Panel on Climate Change (Ed.), *NBER Working paper series* (Vol. 14585). Cambridge University Press. https://doi.org/10.3386/w14585

Besley, T., & Persson, T. (2008b). The Incidence of Civil War: Theory and Evidence. In Intergovernmental Panel on Climate Change (Ed.), *NBER Working paper series* (Vol. 14585). Cambridge University Press. https://doi.org/10.3386/w14585

Binswanger, H. P., & Rosenzweig, M. R. (1981). Contractual arrangements, Employment and wages in rural labor markets: A critical review. In *Studies in employment & rural development series* (Issue SER 67). http://documents.worldbank.org/curated/en/412971467997610342/Contractual-arrangements-employment-and-wages-in-rural-labor-markets-a-critical-review

Blattman, C., & Annan, J. (2010). The Consequences of Child Soldiering. *Review of Economics and Statistics, 92*(4), 882. https://doi.org/10.1162/REST_a_00036

Blattman, C., & Miguel, E. (2010). Civil War. *Journal of Economic Literature, 48*(1), 3–57. https://doi.org/10.1257/jel.48.1.3

Bloem, J. (2019). Good Intentions Gone Bad? The Dodd-Frank Act and Conflict in Africa's Great Lakes Region. In *HiCN*.

Bohnet, H., & Schmitz, C. P. (2019). *Uganda: A role model for refugee integration?* (No. 2; 2019).

Brosché, J., & Höglund, K. (2016). Crisis of governance in South Sudan: Electoral politics and violence in the world's newest nation. *Journal of Modern African Studies, 54*(1), 67–90. https://doi.org/10.1017/S0022278X15000828

Brück, T., D'Errico, M., & Pietrelli, R. (2018). The effects of violent conflict on household resilience and food security: Evidence from the 2014 Gaza conflict. *World Development, 2018*. https://doi.org/10.1016/j.worlddev.2018.05.008

Bundervoet, T., Verwimp, P., & Akresh, R. (2009). Health and civil war in rural Burundi. *Journal of Human Resources, 44*(2), 536–563. https://doi.org/10.3368/jhr.44.2.536

Burke, M., & Young, P. (2009). Social Norms. In A. Bisin, J. Benhabib, & M. Jackson (Eds.), *The Handbook of Social Economics* (pp. 1–51).

Burks, S. V., Carpenter, J. P., & Verhoogen, E. (2003). Playing both roles in the trust game.pdf. *Journal of Economic Behaviour and Organisation, 51*, 195–216. https://doi.org/10.1016/S0167-2681(02)00093-8

Cameron, A. C., Gelbach, J. B., & Miller, D. L. (2007). *Nber Technical Working Paper Series. 90*(August), 414–427. https://pdfs.semanticscholar.org/df0a/ff0cb4db55166abbf5e33696d67698f81d3d.pdf%5Cnhttp://www.mitpressjournals.org/doi/pdf/10.1162/rest.90.3.414

Cesarini, D., Dawes, C. T., Fowler, J. H., Johannesson, M., & Lichtenstein, P. (2008). Heritability of cooperative behaviour in the trust game. *PNAS, 105*(10), 3721–3726. https://doi.org/10.1073/pnas.0710069105

Charness, G., & Rabin, M. (2002). Understanding Social Preferences with Simple Tests. *The Quarterly Journal of Economics, 117*(3), 817–869. http://www.jstor.org/

Chaudhuri, A., Paichayontvijit, T., & Shen, L. (2013a). Gender differences in trust and trustworthiness: Individuals, single sex and mixed sex groups. *Journal of Economic Psychology, 34*, 181–194. https://doi.org/10.1016/j.joep.2012.09.013

Chaudhuri, A., Paichayontvijit, T., & Shen, L. (2013b). Gender differences in trust and trustworthiness: Individuals, single sex and mixed sex groups. *Journal of Economic Psychology, 34*, 181–194. https://doi.org/10.1016/j.joep.2012.09.013

Chen, Y., & Li, S. X. (2009). Group identity and social preferences. *American Economic Review, 99*(1), 431–457. https://doi.org/10.1257/aer.99.1.431

Coggio, T. (2019). Can Uganda's Breakthrough Refugee-Hosting Model Be Sustained? *Migration Policy Institute*, 1–11. https://www.migrationpolicy.org

Collier, P. (1999). On the Economic Consequences of Civil War. *Oxford Economic Papers, 51*(January 1999), 168–183.

Collier, P., & Hoeffler, A. (2004). Greed and grievance in civil war. *Oxford Economic Papers, 56*(2004), 563–595. https://doi.org/10.1093/oep/gpf064

Collier, P., Hoeffler, A., & Söderbom, M. (2004). Collier 2004 – Duration of civil wars. *Journal of Peace Research, 41*(3), 253–273.

Cox, J. C. (2004a). How to identify trust and reciprocity. *Games and Economic Behavior, 46*(2), 260–281. https://doi.org/10.1016/S0899-8256(03)00119-2

Cox, J. C. (2004b). How to identify trust and reciprocity. *Games and Economic Behavior, 8256*(03), 260–281. https://doi.org/10.1016/S0899-8256(03)00119-2

Cramer, C. (2002). Homo Economicus Goes to War: Methodological Individualism, Rational Choice and the Political Economy of War. *World Development, 30*(11), 1845–1864. https://doi.org/10.1016/S0305-750X(02)00120-1

Cunningham, D. E., Gleditsch, K. S., & Salehyan, I. (2009). It Takes Two: A Dyadic Analysis of Civil War Duration and Outcome. *Journal of Conflict Resolution, 53*(4), 570–597. https://www.jstor.org/stable/20684603?seq=1#metadata_info_tab_contents

Cuvelier, J., Van Bockstaal, S., Vlassenroot, K., & Iguma, C. (2014). Analyzing the Impact of the Dodd-Frank Act on Congolese Livelihoods. In *Conflict Prevention and Peace Forum* (Vol. 1, Issue November). https://doi.org/10.1017/CBO9781107415324.004

d'Errico, M., Winters, P., & Romano, D. (2024). Assessing Uganda's Progressive Refugee Policy in the Era of COVID-19: Introduction to the Special Issue. *Journal of Development Studies, 60*(3), 351–359. https://doi.org/10.1080/00220388.2023.2282364

Deininger, K., & Feder, G. (2001). Chapter 6 Land institutions and land markets. In B. Gardner & G. Rausser (Eds.), *Handbook of Agricultural Economics* (2001st ed., Vol. 1, Issue PART A, pp. 287–331). Elsevier Science B.V. https://doi.org/10.1016/S1574-0072(01)10009-5

Denison, R. F., & Muller, K. (2016). The evolution of cooperation. *Scientist*, *30*(1). https://doi.org/10.5840/tpm201467114

Dessalegn, A. G. (2017). The Cause and Consequence of Conflict in South Sudan. *International Journal of Political Science and Development*, *5*(1), 15–21. https://doi.org/10.14662/IJPSD2016.063

Development Pathways. (2018). *Analysis of Refugee Vulnerability in Uganda and Recommendations for Improved Targeting of Food Assistance* (Issue April 2018).

di Montenegro, T. X. (2017). *China's Interest in Africa: Conflict or Stability?* [Florida International University]. https://doi.org/10.25148/etd.FIDC001790

Elwert, G. (2018). Intervention in markets of violence. In *Potentials of disorder* (Issue September 2001, pp. 219–242). Manchester University Press. https://doi.org/10.7765/9781526137586.00017

Eswaran, M., & Kotwal, A. (1985). A Theory of Contractual Structure in Agriculture. *The American Economic Review*, *75*(3), 352–367.

Everett, J. A. C., Faber, N. S., & Crockett, M. (2015). Preferences and beliefs in ingroup favoritism. *Frontiers in Behavioral Neuroscience*, *9*(FEB), 1–21. https://doi.org/10.3389/fnbeh.2015.00015

Everts, E. (2003). Identifying a particular family humor style: A sociolinguistic discourse analysis. *Humor – International Journal of Humor Research*, *16*(4), 752. https://doi.org/10.1515/humr.2003.021

FAO. (2018). *Food Security, Resilience and Well-Being Analysis of Refugees and Host Communities in Northern Uganda.* https://doi.org/10.11975/j.issn.1002-6819.2015.24.025

FAO, & World Food Program. (2018). *Monitoring food security in countries with conflict situations: A joint FAO/WFP update for the United Nations Security Council* (Issue 3).

Fearon, J. D. (1995). Rationalist Explanations for War Author. *International Organization*, *49*(3), 379–414.

Fehr, E. (2009). On the Economics and Biology of Trust. *European Economic Association*, *7*(2–3), 235–266.

Fehr, E., Fischbacher, U., & Gächter, S. (2002). Strong reciprocity, human cooperation, and the enforcement of social norms. *Human Nature*, *13*(1), 1–25. https://doi.org/10.1007/s12110-002-1012-7

Fehr, E., & Schmidt, K. M. (1999). A Theory of Fairness, Competition, and Cooperation. *The Quarterly Journal of Economics*, *114*(3), 817–868. https://doi.org/10.1162/003355399556151

Fershtman, C., & Gneezy, U. (2001a). Discrimination in a Segmented Society: An Experimental Approach. *The Quarterly Journal of Economics*. https://rady.ucsd.edu/faculty/directory/gneezy/pub/docs/discrimination-society.pdf

Fershtman, C., & Gneezy, U. (2001b). Discrimination in a Segmented Society: An Experimental Approach. *The Quarterly Journal of Economics*.

Fisman, B. R., Kariv, S., & Markovits, D. (2007). Individual Preferences for Giving. *The American Economic Review*, *97*(5).

Fisman, R., Jakiela, P., & Kariv, S. (2017). Distributional preferences and political behavior. *Journal of Public Economics*, *155*, 1–10. https://doi.org/10.1016/j.jpubeco.2017.08.010

García, A. D. (2020). Armed groups, IHL and the invisible world: How spiritual beliefs shape warfare. *International Review of the Red Cross*, *102*(915), 1179–1199. https://doi.org/10.1017/S1816383121000229

Gates, S. (2015). Recruitment, Retention, and Religion in Rebel Groups. In *"Peace, Conflict, and Development", ESOP,* (Issue March 2015).

Geanakoplosand, J., Pearce, D., & Ennio, S. (1989). Psychological Games and Sequential Rationality. *Games and Economic Behaviour*, *1*(1989), 60–79.

Gebregziabher, G., & Holden, S. T. (2011). Distress rentals and the land rental market as a safety net: Contract choice evidence from Tigray, Ethiopia. *Agricultural Economics*, *42*(SUPPL. 1), 45–60. https://doi.org/10.1111/j.1574-0862.2011.00551.x

Ghatak, M., & Karaivanov, A. (2014). Contractual structure in agriculture with endogenous matching. *Journal of Development Economics, 110*, 239–249. https://doi.org/10.1016/j.jdeveco.2013.05.005
Ghobarah, H. A., Huth, P., & Russett, B. (2003). and Maim the Shooting Wars Kill Civil People-Long After Stops. *The American Political Science Review, 97*(2), 189–202. http://www.jstor.org/stable/3118203
Glaeser, E. L., Laibson, D. I., Scheinkman, J. A., & Soutter, C. L. (2000). Glaeser et al 2000_article.pdf. *Quarterly Journal of Economics, 115*(3), 811–846.
Grossman, H. (1991). A General Equilibrium Model of Insurrections. In *American Economic Review* (Vol. 81, Issue 4, pp. 912–921). https://doi.org/10.2307/2006650
Guerrero, S. (2009). The Effects of the War in Iraq on Nutrition and Health: An Analysis Using Anthropometric Outcomes of Children. *SSRN Electronic Journal, 14056*. https://doi.org/10.2139/ssrn.1359161
Guerrero Serdan, G. (2009). The Effects of the War in Iraq on Nutrition and Health: An Analysis Using Anthropometric Outcomes of Children. *SSRN Electronic Journal, 14056*. https://doi.org/10.2139/ssrn.1359161
Harris, C., Jenkins, M., & Glaser, D. (2006). Gender Differences in Risk Assessment: Why do women take fewer risks than men? *Judgement and Decision Making, 1*(1), 48–63. http://journal.sjdm.org/jdm06016.pdf
Hartman, A. C., & Morse, B. S. (2018). Violence, Empathy and Altruism: Evidence from the Ivorian Refugee Crisis in Liberia. *British Journal of Political Science*, 1–25. https://doi.org/10.1017/S0007123417000655
Haselhuhn, M. P., Kennedy, J. A., Kray, L. J., Van Zant, A. B., & Schweitzer, M. E. (2015). Gender differences in trust dynamics: Women trust more than men following a trust violation. *Journal of Experimental Social Psychology, 56*, 104–109. https://doi.org/10.1016/j.jesp.2014.09.007
Henrich, J., Boyd, R., & Bowles, S. (2005). "Economic Man" in Cross-Cultural Perspective: Ethnography and Experiments from 15 Small-Scale Societies. *Behavioral and Brain Sciences, 28*(2005), 795–855.
Henrich, J., Ensminger, J., Mcelreath, R., Barr, A., Barrett, C., Bolyanatz, A., Cardenas, J. C., Gurven, M., Gwako, E., Henrich, N., Lesorogol, C., Marlowe, F., Tracer, D., & Ziker, J. (2010). Markets, Religion, Community size, and the Evolution of Fairness and Punishment. *Science, 327*(March 2010), 1480–1484. https://doi.org/10.1126/science.1182238
Henrich, J., McElreath, R., Barr, A., Ensminger, J., Barrett, C., Bolyanatz, A., Cardaroas, J. C., Gurven, M., Gwako, E., Henrich, N., Lesoronol, C., Marlowe, F., Tracer, D., & Ziker, J. (2006a). Costly punishment across human societies. *Science, 312*(5781), 1767–1770. https://doi.org/10.1126/science.1127333
Henrich, J., McElreath, R., Barr, A., Ensminger, J., Barrett, C., Bolyanatz, A., Cardenas, J. C., Gurven, M., Gwako, E., Henrich, N., Lesorogol, C., Marlowe, F., Tracer, D., & Ziker, J. (2006b). Costly punishment across human societies. MATERIAL RESPALDO. *Science (New York, N.Y.), 312*(5781), 1767–1770. https://doi.org/10.1126/science.1127333
Hirshleifer, J. (1995). Theorizing about conflict. In K. Hartley & T. Sandler (Eds.), *Handbook of Defense Economics* (Vol. 1, pp. 165–189). Elsevier. https://doi.org/10.1016/S1574-0013(05)80009-2
Hoeffler, A. (2012). On the Causes of Civil War. In *Oxford Economic Papers* (Vol. 50). Oxford University Press. https://doi.org/10.1093/oxfordhb/9780195392777.013.0009
Holden, S. T., & Otsuka, K. (2014). The roles of land tenure reforms and land markets in the context of population growth and land use intensification in Africa. *Food Policy, 48*, 88–97. https://doi.org/10.1016/j.foodpol.2014.03.005
Hovil, L. (2001). *Refuges and the Security Situation in Adjumani District* (Refugee Law Project, Issue 2).
Jakiela, P. (2011). Using economic experiments to measure informal institutions. In W. University (Ed.), *The Legacy and Work of Douglass C. North: Understanding Institutions and Development*

Economics (pp. 248–265). Department of Economics, Washington University. https://doi.org/10.1017/CBO9781107300361.013

Johnson, N. D., & Mislin, A. A. (2011). Trust games: A meta-analysis. *Journal of Economic Psychology*, *32*(5), 865–889. https://doi.org/10.1016/j.joep.2011.05.007

Joras, U., & Schetter, C. (2004). Hidden ties: Similarities between Research and Policy Approaches to Ethnic Conflicts. In G. Wimmer & U. D. Howowitz (Eds.), *Facing Ethnic Conflicts. Towards a New Realism* (pp. 315–332). Lanham, Rowman & Littlefield.

Jourdan, L. (2011). Mayi-Mayi: Young rebels in Kivu, DRC. *Africa Development*, *36*(3–4), 89–111.

Karlan, D. S. (2005). Using Experimental Economics to Measure Social Capital and Predict Financial Decisions. *American Economic Review*, *95*(5 (Dec., 2005)), 1688–1699. https://www.jstor.org/stable/4132772

Keswell, M., & Carter, M. R. (2014). Poverty and land redistribution. *Journal of Development Economics*, *110*, 250–261. https://doi.org/10.1016/j.jdeveco.2013.10.003

Kimbrough, E. O., & Vostroknutov, A. (2016). Norms Make Preferences Social. *Journal of the European Economic Association*, *14*(3), 608–638. https://doi.org/10.1111/jeea.12152

Kisangani, E. (2003). Conflict in the Democratic Republic of Congo: A mosaic of insurgent groups. *International Journal of World Peace*, *20*(3), 51–80. www.jstor.org/stable/20753410

Kosfeld, M., Heinrichs, M., Zak, P. J., Fischbacher, U., & Fehr, E. (2005). Oxytocin increases trust in humans. *Nature*, *435*(7042), 673–676. https://doi.org/10.1038/nature03701

Kosfeld, M., & Rustagi, D. (2015). Leader punishment and cooperation in groups: Experimental field evidence from commons management in Ethiopia. *American Economic Review*, *105*(2), 747–783. https://doi.org/10.1257/aer.20120700

Kreibaum, M. (2016). Their Suffering, Our Burden? How Congolese Refugees Affect the Ugandan Population. *World Development*, *78*, 262–287. https://doi.org/10.1016/j.worlddev.2015.10.019

Lemarchand, R. (2008). The Burundi Killings of 1972. In *Online Encyclopedia of Mass Violence* (Issue June). https://www.sciencespo.fr/mass-violence-war-massacre-resistance/en/document/burundi-killings-1972.html

Loewenstein, G., & Thompson, L. (1989). Social utility and Decision making in interpersonal contexts. *Journal of Personality and Social Psychology*, *57*(3), 426–441.

Ma, T. (2009). China and Congo's coltan connection. In *Project 2049 Institute*.

Martiniello, G. (2010). African land questions, agrarian transitions and the state: the contradictions of neo-liberal land reforms. *Review of African Political Economy*, *37*(125), 387–389. https://doi.org/10.1080/03056244.2010.511784

Maystadt, J.-F., & Verwimp, P. (2014). Winners and Losers among a Refugee-Hosting Population. *Economic Development and Cultural Change*, *62*(4), 769–809. https://doi.org/10.1086/676458

Melander, E., Pettersson, T., & Themnér, L. (2016). Organized violence, 1989–2015. *Journal of Peace Research*, *53*(5), 727–742. https://doi.org/10.1177/0022343316663032

Merkx, J. (2000). Document. Refugee identities and relief in an African borderland: a study of northern Uganda and southern Sudan. In *New issues in Refugee Research* (Vol. 21, Issue 19). https://doi.org/10.1093/rsq/21.1_and_2.113

Mkandawire, T. (2002). The terrible toll of post-colonial "rebel movements" in Africa: Towards an explanation of the violence against the peasantry. *Journal of Modern African Studies*, *40*(2), 181–215. https://doi.org/10.1017/S0022278X02003889

Mkandawire, T. (2015). Neopatrimonialism and the Political Economy of Economic Performance in Africa: Critical Reflections. *World Politics*, *67*(3), 563–612. https://doi.org/10.1017/S004388711500009X

Ngaruko, F., & Nkirunziza, J. (2000). An economic interpretation of conflict in Burundi. *Journal of African Economies*, *9*(3), 370–409. https://doi.org/10.1093/jae/9.3.370

Nindorera, W. (2012). *The CNDD-FDD in Burundi: The path from armed to political struggle* (Issue 10).

Nkurunziza, J. D. (2015). Timing and Sequencing of Post-Conflict Reconstruction and Peacebuilding in Burundi. In *CRPD Working Paper* (Issue 34). https://doi.org/10.1093/acprof:oso/9780198757276.003.0013

Nkurunziza, J. D. (2022). The origin and persistence of state fragility in Burundi. In *State Fragility, Growth and Development* (Issue April). https://doi.org/10.4324/9781003297697-4
Nshimirimana, F. (2024). *Exclusionary Governance in Burundi:Implications for Democracy and Consolidating Peace.*
Nyadera, I. N. (2018). South Sudan conflict from 2013 to 2018: Rethinking the causes, situation and solutions. *African Journal on Conflict Resolution, 18*(2), 59–86.
O'Brien, A. (2009). Shots in the Dark: The 2008 South Sudan Civilian Disarmament Campaign. In *HSBA Working Paper.*
Odera, L. C. (2013). The Role of Trust as an Informal Institution in the Informal Sector in Africa. *Africa Development, 38*(3–4), 121 – 146.
Peterson, R. (2001). Resistance and Rebellion; Lessons from Eastern Europe. In *Cambrige University Press.* https://doi.org/10.1007/BF02430448
Pham, P. N., Vinck, P., & Stover, E. (2008). The Lord's Resistance Army and Forced Conscription in Northern Uganda. *Human Rights Quarterly, 30*(2008), 404–411.
Poole, L. (2019). *The refugee response in northern Uganda: Resources beyond international humanitarian assistance* (No. 2019; HPG Working Paper, Issue February). www.odi.org/hpg.
Powell, R. (2006). War as a commitment problem. *International Organization, 60*(1), 169–203. https://doi.org/10.1017/S0020818306060061
Rabbie, J. M., Schot, J. C., & Visser, L. (1989). Social identity theory: A conceptual and empirical critique from the perspective of a behavioural interaction model. *European Journal of Social Psychology, 19*(3), 171–202. https://doi.org/10.1002/ejsp.2420190302
Rabellino, D., Morese, R., Ciaramidaro, A., Bara, B. G., & Bosco, F. M. (2016). Third-party punishment: altruistic and anti-social behaviours in in-group and out-group settings. *Journal of Cognitive Psychology, 28*(4), 486–495. https://doi.org/10.1080/20445911.2016.1138961
Rabin, M. (1993). Incorporating fairness into game theory and economics. *The American Economic Review, 83*(5), 1281–1302. http://www.jstor.org/stable/2117561
Raleigh, C., Linke, A., Hegre, H., & Karlsen, J. (2010). Introducing ACLED-Armed Conflict Location and Event Data. *Journal of Peace Research, 47*(5), 651–660.
Refugee law project. (2022). Negotiating peace: Resolution of Conflicts in Uganda's West Nile Region. In *Refugee Law Project Working Paper* (Issue 12). https://doi.org/10.4324/978100331 7487-18
Relief web. (2002). *Rwanda-Uganda: Interahamwe reported present in Uganda.* https://reliefweb.int/report/democratic-republic-congo/rwanda-uganda-interahamwe-reported-present-uganda
Rockmore, M. (2017). The cost of fear: The welfare effect of the risk of violence in Northern Uganda. *World Bank Economic Review, 31*(3), 650–669. https://doi.org/10.1093/wber/lhw025
Rockmore, M. (2020). Conflict-Risk and Agricultural Portfolios: Evidence from Northern Uganda. *The Journal of Development Studies, 2016*, 1–21. https://doi.org/10.1080/00220388.2019.170 3953
Rufanges, C. J., & Aspa, J. M. R. (2016). *Democratic Republic of Congo: A Review of 20 years of war* (Issue April). https://escolapau.uab.cat/img/programas/alerta/alerta/RDCongo_20AnosGuerra_I.pdf
Saferworld. (2010). Karamoja conflict and security assessment. In *Report* (Issue September).
Shemyakina, O. (2011). The effect of armed conflict on accumulation of schooling: Results from Tajikistan. *Journal of Development Economics, 95*(2), 186–200. https://doi.org/10.1016/j.jdeveco.2010.05.002
Sigman, R., & Lindberg, S. I. (2017). Neopatrimonialism and Democracy: An Empirical Investigation of Africa's Political Regimes. *SSRN Electronic Journal, January.* https://doi.org/10.2139/ssrn.3066654
Skaperdas, S. (2008). An economic approach to analyzing civil wars. *Economics of Governance, 9*(1), 25–44. https://doi.org/10.1007/s10101-007-0043-2
State Parties to the 1951 Convention relating to the Status of Refugees and the 1967 Protocol, (2011). https://doi.org/10.1093/rsq/hdn023

Tajfel, H., Billig, M. G., & Bundy, R. (1971). Social categorization and intergroup behaviour. *European Journal of Social Pszchology*, *1*(2), 149–178. https://doi.org/https://doi.org/10.1002/ejsp.2420010202

The Fund For Peace. (2019). *Fragile States Index Annual Report 2019*. www.fundforpeace.org

Titeca, K. (2024). Uganda and the DRC conflict: the interests driving Kampala's involvement. *The Conversation*, 23–26.

Uganda Bureau of Statistics. (2024a). National Population and Housing Census 2024: Preliminary Results. In *National Population and Household Census* (Vol. 256, Issue June).

Uganda Bureau of Statistics. (2024b). National Population and Housing Census 2024. In *Census 2024*. http://libdcms.nida.ac.th/thesis6/2010/b166706.pdf

UN, & African Union. (2011). *Fifth Anniversary of the signing of the Peace, Security and Cooperation Framework (PSCF)* (Vol. 46, Issue 0).

UNDP. (2017). *Summary of Study Uganda's Contribution To*. https://data2.unhcr.org/en/documents/download/64687

UNECA. (2015). *Conflicts in the Democratic Republic of Congo: Causes, impact and implications for the Great Lakes region*. Routledge. https://www.uneca.org/sites/default/files/PublicationFiles/conflits_in_drc_eng_25sept_rev1.pdf

UNECA. (2016). Conflict in the democratic Republic of Congo: Causes, impact and implications for the Great Lakes region. In *Routledge Handbook of Security Studies: Second Edition*. https://doi.org/10.4324/9781315753393

UNHCR. (2018). *South Sudan Regional Refugee Response Plan* (Issue December). http://reporting.unhcr.org/sites/default/files/2018SouthSudanRegionalRefugeeResponsePlan-Jan-Dec2018%28January2018%29_0.pdf

UNHCR. (2019a). *Global Trends Forced Displacemnet in 2018*. www.unhcr.org/5c6fb2d04

UNHCR. (2019b). Uganda Country Refugee Response Plan. *The UN Refugee Agency, Jan 2019–Dec 2020*, 72. http://reporting.unhcr.org/sites/default/files/UgandaCountryRRP2019-20%28January2019%29.pdf

United Nations Development Programme. (2018). *Understanding land dynamics and livelihood in refugee hosting districts of northern Uganda*.

United Nations High Commision for Refugees (UNHCR), & Government of Uganda (GoU). (2019). *Refugee and Host Population by District*. Uganda Comprehensive Refugee Response Portal. https://data2.unhcr.org/en/country/uga

Venugopalan, H. (2016). Understanding the Conflict in Congo. In *ORF ISSUE BRIEF* (Issue May). https://www.orfonline.org/wp-content/uploads/2016/05/ORF_IssueBrief_139_Venugopalan_Final.pdf

Vlassenroot, K., & Van Acker, F. (2001). War as Exit from Exclusion? The Formation of Mayi-Mayi Militias in Eastern Congo. *Afrika Focus*, *17*(1–2), 51–77. https://doi.org/10.21825/af.v17i1-2.5426

von Braun, J., Teklu, T., & Webb, P. (1998). *Famine in Africa. Causes, Response and Prevention*. The John Hopkins Univerisity Press.

Voors, M. J., Nillesen, E. E. M., Verwimp, P., Bulte, E. H., Lensink, R., & Soest, D. P. Van. (2012a). Violent Conflict and Behavior: A field experiment in Burundi. *American Economic Review*, *102*(2), 941–964.

Voors, M. J., Nillesen, E. E. M., Verwimp, P., Bulte, E. H., Lensink, R., & Van Soest, D. P. (2012b). Violent Conflict and Behaviour: a field experiment in Burundi. *Source: The American Economic Review*, *102*(2), 941–964. https://doi.org/10.1257/aer.102.2.941

Wallensteen, P., & Axell, K. (1993). Armed Conflict at the End of the Cold War, 1989–92. *Journal of Peace Research*, *30*(3), 331–346.

Werner, K., & Lambsdorff, J. G. (2019). Emotional Numbing and Lessons Learned after a Violent Conflict – Experimental Evidence from Ambon, Indonesia. *The Journal of Development Studies*, 1–15. https://doi.org/10.1080/00220388.2019.1590550

Whyte, S. R., & Acio, E. (2017). Generations and Access to Land in Postconflict Northern Uganda: Youth Have No Voice in Land Matters. *African Studies Review*, *60*(3), 17–36. https://doi.org/10.1017/asr.2017.120

World Bank. (2015). *Forced Displacement in the Great Lakes Region*. http://hdl.handle.net/10986/21708

World Bank. (2016). *The Uganda Poverty Assessment Report 2016. Farms, cities and good fortune: assessing poverty reduction in Uganda from 2006 to 2013*. http://pubdocs.worldbank.org/en/890971474327477241/Uganda-Poverty-Assessment-Report-2016-Overview.pdf

WorldBank. (2016). *The Uganda Poverty Assessment Report, 2016: Farms, Cities and good fortune: assessing poverty reduction in Uganda from 2006 to 2013*.

Yami, M., & van Asten, P. (2018). Relevance of informal institutions for achieving sustainable crop intensification in Uganda. *Food Security*, *10*(1), 141–150. https://doi.org/10.1007/s12571-017-0754-3

Young, J. (2016). Popular struggles and elite co-optation: the Nuer White Army in South Sudan's Civil War. In E. LeBrun (Ed.), *Small Arms Survey*. Graduate Institute of International and Development studies.

Zhu, H., Filipski, M., Valli, J., Gonzalez, E., Gupta, A., & Taylor, J. E. (2016a). *Economic Impact of Refugee Settlements in Uganda* (Issue November).

Zhu, H., Taylor, J. E., Gupta, A., Filipski, M., Valli, J., & Gonzalez, E. E. (2016b). Economic Impacts of Giving Land to Refugees. In *Agricultural and Applied Economics Association 2018 Annual Meeting*. Agricultural and Applied Economics Association. https://doi.org/10.22004/ag.econ.274212

University of Bonn

The **University of Bonn** is a public research university in Bonn, North Rhine-Westphalia, Germany. It was founded in its present form on 18 October 1818 by Frederick William III. The University of Bonn offers many undergraduate and graduate programs in a range of subjects and has 544 professors. The University of Bonn is a member of the German U15 association of major research-intensive universities in Germany and has the title of "University of Excellence" under the German Universities Excellence Initiative.

Bonn has six Clusters of Excellence, the most of any German university: the Hausdorff Center for Mathematics, the Matter and Light for Quantum Computing cluster, Bonn Center for Dependency and Slavery Studies, PhenoRob: Research for the Future of Crop Production, the Immune Sensory System cluster, and ECONtribute: Markets and Public Policy. The University and State Library Bonn (ULB Bonn) is the central university and archive library of the Rheinische Friedrich-Wilhelms-Universität Bonn and North Rhine-Westphalia; it holds more than five million volumes.

As of October 2020, among its notable alumni, faculty and researchers are 11 Nobel Laureates, 5 Fields Medalists, 12 Gottfried Wilhelm Leibniz Prize winners as well as some of the most gifted minds in Natural Science, e.g. August Kekulé, Heinrich Hertz and Justus von Liebig; eminent mathematicians, such as Karl Weierstrass, Felix Klein, Friedrich Hirzebruch and Felix Hausdorff; major philosophers, such as Friedrich Nietzsche, Karl Marx, and Jürgen Habermas; German poets and writers, for example Heinrich Heine, Paul Heyse and Thomas Mann; painters, like Max Ernst; political theorists, for instance Carl Schmitt and Otto Kirchheimer; statesmen, viz. Konrad Adenauer and Robert Schuman; economists, like Walter Eucken, Ferdinand

A. Adong, *Armed Conflicts and Forced Displacements in the Anthropocene*, The Anthropocene: Politik—Economics—Society—Science 41,
https://doi.org/10.1007/978-3-032-04820-2

Tönnies and Joseph Schumpeter; and furthermore Prince Albert, Pope Benedict XVI and Wilhelm II. The University of Bonn has 32,500 students, and 4,000 of these are international students. Each year about 3,000 undergraduate students graduate. The university also confers about 800 Ph.D.s and about 60 habilitations. More than 90 programs in all fields are offered. Strong fields as identified by the university are mathematics, physics, law, economics, neuroscience, medical genetics, chemical biology, agriculture, Asian and Oriental studies and Philosophy and Ethics. The university has more than 550 professors, an additional academic staff of 3,900 and an administrative staff of over 1,700. The annual budget was more than 570 million euros in 2016.

From the foundation in 1818–1928 the University of Bonn had five faculties, that is, the Faculty of Catholic Theology, the Faculty of Protestant Theology, the Faculty of Law and the Faculty of Arts and Science. In 1928, the Faculty of Law and the Department of Economics, that until then was part of the Faculty of Arts and Science, merged into the new Faculty of Law and Economics. In 1934 the until then independent Agricultural University Bonn-Poppelsdorf (German: *Landwirtschaftliche Hochschule Bonn-Poppelsdorf*) was merged into the University of Bonn as the Faculty of Agricultural Science. In 1936, the science departments were separated from the Faculty of Arts and Science. Today the university is divided into seven faculties.

The Center for Development Research (ZEF)

The Center for Development Research – ZEF – is an internationally and interdisciplinary oriented research institute of the Rheinische Friedrich-Wilhelms-Universität Bonn. The research activities of ZEF focus on three core areas: economic development and technological change, ecology and management of natural resources, and political and cultural change. The ZEF attaches central importance to scientific training and postgraduate studies, in particular those of junior scientists from developing and transforming countries. Since October 1999, ZEF has offered the three-year study course "International Doctoral Studies Program for Development" exclusively in English. ZEF cooperates with ZEI under one roof in the International Science Forum Bonn IWB.

The Center for Development Research (ZEF) was founded in 1995 and started its actual research activities in 1997. ZEF's research aims at finding solutions to development-related issues. The three departmental heads form the ZEF Board of Directors. The Director of UNU-EHS is an ex-officio member of the directorate. ZEF is an institute affiliated to the University of Bonn by being directly subordinated to the University's senate. The three departments cooperate closely with the University's respective faculties. The work of the Center is supported by an external, international Advisory Board, which was inaugurated in 1999. On the strength of its members' professional competence and reputation, the Board has the task and responsibility of monitoring and evaluating ZEF's activities as well as advising and supporting the Center in its current work and future strategy.

By covering three main research areas, which are interrelated through interdisciplinary research projects, ZEF offers a broad and integrated perspective on development. Since development is rarely constrained by a single problem within a single

A. Adong, *Armed Conflicts and Forced Displacements in the Anthropocene*, The Anthropocene: Politik—Economics—Society—Science 41,
https://doi.org/10.1007/978-3-032-04820-2

discipline, ZEF works on cross-cutting themes of central importance for the developing world. The research programs build on the methods and analytical styles of the disciplinary research areas and link and integrate knowledge and capacities from these different areas. ZEF's three research departments are:

- Political and Cultural Change (ZEF A)
- Economic and Technological Change (ZEF B)
- Ecology and Natural Resources Management (ZEF C)

The results of ZEF's research are published in its own book series, in the ZEF Discussion Papers on Development Policy, in renowned academic journals, and in books. Through its Bonn Interdisciplinary Graduate School for Development Research (BiGS – DR), ZEF contributes to strengthening the international development research community in Germany, Europe and the developing world. The program is educating highly qualified academic staff, advisers, and managers for both the private and public sectors. In its interdisciplinarity, size and concept the program is unique and has become an internationally renowned institution.

ZEF maintains an active dialogue with representatives from governmental and non-governmental bodies, as well as with national and international organizations for science and development cooperation and with the private and business sectors. The Center organizes international conferences and expert rounds on development issues and is involved in processes with a policy impact on topics such as biodiversity and land degradation. To reach out to a non-scientific audience, ZEF organizes lecture series and publishes policy briefs and a newsletter as well as an annual report.

Collaboration with outstanding academics and scientists from research centers in developing countries as well as other countries all over the world is an important part of the partnership effort. About 50% of ZEF's staff is recruited internationally. ZEF strives to involve both private sector and government organizations in development cooperation to help them benefit from its activities. www.zef.de.

Makerere University in Kampala

Makerere University (**Mak**) is Uganda's largest and oldest institution of higher learning, first established as a technical school in 1922, and the oldest currently active University in East Africa. It became an independent national university in 1970. Its establishment marked the beginning of higher education in Uganda and the East African region. Some of the courses offered at the time of its establishment included medical care, agriculture, veterinary sciences, and teacher training. From being a technical school, it expanded over the years to become a center for higher education in East Africa in 1935 and an institution of higher education offering post-school certificate courses in 1937. In 1949, it became a University College affiliated with the University of London as its mother institution, offering courses that led to the award of degrees. It was detached from the University of London in 1963 and transferred to the University of East Africa, and it started offering degrees. On July 1, Makerere transformed into an independent national university of the Republic of Uganda, offering undergraduate and postgraduate courses and having its own awards. Today, Makerere University offers programs for about 36,000 undergraduates and 4,000 postgraduates (both nationals and internationals). The University also remains an active research center.

In July 2011, the University transitioned from a Faculty-Based to a collegiate system, with nine constituent colleges, which later expanded to ten on July 1, 2014. All colleges operate as semi-autonomous units. These colleges include College of Natural Sciences (CONAS), College of Health Sciences (CHS), College of Engineering Art and Design (CEDAT), College of Agriculture and Environmental Studies (CAES), College Of Business and Management Sciences (CoBAMS), College of Humanities and Social Sciences (CHUSS), College of Computing and Information Sciences (COCIS), College of Veterinary Medicine, Animal Resources and Biosecurity (COVAB), College of Education and External Studies (CEES), Makerere University Business School (MUBS) and the school of law. Additionally, Makerere has another campus in Eastern Uganda, located in Jinja City.

A. Adong, *Armed Conflicts and Forced Displacements in the Anthropocene*, The Anthropocene: Politik—Economics—Society—Science 41,
https://doi.org/10.1007/978-3-032-04820-2

The University offers several programs. At the undergraduate level, Makerere University has 145 programmes which include 11 Diplomas and 134 Bachelors programmes.[1] The University also offers over 139 Postgraduate Programmes, which include 17 (Seventeen) Postgraduate Diplomas and 135 Master's Degree programmes. All academic units have the provision to offer doctoral degrees, either by research only or by a combination of coursework and dissertation.

Makerere University is the alma mater of many post-independence African leaders, including Ugandan president Milton Obote and Tanzanian presidents Julius Nyerere and Benjamin Mkapa. The former president of the Democratic Republic of the Congo, Joseph Kabila, and the former Kenyan president, the late Mwai Kibaki, are also Makerere alumni.

In the years immediately after Uganda's independence, Makerere University was a focal point for the literary activity that was central to African nationalist culture. Many prominent writers, including Nuruddin Farah, Ali Mazrui, David Rubadiri, Okello Oculi, Ngũgĩ wa Thiong'o, John Ruganda, Paul Theroux, Nobel Prize laureate V. S. Naipaul, and Peter Nazareth, were at Makerere University at one point in their writing and academic careers.

[1] https://mak.ac.ug/about/facts-figures.

Biography

Annet Adong holds a Ph.D. in Development and Agricultural Economics from the University of Bonn, Germany, a Master's in Development and Natural Resource Economics from the University of Life Sciences in Norway, and a B.Sc. in Agriculture Economics from Makerere University, Uganda. Annet's research is at the intersection of Agriculture, Conflicts, and Forced Displacements in Sub-Saharan Africa. She has published her work in the *Journal of World Development*, the *Journal of World Effectiveness*, and *Food Policy*. She has also consulted for Organizations such as the World Bank, the Food and Agricultural Organization, and the International Food Policy Research Institute (IFPRI). She received a Post Doctoral Fellowship with IMMANA, Tuft University in 2022. She belongs to several research networks, including EGAP, the East African Social Science Translation, the Network for Impact Evaluators in Uganda, and AGRODEP

A. Adong, *Armed Conflicts and Forced Displacements in the Anthropocene*, The Anthropocene: Politik—Economics—Society—Science 41,
https://doi.org/10.1007/978-3-032-04820-2

Adong, A.; Kornher, L.; Chichaibelu, B.B.; Arslan, A. (2024). The Hidden Costs of Coffee Production in the Eastern Africa Value Chains. Background paper to the FAO flagship, The State of Food and Agriculture 2024 – Value-driven Transformation of Agrifood Systems. https://openknowledge.fao.org/items/78ec67c8-8b21-403d-86d1-462dfdab9a64

Acemoglu, D., Vindigni, A., & Ticchi, D. (2010). Persistence of Civil Wars. *European Economic Association*, *8*(May), 664–676.

Adelman, S., & Peterman, A. (2014). Resettlement and gender dimensions of land rights in post-conflict Northern Uganda. *World Development*, *64*, 583–596. https://doi.org/10.1016/j.worlddev.2014.06.031

Ager, A., & Strang, A. (2008). Understanding Integration: A Conceptual Framework. *Journal of Refugee Studies*, *21*(2), 166–191. https://doi.org/10.1093/jrs/fen016

Ahabwe, G., & Depio, S. (2019). *How Effective is the Self-Reliance Agenda in Uganda's* (Issue 107).

Akerlof, G. A., & Kranton, R. E. (2000). Economics and Identity. *Economics and Identity*, *CXV*(3), 715–753.

Akresh, R., Lucchetti, L., & Thirumurthy, H. (2012). Wars and child health: Evidence from the Eritrean – Ethiopian conflict. *Journal of Development Economics*, *99*(2), 330–340. https://doi.org/10.1016/j.jdeveco.2012.04.001

Allen, D., & Lueck, D. (1992). Contract Choice in Modern Agriculture: Cash Rent versus Cropshare. *The Journal of Law and Economics*, *35*(2), 397–426. http://www.jstor.com/stable/725546

Allen, T. (1991). Understanding Alice: Uganda's Holy spirit Movement in Context. *Journal of the International African Institute*, *61*(3), 370–399. https://www.jstor.org/stable/1160031?seq=1#metadata_info_tab_contents

Allen, T., & Koen, V. (2010). *The Lord's Resistance Army: Myth and Reality* (T. Allen & K. Vlassenroot (eds.); Issue November). Zed Books Ltd. http://www.zedbooks.co.uk/

Andreoni, J., & Bernheim, D. (2009). Social image and the 50–50 norm: a theoretical and experimental analysis of audience effects. *Econometrica*, *77*(5), 1607–1636. https://doi.org/10.3982/ECTA7384

Andreoni, J., & Miller, J. (2002). Giving According to GARP: An Experimental Test of the Consistency of Preferences for Altruism. *Econometrica*, *70*(2), 737–753.

Annan, J., Blattman, C., Mazurana, D., & Carlson, K. (2011). Civil war, reintegration, and gender in northern Uganda. *Journal of Conflict Resolution*, *55*(6), 877–908. https://doi.org/10.1177/0022002711408013

Ashraf, N., Gine, X., & Karlan, D. (2009). Finding missing markets (and a disturbing epilogue): Evidence from an export crop adoption and marketing intervention in Kenya. *American Journal of Agricultural Economics*, *91*(November), 973–990. https://doi.org/10.1111/j.1467-8276.2009.01319.x

Ashraf, N., Bohnet, I., & Piankov, N. (2006). Decomposing trust and trustworthiness. *Experimental Economics*, *9*(3), 193–208. https://doi.org/10.1007/s10683-006-9122-4

Bakwesegha, C., Brubaker, R., Connor, W., Ellis, A., Esman, M., Hannan, H., Hechter, M., Kalin, W., Lemarchand, R., Lund, Michaels, S., van der Stoel, M.,

Miall, H., Zartmann, William, I., Ropers, N., Rothchild, D., Tishkov, Valery, A., Vinas, A., & Waldman, P. (2004). Facing Ethnic Conflicts: Toward a New Realism. In G. Wimmer (Ed.), *Toward a new realism*. Rowman & Littlefield Publishers, 2004. https://books.google.de/books?id=DdtOAQAAQBAJ&dq=conrad+schetter+conflict&lr=&source=gbs_navlinks_s

Barr, A. (2003). Trust and expected trustworthiness: Experimental evidence from Zimbabwean villages. *Economic Journal, 113*(489), 614–630. https://doi.org/10.1111/1468-0297.t01-1-00150

Bauer, M., Blattman, C., Chytilová, J., Henrich, J., Miguel, E., & Mitts, T. (2016). Can War Foster Cooperation? *Journal of Economic Perspectives, 30*(3), 249–274. https://doi.org/10.1257/jep.30.3.249

Bauer, M., Fiala, N., & Levely, I. (2018). Trusting Former Rebels: An Experimental Approach to Understanding Reintegration after Civil War. *Economic Journal, 128*(613), 1786–1819. https://doi.org/10.1111/ecoj.12503

Baumgartner, T., Götte, L., Gügler, R., & Fehr, E. (2012). The mentalizing network orchestrates the impact of parochial altruism on social norm enforcement. *Human Brain Mapping, 33*(6), 1452–1469. https://doi.org/10.1002/hbm.21298

Bellemare, C., & Kröger, S. (2007). On representative social capital. *European Economic Review, 51*(1), 183–202. https://doi.org/10.1016/j.euroecorev.2006.03.006

Bellows, J., & Miguel, E. (2006). War and institutions: New evidence from Sierra Leone. *American Economic Review, 96*(2), 394–399. https://doi.org/10.1257/000282806777212323

Bellows, J., & Miguel, E. (2009). War and local collective action in Sierra Leone. *Journal of Public Economics, 93*(11–12), 1144–1157. https://doi.org/10.1016/j.jpubeco.2009.07.012

Bennett, D. S., & Stam, A. C. (2016). The Duration of Interstate Wars, 1816–1985 Author(s): D. Scott Bennett and Allan C. Stam III Source: The American Political Science Review, Vol. 90, No. 2 (Jun., 1996), pp. 239–257 Published by: American Political Science Association Stabl. *The American Political Science Review, 90*(2), 239–257.

Berg, J., Dickhaut, J., & McCabe, K. (1995). Trust, reciprocity, and social history. *Games and Economic Behavior, 10*(1), 122–142. https://doi.org/10.1006/game.1995.1027

Bernhard, H., Fischbacher, U., & Fehr, E. (2006). Parochial altruism in humans. *Nature, 442*(7105), 912–915. https://doi.org/10.1038/nature04981

Besley, T., & Persson, T. (2008a). The Incidence of Civil War: Theory and Evidence. In Intergovernmental Panel on Climate Change (Ed.), *NBER Working paper series* (Vol. 14585). Cambridge University Press. https://doi.org/10.3386/w14585

Besley, T., & Persson, T. (2008b). The Incidence of Civil War: Theory and Evidence. In Intergovernmental Panel on Climate Change (Ed.), *NBER Working paper series* (Vol. 14585). Cambridge University Press. https://doi.org/10.3386/w14585

Binswanger, H. P., & Rosenzweig, M. R. (1981). Contractual arrangements, Employment and wages in rural labor markets: A critical review. In *Studies in employment & rural development series* (Issue SER 67). http://documents.worldbank.org/curated/en/412971467997610342/Contractual-arrangements-employment-and-wages-in-rural-labor-markets-a-critical-review

Blattman, C., & Annan, J. (2010). The Consequences of Child Soldiering. *Review of Economics and Statistics, 92*(4), 882. https://doi.org/10.1162/REST_a_00036

Blattman, C., & Miguel, E. (2010). Civil War. *Journal of Economic Literature, 48*(1), 3–57. https://doi.org/10.1257/jel.48.1.3

Bloem, J. (2019). Good Intentions Gone Bad? The Dodd-Frank Act and Conflict in Africa's Great Lakes Region. In *HiCN*.

Bohnet, H., & Schmitz, C. P. (2019). *Uganda: A role model for refugee integration?* (No. 2; 2019).

Brosché, J., & Höglund, K. (2016). Crisis of governance in South Sudan: Electoral politics and violence in the world's newest nation. *Journal of Modern African Studies, 54*(1), 67–90. https://doi.org/10.1017/S0022278X15000828

Brück, T., D'Errico, M., & Pietrelli, R. (2018). The effects of violent conflict on household resilience and food security: Evidence from the 2014 Gaza conflict. *World Development, 2018*. https://doi.org/https://doi.org/10.1016/j.worlddev.2018.05.008

Bundervoet, T., Verwimp, P., & Akresh, R. (2009). Health and civil war in rural Burundi. *Journal of Human Resources, 44*(2), 536–563. https://doi.org/10.3368/jhr.44.2.536

Burke, M., & Young, P. (2009). Social Norms. In A. Bisin, J. Benhabib, & M. Jackson (Eds.), *The Handbook of Social Economics* (pp. 1–51).

Burks, S. V., Carpenter, J. P., & Verhoogen, E. (2003). Playing both roles in the trust game.pdf. *Journal of Economic Behaviour and Organisation, 51*, 195–216. https://doi.org/10.1016/S0167-2681(02)00093-8

Cameron, A. C., Gelbach, J. B., & Miller, D. L. (2007). *Nber Technical Working Paper Series. 90*(August), 414–427. https://pdfs.semanticscholar.org/df0a/ff0cb4db55166abbf5e33696d67698f81d3d.pdf%5Cnhttp://www.mitpressjournals.org/doi/pdf/10.1162/rest.90.3.414

Cesarini, D., Dawes, C. T., Fowler, J. H., Johannesson, M., & Lichtenstein, P. (2008). Heritability of cooperative behaviour in the trust game. *PNAS, 105*(10), 3721–3726. https://doi.org/10.1073/pnas.0710069105

Charness, G., & Rabin, M. (2002). Understanding Social Preferences with Simple Tests. *The Quarterly Journal of Economics, 117*(3), 817–869. http://www.jstor.org/

Chaudhuri, A., Paichayontvijit, T., & Shen, L. (2013a). Gender differences in trust and trustworthiness: Individuals, single sex and mixed sex groups. *Journal of Economic Psychology, 34*, 181–194. https://doi.org/10.1016/j.joep.2012.09.013

Chaudhuri, A., Paichayontvijit, T., & Shen, L. (2013b). Gender differences in trust and trustworthiness: Individuals, single sex and mixed sex groups. *Journal of Economic Psychology, 34*, 181–194. https://doi.org/10.1016/j.joep.2012.09.013

Chen, Y., & Li, S. X. (2009). Group identity and social preferences. *American Economic Review*, *99*(1), 431–457. https://doi.org/10.1257/aer.99.1.431

Coggio, T. (2019). Can Uganda's Breakthrough Refugee-Hosting Model Be Sustained? *Migration Policy Institute*, 1–11. https://www.migrationpolicy.org

Collier, P. (1999). On the Economic Consequences of Civil War. *Oxford Economic Papers*, *51*(January 1999), 168–183.

Collier, P., & Hoeffler, A. (2004). Greed and grievance in civil war. *Oxford Economic Papers*, *56*(2004), 563–595. https://doi.org/10.1093/oep/gpf064

Collier, P., Hoeffler, A., & Söderbom, M. (2004). Collier 2004 – Duration of civil wars. *Journal of Peace Research*, *41*(3), 253–273.

Cox, J. C. (2004a). How to identify trust and reciprocity. *Games and Economic Behavior*, *46*(2), 260–281. https://doi.org/10.1016/S0899-8256(03)00119-2

Cox, J. C. (2004b). How to identify trust and reciprocity. *Games and Economic Behavior*, *8256*(03), 260–281. https://doi.org/10.1016/S0899-8256(03)00119-2

Cramer, C. (2002). Homo Economicus Goes to War: Methodological Individualism, Rational Choice and the Political Economy of War. *World Development*, *30*(11), 1845–1864. https://doi.org/10.1016/S0305-750X(02)00120-1

Cunningham, D. E., Gleditsch, K. S., & Salehyan, I. (2009). It Takes Two: A Dyadic Analysis of Civil War Duration and Outcome. *Journal of Conflict Resolution*, *53*(4), 570–597. https://www.jstor.org/stable/20684603?seq=1#metadata_info_tab_contents

Cuvelier, J., Van Bockstaal, S., Vlassenroot, K., & Iguma, C. (2014). Analyzing the Impact of the Dodd-Frank Act on Congolese Livelihoods. In *Conflict Prevention and Peace Forum* (Vol. 1, Issue November). https://doi.org/10.1017/CBO9781107415324.004

d'Errico, M., Winters, P., & Romano, D. (2024). Assessing Uganda's Progressive Refugee Policy in the Era of COVID-19: Introduction to the Special Issue. *Journal of Development Studies*, *60*(3), 351–359. https://doi.org/10.1080/00220388.2023.2282364

Deininger, K., & Feder, G. (2001). Chapter 6 Land institutions and land markets. In B. Gardner & G. Rausser (Eds.), *Handbook of Agricultural Economics* (2001st ed., Vol. 1, Issue PART A, pp. 287–331). Elsevier Science B.V. https://doi.org/10.1016/S1574-0072(01)10009-5

Denison, R. F., & Muller, K. (2016). The evolution of cooperation. *Scientist*, *30*(1). https://doi.org/10.5840/tpm201467114

Dessalegn, A. G. (2017). The Cause and Consequence of Conflict in South Sudan. *International Journal of Political Science and Development*, *5*(1), 15–21. https://doi.org/10.14662/IJPSD2016.063

Development Pathways. (2018). *Analysis of Refugee Vulnerability in Uganda and Recommendations for Improved Targeting of Food Assistance* (Issue April 2018).

di Montenegro, T. X. (2017). *China's Interest in Africa: Conflict or Stability?* [Florida International University]. https://doi.org/10.25148/etd.FIDC001790

Elwert, G. (2018). Intervention in markets of violence. In *Potentials of disorder* (Issue September 2001, pp. 219–242). Manchester University Press. https://doi.org/10.7765/9781526137586.00017

Eswaran, M., & Kotwal, A. (1985). A Theory of Contractual Structure in Agriculture. *The American Economic Review*, *75*(3), 352–367.

Everett, J. A. C., Faber, N. S., & Crockett, M. (2015). Preferences and beliefs in ingroup favoritism. *Frontiers in Behavioral Neuroscience*, *9*(FEB), 1–21. https://doi.org/10.3389/fnbeh.2015.00015

Everts, E. (2003). Identifying a particular family humor style: A sociolinguistic discourse analysis. *Humor – International Journal of Humor Research, 16*(4), 752. https://doi.org/10.1515/humr.2003.021

FAO. (2018). *Food Security, Resilience and Well-Being Analysis of Refugees and Host Communities in Northern Uganda.* https://doi.org/10.11975/j.issn.1002-6819.2015.24.025

FAO, & World Food Program. (2018). *Monitoring food security in countries with conflict situations: A joint FAO/WFP update for the United Nations Security Council* (Issue 3).

Fearon, J. D. (1995). Rationalist Explanations for War Author. *International Organization, 49*(3), 379–414.

Fehr, E. (2009). On the Economics and Biology of Trust. *European Economic Association, 7*(2–3), 235–266.

Fehr, E., Fischbacher, U., & Gächter, S. (2002). Strong reciprocity, human cooperation, and the enforcement of social norms. *Human Nature, 13*(1), 1–25. https://doi.org/10.1007/s12110-002-1012-7

Fehr, E., & Schmidt, K. M. (1999). A Theory of Fairness, Competition, and Cooperation. *The Quarterly Journal of Economics, 114*(3), 817–868. https://doi.org/10.1162/003355399556151

Fershtman, C., & Gneezy, U. (2001a). Discrimination in a Segmented Society: An Experimental Approach. *The Quarterly Journal of Economics.* https://rady.ucsd.edu/faculty/directory/gneezy/pub/docs/discrimination-society.pdf

Fershtman, C., & Gneezy, U. (2001b). Discrimination in a Segmented Society: An Experimental Approach. *The Quarterly Journal of Economics.*

Fisman, B. R., Kariv, S., & Markovits, D. (2007). Individual Preferences for Giving. *The American Economic Review, 97*(5).

Fisman, R., Jakiela, P., & Kariv, S. (2017). Distributional preferences and political behavior. *Journal of Public Economics, 155*, 1–10. https://doi.org/10.1016/j.jpubeco.2017.08.010

García, A. D. (2020). Armed groups, IHL and the invisible world: How spiritual beliefs shape warfare. *International Review of the Red Cross, 102*(915), 1179–1199. https://doi.org/10.1017/S1816383121000229

Gates, S. (2015). Recruitment, Retention, and Religion in Rebel Groups. In *"Peace, Conflict, and Development", ESOP,* (Issue March 2015).

Geanakoplosand, J., Pearce, D., & Ennio, S. (1989). Psychological Games and Sequential Rationality. *Games and Economic Behaviour, 1*(1989), 60–79.

Gebregziabher, G., & Holden, S. T. (2011). Distress rentals and the land rental market as a safety net: Contract choice evidence from Tigray, Ethiopia. *Agricultural Economics, 42*(SUPPL. 1), 45–60. https://doi.org/10.1111/j.1574-0862.2011.00551.x

Ghatak, M., & Karaivanov, A. (2014). Contractual structure in agriculture with endogenous matching. *Journal of Development Economics, 110*, 239–249. https://doi.org/10.1016/j.jdeveco.2013.05.005

Ghobarah, H. A., Huth, P., & Russett, B. (2003). and Maim the Shooting Wars Kill Civil People-Long After Stops. *The American Political Science Review, 97*(2), 189–202. http://www.jstor.org/stable/3118203

Glaeser, E. L., Laibson, D. I., Scheinkman, J. A., & Soutter, C. L. (2000). Glaeser et al 2000_article.pdf. *Quarterly Journal of Economics, 115*(3), 811–846.

Grossman, H. (1991). A General Equilibrium Model of Insurrections. In *American Economic Review* (Vol. 81, Issue 4, pp. 912–921). https://doi.org/10.2307/2006650

Guerrero, S. (2009). The Effects of the War in Iraq on Nutrition and Health: An Analysis Using Anthropometric Outcomes of Children. *SSRN Electronic Journal, 14056*. https://doi.org/10.2139/ssrn.1359161

Guerrero Serdan, G. (2009). The Effects of the War in Iraq on Nutrition and Health: An Analysis Using Anthropometric Outcomes of Children. *SSRN Electronic Journal, 14056*. https://doi.org/10.2139/ssrn.1359161

Harris, C., Jenkins, M., & Glaser, D. (2006). Gender Differences in Risk Assessment: Why do women take fewer risks than men? *Judgement and Decision Making, 1*(1), 48–63. http://journal.sjdm.org/jdm06016.pdf

Hartman, A. C., & Morse, B. S. (2018). Violence, Empathy and Altruism: Evidence from the Ivorian Refugee Crisis in Liberia. *British Journal of Political Science*, 1–25. https://doi.org/10.1017/S0007123417000655

Haselhuhn, M. P., Kennedy, J. A., Kray, L. J., Van Zant, A. B., & Schweitzer, M. E. (2015). Gender differences in trust dynamics: Women trust more than men following a trust violation. *Journal of Experimental Social Psychology, 56*, 104–109. https://doi.org/10.1016/j.jesp.2014.09.007

Henrich, J., Boyd, R., & Bowles, S. (2005). "Economic Man" in Cross-Cultural Perspective: Ethnography and Experiments from 15 Small-Scale Societies. *Behavioral and Brain Sciences, 28*(2005), 795–855.

Henrich, J., Ensminger, J., Mcelreath, R., Barr, A., Barrett, C., Bolyanatz, A., Cardenas, J. C., Gurven, M., Gwako, E., Henrich, N., Lesorogol, C., Marlowe, F., Tracer, D., & Ziker, J. (2010). Markets, Religion, Community size, and the Evolution of Fairness and Punishment. *Science, 327*(March 2010), 1480–1484. https://doi.org/10.1126/science.1182238

Henrich, J., McElreath, R., Barr, A., Ensminger, J., Barrett, C., Bolyanatz, A., Cardaroas, J. C., Gurven, M., Gwako, E., Henrich, N., Lesoronol, C., Marlowe, F., Tracer, D., & Ziker, J. (2006a). Costly punishment across human societies. *Science, 312*(5781), 1767–1770. https://doi.org/10.1126/science.1127333

Henrich, J., McElreath, R., Barr, A., Ensminger, J., Barrett, C., Bolyanatz, A., Cardenas, J. C., Gurven, M., Gwako, E., Henrich, N., Lesorogol, C., Marlowe, F., Tracer, D., & Ziker, J. (2006b). Costly punishment across human societies. MATERIAL RESPALDO. *Science (New York, N.Y.), 312*(5781), 1767–1770. https://doi.org/10.1126/science.1127333

Hirshleifer, J. (1995). Theorizing about conflict. In K. Hartley & T. Sandler (Eds.), *Handbook of Defense Economics* (Vol. 1, pp. 165–189). Elsevier. https://doi.org/10.1016/S1574-0013(05)80009-2

Hoeffler, A. (2012). On the Causes of Civil War. In *Oxford Economic Papers* (Vol. 50). Oxford University Press. https://doi.org/10.1093/oxfordhb/9780195392777.013.0009

Holden, S. T., & Otsuka, K. (2014). The roles of land tenure reforms and land markets in the context of population growth and land use intensification in Africa. *Food Policy, 48*, 88–97. https://doi.org/10.1016/j.foodpol.2014.03.005

Hovil, L. (2001). *Refuges and the Security Situation in Adjumani District* (Refugee Law Project, Issue 2).

Jakiela, P. (2011). Using economic experiments to measure informal institutions. In W. University (Ed.), *The Legacy and Work of Douglass C. North: Understanding Institutions and Development Economics* (pp. 248–265). Department of Economics, Washington University. https://doi.org/10.1017/CBO9781107300361.013

Johnson, N. D., & Mislin, A. A. (2011). Trust games: A meta-analysis. *Journal of Economic Psychology, 32*(5), 865–889. https://doi.org/10.1016/j.joep.2011.05.007

Joras, U., & Schetter, C. (2004). Hidden ties: Similarities between Research and Policy Approaches to Ethnic Conflicts. In G. Wimmer & U. D. Howowitz (Eds.), *Facing Ethnic Conflicts. Towards a New Realism* (pp. 315–332). Lanham, Rowman & Littlefield.

Jourdan, L. (2011). Mayi-Mayi: Young rebels in Kivu, DRC. *Africa Development, 36*(3–4), 89–111.

Karlan, D. S. (2005). Using Experimental Economics to Measure Social Capital and Predict Financial Decisions. *American Economic Review, 95*(5 (Dec., 2005)), 1688–1699. https://www.jstor.org/stable/4132772

Keswell, M., & Carter, M. R. (2014). Poverty and land redistribution. *Journal of Development Economics, 110*, 250–261. https://doi.org/10.1016/j.jdeveco.2013.10.003

Kimbrough, E. O., & Vostroknutov, A. (2016). Norms Make Preferences Social. *Journal of the European Economic Association, 14*(3), 608–638. https://doi.org/10.1111/jeea.12152

Kisangani, E. (2003). Conflict in the Democratic Republic of Congo: A mosaic of insurgent groups. *International Journal of World Peace, 20*(3), 51–80. www.jstor.org/stable/20753410

Kosfeld, M., Heinrichs, M., Zak, P. J., Fischbacher, U., & Fehr, E. (2005). Oxytocin increases trust in humans. *Nature, 435*(7042), 673–676. https://doi.org/10.1038/nature03701

Kosfeld, M., & Rustagi, D. (2015). Leader punishment and cooperation in groups: Experimental field evidence from commons management in Ethiopia. *American Economic Review, 105*(2), 747–783. https://doi.org/10.1257/aer.20120700

Kreibaum, M. (2016). Their Suffering, Our Burden? How Congolese Refugees Affect the Ugandan Population. *World Development*, *78*, 262–287. https://doi.org/10.1016/j.worlddev.2015.10.019

Lemarchand, R. (2008). The Burundi Killings of 1972. In *Online Encyclopedia of Mass Violence* (Issue June). https://www.sciencespo.fr/mass-violence-war-massacre-resistance/en/document/burundi-killings-1972.html

Loewenstein, G., & Thompson, L. (1989). Social utility and Decision making in interpersonal contexts. *Journal of Personality and Social Psychology*, *57*(3), 426–441.

Ma, T. (2009). China and Congo's coltan connection. In *Project 2049 Institute*.

Martiniello, G. (2010). African land questions, agrarian transitions and the state: the contradictions of neo-liberal land reforms. *Review of African Political Economy*, *37*(125), 387–389. https://doi.org/10.1080/03056244.2010.511784

Maystadt, J.-F., & Verwimp, P. (2014). Winners and Losers among a Refugee-Hosting Population. *Economic Development and Cultural Change*, *62*(4), 769–809. https://doi.org/10.1086/676458

Melander, E., Pettersson, T., & Themnér, L. (2016). Organized violence, 1989–2015. *Journal of Peace Research*, *53*(5), 727–742. https://doi.org/10.1177/0022343316663032

Merkx, J. (2000). Document. Refugee identities and relief in an African borderland: a study of northern Uganda and southern Sudan. In *New issues in Refugee Research* (Vol. 21, Issue 19). https://doi.org/10.1093/rsq/21.1_and_2.113

Mkandawire, T. (2002). The terrible toll of post-colonial "rebel movements" in Africa: Towards an explanation of the violence against the peasantry. *Journal of Modern African Studies*, *40*(2), 181–215. https://doi.org/10.1017/S0022278X02003889

Mkandawire, T. (2015). Neopatrimonialism and the Political Economy of Economic Performance in Africa: Critical Reflections. *World Politics*, *67*(3), 563–612. https://doi.org/10.1017/S004388711500009X

Ngaruko, F., & Nkirunziza, J. (2000). An economic interpretation of conflict in Burundi. *Journal of African Economies*, *9*(3), 370–409. https://doi.org/10.1093/jae/9.3.370

Nindorera, W. (2012). *The CNDD-FDD in Burundi: The path from armed to political struggle* (Issue 10).

Nkurunziza, J. D. (2015). Timing and Sequencing of Post-Conflict Reconstruction and Peacebuilding in Burundi. In *CRPD Working Paper* (Issue 34). https://doi.org/10.1093/acprof:oso/9780198757276.003.0013

Nkurunziza, J. D. (2022). The origin and persistence of state fragility in Burundi. In *State Fragility, Growth and Development* (Issue April). https://doi.org/10.4324/9781003297697-4

Nshimirimana, F. (2024). *Exclusionary Governance in Burundi: Implications for Democracy and Consolidating Peace*.

Nyadera, I. N. (2018). South Sudan conflict from 2013 to 2018: Rethinking the causes, situation and solutions. *African Journal on Conflict Resolution*, *18*(2), 59–86.

O'Brien, A. (2009). Shots in the Dark: The 2008 South Sudan Civilian Disarmament Campaign. In *HSBA Working Paper*.

Odera, L. C. (2013). The Role of Trust as an Informal Institution in the Informal Sector in Africa. *Africa Development*, *38*(3–4), 121–146.

Peterson, R. (2001). Resistance and Rebellion; Lessons from Eastern Europe. In *Cambrige University Press*. https://doi.org/10.1007/BF02430448

Pham, P. N., Vinck, P., & Stover, E. (2008). The Lord's Resistance Army and Forced Conscription in Northern Uganda. *Human Rights Quarterly*, *30*(2008), 404–411.

Poole, L. (2019). *The refugee response in northern Uganda: Resources beyond international humanitarian assistance* (No. 2019; HPG Working Paper, Issue February). www.odi.org/hpg.

Powell, R. (2006). War as a commitment problem. *International Organization*, *60*(1), 169–203. https://doi.org/10.1017/S0020818306060061

Rabbie, J. M., Schot, J. C., & Visser, L. (1989). Social identity theory: A conceptual and empirical critique from the perspective of a behavioural interaction model. *European Journal of Social Psychology*, *19*(3), 171–202. https://doi.org/10.1002/ejsp.2420190302

Rabellino, D., Morese, R., Ciaramidaro, A., Bara, B. G., & Bosco, F. M. (2016). Third-party punishment: altruistic and anti-social behaviours in in-group and out-group settings. *Journal of Cognitive Psychology*, *28*(4), 486–495. https://doi.org/10.1080/20445911.2016.1138961

Rabin, M. (1993). Incorporating fairness into game theory and economics. *The American Economic Review*, *83*(5), 1281–1302. http://www.jstor.org/stable/2117561

Raleigh, C., Linke, A., Hegre, H., & Karlsen, J. (2010). Introducing ACLED- Armed Conflict Location and Event Data. *Journal of Peace Research*, *47*(5), 651–660.

Refugee law project. (2022). Negotiating peace: Resolution of Conflicts in Uganda's West Nile Region. In *Refugee Law Project Working Paper* (Issue 12). https://doi.org/10.4324/9781003317487-18

Relief web. (2002). *Rwanda-Uganda: Interahamwe reported present in Uganda*. https://reliefweb.int/report/democratic-republic-congo/rwanda-uganda-interahamwe-reported-present-uganda

Rockmore, M. (2017). The cost of fear: The welfare effect of the risk of violence in Northern Uganda. *World Bank Economic Review*, *31*(3), 650–669. https://doi.org/10.1093/wber/lhw025

Rockmore, M. (2020). Conflict-Risk and Agricultural Portfolios: Evidence from Northern Uganda. *The Journal of Development Studies*, *2016*, 1–21. https://doi.org/10.1080/00220388.2019.1703953

Rufanges, C. J., & Aspa, J. M. R. (2016). *Democratic Republic of Congo: A Review of 20 years of war* (Issue April). https://escolapau.uab.cat/img/programas/alerta/alerta/RDCongo_20AnosGuerra_I.pdf

Saferworld. (2010). Karamoja conflict and security assessment. In *Report* (Issue September).

Shemyakina, O. (2011). The effect of armed conflict on accumulation of schooling: Results from Tajikistan. *Journal of Development Economics*, *95*(2), 186–200. https://doi.org/10.1016/j.jdeveco.2010.05.002

Sigman, R., & Lindberg, S. I. (2017). Neopatrimonialism and Democracy: An Empirical Investigation of Africa's Political Regimes. *SSRN Electronic Journal*, *January*. https://doi.org/10.2139/ssrn.3066654

Skaperdas, S. (2008). An economic approach to analyzing civil wars. *Economics of Governance*, *9*(1), 25–44. https://doi.org/10.1007/s10101-007-0043-2

State Parties to the 1951 Convention relating to the Status of Refugees and the 1967 Protocol, (2011). https://doi.org/10.1093/rsq/hdn023

Tajfel, H., Billig, M. G., & Bundy, R. (1971). Social categorization and intergroup behaviour. *European Journal of Social Pszchology*, *1*(2), 149–178. https://doi.org/https://doi.org/10.1002/ejsp.2420010202

The Fund For Peace. (2019). *Fragile States Indcx Annual Report 2019*. www.fundforpeace.org

Titeca, K. (2024). Uganda and the DRC conflict: the interests driving Kampala's involvement. *The Conversation*, 23–26.

Uganda Bureau of Statistics. (2024a). National Population and Housing Census 2024: Preliminary Results. In *National Population and Household Census* (Vol. 256, Issue June).

Uganda Bureau of Statistics. (2024b). National Population and Housing Census 2024. In *Census 2024*. http://libdcms.nida.ac.th/thesis6/2010/b166706.pdf

UN, & African Union. (2011). *Fifth Anniversary of the signing of the Peace, Security and Cooperation Framework (PSCF)* (Vol. 46, Issue 0).

UNDP. (2017). *Summary of Study Uganda's Contribution To*. https://data2.unhcr.org/en/documents/download/64687

UNECA. (2015). *Conflicts in the Democratic Republic of Congo: Causes, impact and implications for the Great Lakes region*. Routledge. https://www.uneca.org/sites/default/files/PublicationFiles/conflits_in_drc_eng_25sept_rev1.pdf

UNECA. (2016). Conflict in the democratic Republic of Congo: Causes, impact and implications for the Great Lakes region. In *Routledge Handbook of Security Studies: Second Edition*. https://doi.org/10.4324/9781315753393

UNHCR. (2018). *South Sudan Regional Refugee Response Plan* (Issue December). http://reporting.unhcr.org/sites/default/files/2018SouthSudanRegionalRefugeeResponsePlan-Jan-Dec2018%28January2018%29_0.pdf

UNHCR. (2019a). *Global Trends Forced Displacemnet in 2018*. www.unhcr.org/5c6fb2d04

UNHCR. (2019b). Uganda Country Refugee Response Plan. *The UN Refugee Agency*, *Jan 2019–Dec 2020*, 72. http://reporting.unhcr.org/sites/default/files/UgandaCountryRRP2019-20%28January2019%29.pdf

United Nations Development Programme. (2018). *Understanding land dynamics and livelihood in refugee hosting districts of northern Uganda*.

United Nations High Commision for Refugees (UNHCR), & Government of Uganda (GoU). (2019). *Refugee and Host Population by District*. Uganda Comprehensive Refugee Response Portal. https://data2.unhcr.org/en/country/uga

Venugopalan, H. (2016). Understanding the Conflict in Congo. In *ORF ISSUE BRIEF* (Issue May). https://www.orfonline.org/wp-content/uploads/2016/05/ORF_IssueBrief_139_Venugopalan_Final.pdf

Vlassenroot, K., & Van Acker, F. (2001). War as Exit from Exclusion? The Formation of Mayi-Mayi Militias in Eastern Congo. *Afrika Focus*, *17*(1–2), 51–77. https://doi.org/10.21825/af.v17i1-2.5426

von Braun, J., Teklu, T., & Webb, P. (1998). *Famine in Africa. Causes, Response and Prevention.* The John Hopkins Univerisity Press.

Voors, M. J., Nillesen, E. E. M., Verwimp, P., Bulte, E. H., Lensink, R., & Soest, D. P. Van. (2012a). Violent Conflict and Behavior: A field experiment in Burundi. *American Economic Review*, *102*(2), 941–964.

Voors, M. J., Nillesen, E. E. M., Verwimp, P., Bulte, E. H., Lensink, R., & Van Soest, D. P. (2012b). Violent Conflict and Behaviour: a field experiment in Burundi. *Source: The American Economic Review*, *102*(2), 941–964. https://doi.org/10.1257/aer.102.2.941

Wallensteen, P., & Axell, K. (1993). Armed Conflict at the End of the Cold War, 1989-92. *Journal of Peace Research*, *30*(3), 331–346.

Werner, K., & Lambsdorff, J. G. (2019). Emotional Numbing and Lessons Learned after a Violent Conflict – Experimental Evidence from Ambon, Indonesia. *The Journal of Development Studies*, 1–15. https://doi.org/10.1080/00220388.2019.1590550

Whyte, S. R., & Acio, E. (2017). Generations and Access to Land in Postconflict Northern Uganda: Youth Have No Voice in Land Matters. *African Studies Review*, *60*(3), 17–36. https://doi.org/10.1017/asr.2017.120

World Bank. (2015). *Forced Displacement in the Great Lakes Region.* http://hdl.handle.net/10986/21708

World Bank. (2016). *The Uganda Poverty Assessment Report 2016. Farms, cities and good fortune: assessing poverty reduction in Uganda from 2006 to 2013.* http://pubdocs.worldbank.org/en/890971474327477241/Uganda-Poverty-Assessment-Report-2016-Overview.pdf

WorldBank. (2016). *The Uganda Poverty Assessment Report, 2016: Farms, Cities and good fortune: assessing poverty reduction in Uganda from 2006 to 2013.*

Yami, M., & van Asten, P. (2018). Relevance of informal institutions for achieving sustainable crop intensification in Uganda. *Food Security*, *10*(1), 141–150. https://doi.org/10.1007/s12571-017-0754-3

Young, J. (2016). Popular struggles and elite co-optation: the Nuer White Army in South Sudan's Civil War. In E. LeBrun (Ed.), *Small Arms Survey*. Graduate Institute of International and Development studies.

Zhu, H., Filipski, M., Valli, J., Gonzalez, E., Gupta, A., & Taylor, J. E. (2016a). *Economic Impact of Refugee Settlements in Uganda* (Issue November).

Zhu, H., Taylor, J. E., Gupta, A., Filipski, M., Valli, J., & Gonzalez, E. E. (2016b). Economic Impacts of Giving Land to Refugees. In *Agricultural and Applied Economics Association 2018 Annual Meeting*. Agricultural and Applied Economics Association. https://doi.org/10.22004/ag.econ.274212

Adong, A., Kornher, L., Kirui,O., & von Braun, J. (2021). Conflict Exposure and Food Consumption Pathways During and After Conflict: Evidence from Northern Uganda. World Development. https://doi.org/10.1016/j.worlddev.2021.105636

Adong, A., Tinker, J., Levine, D., Mbowa, S. (2020). Encouraging Fertilizer Adoption through a Risk-Free Sales Offer: A Randomized Control Trial in Uganda: Development Perspectives. https://doi.org/10.1016/j.wdp.2020.100230

Adong, A. (2014). Impact of Households' Membership of Farmer Groups on the Adoption of Agricultural Technologies in Uganda: Evidence from the Uganda Census of Agriculture 2008/09. Agricultural Economics Research, Policy and Practice in Southern Africa (AGREKON). https://doi.org/10.1080/03031853.2014.915485

Hernandez, M.A., Paz, F., Adeoti, A.I., Adong, A., Jumbe, C.B.L., Lagat, K.A., Kaiyatsa, S. (2018). Overview of the Fertilizer Supply Chain and Market Structure in Africa: A Cross-Country Assessment; Project Note, International Food Policy Research Center, 2018

Address: Annet ADONG (Ph.D.), Center for Population and Applied Statistics, Makerere University, Kampala, Uganda.

Email: annetteadong@gmail.com or annetteadong@yahoo.com

Website: https://nieraglobal.org/team/details/annet-adong

The Hans Günter Brauch Foundation on Peace and Ecology in the Anthropocene

The Hans Günter Brauch Foundation for Peace and Ecology in the Anthropocene (HGBS) is a foundation under civil law which has its registered office in 74821 Mosbach in Baden-Württemberg.

Aims and Purposes of this Foundation

The purpose of the Foundation is to promote science and research, education and upbringing, international peace and environmental protection, in particular peace research, ecology and the interrelationships of peace and ecology (peace ecology) in the Anthropocene, the new epoch in the history of the Earth.

The Purpose of the Foundation Shall be Realised Through

(a) Promoting local competitions on questions of the transition to sustainability and peace at general-education grammar schools in the Neckar-Odenwald County, which will be awarded annually to each school from 2022 onwards.
(b) An international science prize for peace and ecology that will be awarded from 2023 onwards with the prize for students.
(c) Maintenance of a foundation house with archives, library and the foundation office (after the founder's death).
(d) Conducting scientific events, research projects and their publication on peace research and ecology (currently not possible).

Members of the Governing Board

- **Dr. Hans Günter Brauch (1947), Mosbach, Germany**, Chairman of the Board Political Scientist,

A. Adong, *Armed Conflicts and Forced Displacements in the Anthropocene*,
The Anthropocene: Politik—Economics—Society—Science 41,
https://doi.org/10.1007/978-3-032-04820-2

- **Prof. Dr. Úrsula Oswald Spring (1946), Mexico, Switzerland)**, Deputy Board Chair, UNAM, CRIM, Cuernavaca, Mexico,
- **Dr. Hans Friedrich Happes, MA (1953)**, Deputy Board Chair, former headmaster, Nicolaus-Kistner Grammar School in Mosbach (Ret.),
- **Georg Nelius (1949)**, Member of the Board, former SPD member of the State Parliament (2007–2021), Deputy Mayor of Mosbach, Chair of the SPD Faction in the Town Council. Member of the County Council, Neckar-Odenwald Council.

International Science Prize for Peace and Ecology in the Anthropocene

Starting in July 2023, an international science prize has been awarded annually by the *Hans Günter Brauch Foundation for Peace and Ecology in the Anthropocene* (HGBF) in Mosbach, Baden-Württemberg in South Germany that combines:

- *Peace and Ecology* as two distinct research programs in the social sciences that evolved since the 1950s and 1970s and that have coexisted without a joint research perspective.
- *Peace Research* emerged between World War I and World War II in the idealist or Kantian tradition of international relations that offered critiques of the new realist tradition in international law and politics that prevailed after World War II.
- *Peace Research* started in North America and Scandinavia and spread in the 1970s to other parts of the world after the *International Peace Research Association* (IPRA) had been established in 1964. J. W. Burton was one of the founding fathers.
- The '*ecology concept*' was coined in the 1860s by Ernst Häckel, a German biologist. Since World War II the concept widened as 'deep ecology', 'human ecology', 'political ecology', 'social ecology', 'geoecology' and 'ecofeminism'.
- In political science and international relations *ecological perspectives, environmental studies* started in the 1960s and *research on global environmental change* followed in the 1980s.
- *Peace Research and Environmental Studies* have coexisted as two research programs with little conceptual, theoretical and empirical interchange.
- *Paul J. Crutzen*, Nobel Laureate in Chemistry, propagated the term *Anthropocene* in February 2000 as a *New Epoch in Earth's History.*
- *The Anthropocene Working Group (AWG)* proposed in 2019 as its start the years 1945 (first nuclear weapon test in Alomogordo) and 1950 (start of the Great Acceleration).

The *Hans Günter Brauch Foundation* (HGBF) *on Peace and Ecology in the Anthropocene* (PEA) was established on 8 May 2020 on the occasion of the 75th anniversary of the end of World War II and of the liberation from Fascism to combine a joint peace research and ecology perspective on the new challenges facing humankind's survival in the Anthropocene.

The *HGBF on Peace and Ecology in the Anthropocene* supports *globally scientific research* and *locally education* in secondary schools in the county where the founder was born and has lived. The HGBF funds *local educational prizes* for grammar or high school students and globally this *international science prize*. Both prizes will be awarded jointly to enhance the exchange of scientific results to secondary schools and the cooperation between scientists and pupils.

Between peace and security issues on the one hand and environment and sustainable development problems on the other, various relationships and linkages have been addressed in the social science literature since the 1960s in the Anthropocene Epoch:

- early conceptual debate on linkages between peace and the environment (since 1980s);
- conceptual discussion on environmental and ecological security (since 1989);
- research on the impacts of weapons and wars on the environment (Westing et al.);
- impact of environmental degradation and stress on environmental conflict (Baechler, Homer-Dixon);
- environmental peace-making (Conca) and role of the environment in post-conflict peacebuilding;
- emerging discourse and policy debate on climate change and conflicts (since 1989);
- early approaches to peace ecology and their shortcomings (Kyrou, Amster, Oswald/Brauch);
- theoretical and empirical work on sustainability transition, transformation of the economy, society and political realm and climate neutrality.

These manifold research themes have not yet resulted in a peace ecology research program in the Anthropocene Epoch. The theme of *the first international Science Prize of the HGB-Foundation was:* Climate Change and Conflicts in 2023. The first recipient is PD Prof. Dr. Tobias Ide (senior lecturer, Murdoch University, Perth (Australia) who also teaches at the University of Hiroshima (Japan) and at the TH in Braunschweig (Germany). International Recognitions were awarded to Dr. Tom Deligiannis, Laurier University (Canada) and Dr. Richard Marcantonio, Notre Dame University (USA).

The theme of *the second international Science Prize of the HGB-Foundation* in 2024 *was*: Ecocide: Impacts of Wars and/or Climate Change on Food Security since 1945. The second recipients were Prof. Dr. Gregory Thaler, Oxford University, Oxford, UK, and Dr. Victor Tsilonis, international lawyer, Greece. International Recognitions were awarded to Dr. Annet Adong (Uganda), Dr. Melissa Roxana Quispe-Zuniga (Peru), and Dr. Christo Idowu Odeymi (Nigeria).

The third international science prize in 2025 will be awarded to Dr. Angela J. Lederach, Assistant, Chapman University, California, USA for her book: *Feel the Grass Grow: Ecologies of Slow Peace* (Stanford University Press, 2023) and to Dr. Matthew Gillett, Senior Lecturer (Associate Professor), *University of Essex* (NZ, UK) for his book: *Prosecuting Environmental Harm before the International Criminal Court* (Cambridge University Press, 2022). An international scientific recognition will be awarded *to Dr. Anselm Vogler for his Ph.D. thesis* (2025): *Navigating External and Existential Threats: National-Level Policy Responses to Climate Security*, Hamburg University, Germany; Dr. Barbara Magalhães Teixeira (2024) for her thesis at Lund University on: *The Nature of Peace and the Continuum of Violence in Environmental Conflicts*, and Dr. ASM Mostafizur Rahman, Heidelberg University, for his thesis (2024) on *Garments and Growth – State, Ideas, Policy Learning, and Globalization in Bangladesh.*

Chairman of the Board of Trustees (*Kuratorium*) of the HGB-Foundation: Lord Mayor of the town of Mosbach, Julian Stipp. Mosbach has been a member of Mayors for Peace since 2021.

See at: http://hgb-stiftung.org/index.html and http://hgb-stiftung.de/index.html.

List of Books edited by Hans Günter Brauchin the Hexagon Series

https://www.springer.com/series/8090 and http://www.afes-press-books.de/html/hexagon.htm

List of Books in the APESS Series

https://www.springer.com/series/15232 and http://www.afes-press-books.de/html/APESS.htm

List of Books in the ESDP Series

https://www.springer.com/series/10357 and http://www.afes-press-books.de/html/SpringerBriefs_ESDP.htm

List of Books in the PSP Series

https://www.springer.com/series/10970 and http://www.afes-press-books.de/html/SpringerBriefs_PSP.htm

List of Books in the PAHSEP Series

https://www.springer.com/series/15230 and http://www.afes-press-books.de/html/PAHSEP.htm

Open Access Books Published in These Five Series

List of Open Access Books in the Hexagon Series

HESP 1: Truong, Thanh-Dam; Gasper, Des; Handmaker, J., Bergh, S.I. (Eds.): Migration, Gender and Social Justice – Perspectives on Human Insecurity. Hexagon Series on Human and Environmental Security and Peace, vol. 9 (Heidelberg – New York – Dordrecht – London: Springer, 2013); at: https://link.springer.com/book/10.1007/978-3-642-28012-2

HESP 2: Jeroen Kool, Saeb Bamya, Samer Talozi, EcoPeace, Tel Aviv, Israel – Bethlehem, Palestine – Amman, Jordan: *Sustainable Development in the Jordan River Valley: Final Report of the Regional NGO Master Plan.* Hexagon Series on Human and Environmental Security and Peace, vol. 13 (Berlin – Heidelberg – New York: Springer, 2016); at: https://link.springer.com/book/10.1007/978-3-319-30036-8.

List of Open Access Books in the APESS Series

APESS 1: Maja Göpel: *The Great Mindshift: How a New Economic Paradigm and Sustainability Transformations go Hand in Hand* (Cham – Heidelberg – New York – Dordrecht – London: Springer International Publishing, 2017); at: https://link.springer.com/ book/10.1007/978-3-319-43766-8.

APESS 2: Carl Middleton, Vanessa Lamb (Eds.) (Eds.): *Knowing the Salween River: Resource Politics of a Contested Transboundary River* (Cham: Springer International Publishing, 2019); at: https://link.springer.com/book/10.1007/978-3-319-77440-4.

APESS 3: S. Benner, G. Lax, G., P.J. Crutzen, , U. Pöschl,, J. Lelieveld, H.G. Brauch (Eds.). *Paul J. Crutzen and the Anthropocene: A New Epoch in Earth's History* (Cham: Springer International Publishing, 2021); at: https://link.springer.com/book/ 10.1007/978-3-030-82202-6.

APESS 4: H.G. Brauch (Eds.): *Towards Rethinking Politics, Policy and Polity in the Anthropocene – Multidisciplinary Perspectives* (Cham: Springer International Publishing, 2021); at: https://link.springer.com/book/10.1007/978-3-031-71807-6.

List of Open Access Books in the ESDP Series

ESDP 1: So far no Open Access Volume is available in this book series.

List of Books in the PSP Series

PSP 1: Paul J. Crutzen, Hans Günter Brauch (Eds.): *Paul J. Crutzen: A Pioneer on Atmospheric Chemistry and Climate Change in the Anthropocene.* Springer Briefs on Pioneers in Science and Practice No. 50 (Cham – Heidelberg – New York – Dordrecht – London: Springer International Publishing, 2016; at: https://link.springer.com/book/10.1007/978-3-319-27460-7.

PSP 2: Nils Petter Gleditsch: *Pioneer in the Analysis of War and Peace* – Presented by Peter Wallensteen. Springer Briefs on Pioneers in Science and Practice No. 29 (Cham – Heidelberg – New York – Dordrecht – London: Springer, 2016); at: https:// link.springer.com/book/10.1007/978-3-319-03820-9.

PSP 3: Gleditsch, Nils Petter (Ed.): *R. J. Rummel: An Assessment of His Many Contributions.* Springer Briefs on Pioneers in Science and Practice, vol. 37 (Cham – Heidelberg – New York – Dordrecht – London: Springer-Verlag, 2017); at: https:// link.springer.com/book/10.1007/978-3-319-54463-2.

List of Books in the PAHSEP Series

PAHSEP 1: Nils Petter Gleditsch (Ed.): *Lewis Fry Richardson: His Intellectual Legacy and Influence in the Social Sciences.* Pioneers in Arts, Humanities, Science, Engineering, Practice (PAHSEP), No. 27 (Cham: Springer International Publishing, 2020); at: https://link.springer.com/book/10.1007/978-3-030-31589-4.

MIX
Papier aus verantwortungsvollen Quellen
Paper from responsible sources
FSC® C105338

If you have any concerns about our products,
you can contact us on
ProductSafety@springernature.com

In case Publisher is established outside the EU,
the EU authorized representative is:
Springer Nature Customer Service Center GmbH
Europaplatz 3, 69115 Heidelberg, Germany

Printed by Libri Plureos GmbH
in Hamburg, Germany